Paolo Lazzarin

ONE HUNDRED & ONE
Beautiful TOWNS *in Italy*

SHOPS & CRAFTS

RIZZOLI
NEW YORK

VALLE D'AOSTA

PIEDMONT

LOMBARDY

TRENTINO—ALTO ADIGE

FRIULI—VENEZIA GIULIA

VENETO

EMILIA—ROMAGNA

LIGURIA

MARCHE

TUSCANY

UMBRIA

ABRUZZO

MOLISE

LAZIO

SARDINIA

PUGLIA

CAMPANIA

BASILICATA

CALABRIA

SICILY

22

REGIONAL CONTENTS

ALPHABETICAL CONTENTS

PREFACE

A book of this kind could turn out to be a mere selection of colorful shop windows, however, this book represents Italy's lively productivity, both in the field of crafts, with the presentation of objects of art, as well as industries in which the country has excelled, such as fashion, design, and automobiles. This puts Italy at the forefront during a moment in time when Western economies and the pressing competition of the Asian market seem to be allied in an attempt to suffocate the production of objects that have a story to tell and a personality to defend. It is culturally and economically fortunate that the ceramics of Capodimonte are still of interest, and that qualified collectors can distinguish at a glance between those of Faenza or Grottaglie; both are beautiful and intrinsically unique. Much the same can be said for Cogne lace, Piedmont brocades, Biella textiles, Como silks, the industrial designs coming out of Milan, and the automobile industry of Emilia.

Many of these activities are concentrated in economically important "districts." Sometimes they are spread over large areas, such as the production of shoes and sportswear in Treviso, or the luxury footwear industry in the Marche, furniture-making in Brianza, or textile production in Prato. Other crafts occupy small villages or entire districts of a town, such as knife manufacturing in Maniago, the crafting of nativity figures to the east of Spaccanapoli in Naples, alabaster in Volterra, and ocarinas in Budrio. This is a modern marketing and production concept, but the concentration of one kind of product in a single location often either has a historical background or is linked to the availability of raw materials in the area. Sometimes it is the legacy of the ancient consortiums that in the past benefited from important privileges, for example, the goldsmiths of Naples.

This volume gathers together the most distinctive and time-honored objects from every field of craftsmanship, leaving out the products—and there are many of them—that are sold as common souvenirs throughout Italy. The search for the highest-quality items is a monumental task and no dark alleyway was left unexplored in the quest to find the most interesting, intriguing, and original items Larger cities, such as Rome and Milan, have been allocated more pages because they are easier to reach and because of the wealth and variety of items they have to offer.

The craftsmanship that was born out of the need to produce objects for everyday use is not only doomed to disappear but has already disappeared, and has been substituted by mass-produced goods at lower costs. The production of goods whose form and function blend has survived and is destined to grow. These are the beautiful articles we can look at and touch and that deserve our attention not only for what they are but also for what they represent. There are thousands of artisans plying their trades along the length of the Italian peninsula, producing objects of rare cultural significance. These items are wonderfully unique, as are the hands and minds of the people who produce them—simple as a terracotta piece from Puglia or rare and refined as filigree from Liguria.

Italian craftsmanship has been handed down from generation to generation over the centuries, yet artisans continue to reinvent ways to express themselves and make a living at the same time. In both cases it is possible to admire the skill of a person or of a people, as well as the culture and history from which art is produced. Buying an object of this kind means taking home a memory from the most authentic part of Italy.

A lush display of ranunculus in the nature park in the Friuli Dolomites with the peaks of the Urtisiel and Pecoli mountains in the background.

AOSTA

THE POMEGRANATE TREE

IF YOU WERE TO DRAW A LINE ON A MAP OF THE VALLE D'AOSTA joining the peak of Mont Blanc with those of Monte Rosa and the Gran Paradiso, it would form an equilateral triangle with the point facing south. At the center of this triangle would be a small rectangle, created from the perimeter of the walls within which the ancient Romans built the *Augusta Praetoria* two thousand years ago. These mysterious and magical geometries have led some people to think that Aosta is the mythical Shangri-La, the city were time stood still and that legend would have us believe is lost in the peaks of the Himalayas. In truth, Aosta does not stand still; it moves with the times, modern and practical. It is crossed by a highway that penetrates into the bowels of Mont Blanc, and like a generous artery, enables the flow of vital lifeblood between the north and south of Europe. Aosta, however, is still profoundly tied to its past and conserves its traditions. Scattered in every village of the valley there are craftsmen who work in metal, wood, and textiles. In the middle course of the river Dora, facing Verrès, stands the castle of Issogne, one of the most emblematic princely residences of the fifteenth century, connected to the fortunes of the Challant family, lords of the valley. It is worth a visit, even if it is only to see the masterpiece that stands on the well in the central courtyard: a wrought-iron pomegranate tree, a gift from the then prior of Aosta to Filiberto of Challant and his bride, Louise d'Arberg. The Fontana del Melograno (Pomegranate Fountain) was forged in the sixteenth century and is one of the most refined objects of its kind in the world. It is witness to the ability of the craftsmen of the period who, with iron from the mines of Cogne, made weapons and tools, but also the balustrades and grilles that still decorate many noble houses in the Valle d'Aosta. The mines are not active today, but nearby at Verrès and in other small centers in the valley, there are still many forges that produce fire dogs, lanterns, candelabra, locks, hangers, signs, and ornamental objects that recall examples of the Gothic art of the valley. Iron is not the only material with which the craftsmen of the region display their ability. Wooden objects for everyday use are witness to their artistry: walnut furniture finely decorated in Swiss oak or poplar, the softest woods for carving. The *sabot* is typical of the valley: clogs that are hardwearing for men and elegant for women. Wooden drinking vessels and friendship cups, toys in the shape of animals— long-necked chickens, fat cows without legs, and mules on wheels— are all typical of the region.

facing page
The cast iron tree of the Pomegranate Fountain (a symbol of prosperity) in the courtyard of the Castle of Issogne.

below
A craftsman fashions a pair of clogs at the Sant'Orso Fair.

Craft fairs are held at Donnas on the third week of January, at Pré-St.-Didier in December, and at Rhêmes-Notre-Dame in July. There is a local antiques fair at Entreves every Monday in August. Wooden objects are made in many villages of the valley. Luciano Savin at Verrès works in iron. Lace (called dentelles) is made at Cogne, where there is also a school for lace-making. The designs are inspired by stylized animals, flowers, and objects of everyday use. Lace can be found in other villages in the valley, such as Champorcher.

A fair dedicated to the legendary Saint Orso, who lived in the sixth century, is held every year in the historic center of Aosta on January 30 and 31. The origins of this fair date back to the year 1000, and in 1243 precise laws were passed to favor commercial exchanges of agricultural equipment, tools, textiles, and jewelry among the villages of the valley and also with neighboring regions such as Piedmontese Savoy and Swiss Vallese. Every Saint Orso fair is a window on the art and craftsmanship of the valley, with more than a thousand exhibitors offering sleighs and baskets, ladles and bowls, clogs and friendship cups, snuff boxes and crucifixes, toys and large statues of granite or soapstone, lace and wrought-iron objects.

ALESSANDRIA

THE BORSALINO

GIUSEPPE BORSALINO, WHO HAD BEEN FOND OF WEARING HATS ever since he was a child, founded a millinery factory in Alessandria that would come to produce some of the finest and most elegant fedoras in Europe. At the age of fourteen Borsalino left his home in the fields of Valenza to become an apprentice hatter and, two years later, moved to France, a country that was thought to be the home of millinery. Here he learned to brush felt and weigh it, to baste and shave, iron and trim. Having learned his art, he returned to Alessandria in 1857, took over a small factory, and opened a hat-making shop in the center of town. The Borsalino shop started out with ten workers, producing fifty hats a day, and by 1900, the year of its founder's death, production had reached 750,000 hats annually, the greater part of which was exported. "Il Borsalino," or the Borsalino fedora, became famous in Germany even before its popularity spread throughout Italy. The milliner's son, Teresio, inherited the factory and continued his father's work and Alessandria became the classic example of a one-company town. The factory soon expanded, encompassing nearly 600,000 square feet and employing 2,500 workers, and production increased: by 1913 it had reached two million hats per year, half of which were exported. The Borsalino fedora became synonymous with style and was considered an essential element to the classic businessman's suit, but was also worn by gangsters, con men, and the movie stars who depicted them: Paul Newman donned one in *The Sting*; Humphrey Bogart and Frank Sinatra could not be separated from theirs; and, during the height of Al Capone's influence as a crime lord, gangsters in New York City and Chicago donned Borsalinos. A gradual reorganization of the factory took place in the 1940s, but the fame of the brand continued. In fact, it inspired the 1970 film *Borsalino* starring Jean-Paul Belmondo and Alain Delon. Today, the classic Borsalino fedora is made just as it was a hundred years ago, with a wooden block, cast iron and steam press. The forty stages are scrupulously followed, and from the brushing of the felt to the packing of the final product lasts seven weeks. Today, Giuseppe Borsalino is known not only for the celebrated felt hat but for the refined straw Montecristo Panama as well. There are more fashionable models, made particularly for women, with trimmings in lace and jacquard, and there is a Borsalino line of accessories, including scarves, belts, and head squares. The factory has also been making hats for the Orthodox Jewish community for fifty years. Fifty thousand hats with large brims (9 centimeters instead of the classic 6 centimeters) are sold each year to Orthodox Jewish shops in Jerusalem and in Brooklyn, New York.

facing page
The famous Borsalino panama and felt hats are made from waterproof fabrics. Stripes are popular for the summer.

below
The bell tower of the Cathedral at Alessandria.

The Borsalino showroom is located in the center of Milan, and here, apart from the hats, various accessories from the company's line can be found. Other towns known for their manufacture of hats of every kind are Montappone, called Italy's hat capital, and Ghiffa; in both towns visitors can learn about the history of millinery at local museums. Alessandria is also especially known for the handicraft of interior design ornaments and plates and picture frames in silver.

In New York, on September 11, 2005, after a memorial service honoring those who died in the World Trade Center tragedy, powerful bands of blue light were projected up into the sky, recreating the silhouettes of the Twin Towers. Space Cannon, a company whose headquarters are located just outside Alessandria, had made it possible for the towers to shine once more. The company specializes in grand events, special lighting for parks and gardens, and "painting" buildings of any size with light. Space Cannon carried out the illumination in Suanyaa, China, of the world's largest statue of Buddha; Taipei City's Taipei 101 skyscraper, the tallest building in the world; Atlantic City's sports complex; the Panda Hypermarket in Saudi Arabia; the Olympia Museum in Athens, Greece; and the venues of the 2000 Olympic Games in Sydney, Australia.

A S T I

TAPESTRIES FIT FOR A PALACE

Seen at dawn from the low hills surrounding the town, the valley of Asti evokes the sea, with turquoise colored waves painted by the copper sulfate that covers the endless vineyards from which the city draws its lifeblood. Barbera, Grignolino, Moscato: wine has always been Asti's greatest source of pride and profit, and the surrounding countryside is covered with vineyards that stretch to the perimeter of the Roman walls. Although Asti is known as the "city of 100 towers," in imperial Roman times 120 towers rose from the ramparts, asserting the town's might and prosperity. Today twelve towers remain from the original 120, among them the well-preserved Torre Rossa, which has been partly restored. The *recinto dei nobili*, the perimeter of the nobles, stretches from the Bishopric to Piazza Catena, and is separated by the *recinto dei Borghigiani*, which spreads out externally showing off the increasing opulence of the city. Emblematic baroque vine ornaments decorate the pillars supporting the nave of the grandiose cathedral, and for this it is nicknamed "the vineyard." The great Vittorio Alfieri piazza has become the city center. A crowded market unfolds under the porticoes, but in the nobles' quarter only the most significant and ancient monuments remain, silent in the cobblestone streets. The Rotonda, or Baptistery of San Pietro is built on the remains of a little Roman temple, with pillars made from the red brick so characteristic of the old city. Beside it stand a cloister and a chapel dedicated to San Pietro Consavia, who might not have existed, but to whom is attributed a miracle in the year 1000.

Besides its wine, Asti is famous for its fine handwoven tapestries made near the center of town in the ancient Certosa di Valmanera. During World War II this charterhouse was transformed by Ugo Scassa into a successful center for tapestry weaving, as he rediscovered the ancient techniques used in the Middle Ages when the art of tapestry reached its greatest splendor. Some years later, Vittoria Montalbano opened another tapestry-making center in the rooms of the Michelerio, in the historic center of Asti. Due in large part to the management of the painter Valerio Miroglio this, too, was able to produce work of the highest quality. The making of tapestries requires the most refined and precious weaving techniques. Its origins are recent in Asti, but it has reached a high level in only a few years. Scassa began his business by weaving carpets depicting famous paintings by artists such as Andy Warhol. He then began making tapestries with the ancient technique of *ad alto liccio* (on a vertical loom). Of the 220 impressive tapestries created to date by Scassa many hang in the reception rooms of gracious houses and grand hotels.

Detail of an external chapel of the Gothic cathedral of Santa Maria Assunta.

The Certosa di Valmanera was founded in the eleventh century for the monks of Vallombroso and was then passed to the Carthusians who lived there until Napoleon closed it at the beginning of the nineteenth century. The abandoned and partly destroyed buildings were recovered at the beginning of the twentieth century and were later transformed into a factory for tapestry-making. The Certosa is one of the largest manufacturers of tapestries in Italy and contains a museum housing a collection of dozens of tapestries made from the designs of important modern painters, including de Chirico, Guttuso, Ernst, Kandinsky, Klee, Matisse, and Miro. The School of Professional Weavers enables the art of maestro Ugo Scassa and his collaborators to be kept alive.

The manufacture of tapestries is not widespread in Italy owing to low demand, but the same technique is used to make cushions and bed covers. Pieces that are real works of art can be purchased at the Arazzeria Scassa or at Vittoria Montalbano. Other small workshops for the production of tapestries can be found in Umbria, or at Sant'Agnello in Campania, and Mogoro in Sardinia.

facing page
Tapestry of Paul Klee's *Landscape with Yellow Birds*, created at the Arazzeria Scassa. Tapestries are made here on antique frames using the "high loop" technique.

BIELLA

ELEGANT ATTIRE

THE CLOTH INDUSTRY IN ITALY CENTERS AROUND THE THREE TOWNS OF Como, Biella, and Prato, each with their own areas of expertise: silk in Como, high-quality wool in Biella, and textile processing and distribution in Prato. Biella, once known as Bugella to the ancient Romans, flourished during the Middle Ages as a center for sheep farming. The town's geographical location in the region of Piedmont, characterized by high mountain pastures and rushing streams, was ideal for sheep grazing and the washing of fleece and powering of mills. The cultivation of hemp was also widespread throughout Piedmont, and until industrialization and the introduction of the mechanical loom in the nineteenth century many families wove their own clothes and household linens at home. Biella's textile industry centered on wool and thrived along the riverbanks of the pre-Alps, where flocks of sheep would graze. Men, women, and often children were employed under less than pleasant conditions and in crowded warehouses in order to work the wool. Some of the factories in which the first seedlings of the industrialization of the cloth industry were planted are now part of a tour exploring early modernization in Biella. At the beginning of the nineteenth century the production of wool was concentrated around Biella and Mosso Santa Maria, from whence it spread to other villages in the region. Today Biella is a province covering less than 1,000 square kilometers and with a population of more than 150,000 inhabitants. Roughly a thousand large and small companies, mainly family owned and operated, dot the surrounding area and specialize in textile manufacture. It is the most highly skilled center for wool production in the world. It only contributes 7 percent of the production of Italian textiles, but this is where we find the best wool (cashmere, alpaca, and mohair) as well as cotton and synthetic fibers. The famous Japanese commercial chain Isetan has recently proposed a collection of clothes to be made with Biella textiles and branded "Biella, the Art of Excellence." The collection would be sold exclusively in the prestigious Shinjuku shopping center in Tokyo. Ermenegildo Zegna was founded in 1910 at Trivero and is among the most famous of designer companies producing high-quality textiles. Zegna has become a giant in the world of ready-to-wear clothes with branches all over the world and boutiques in London, Berlin, New York, Tokyo, Beijing, and Beverly Hills. Today, Zegna is also well known for made-to-measure clothes that cost slightly more than the ready-to-wear pieces and are made with fabrics chosen from the 450 lines that the company produces.

Balls of colorful fine wool.

facing page
The old Biella wool mills along the Cervo River.

Nearby fashion outlets offer excellent bargains on the latest style whims. For fabrics and clothing visit the Cerruti di Biella wool factory or the Centro Zegna in Trivero; for knitted goods, Tollegeno and Liabel; for sports and casual clothes, the Fila store in Verrone; and for a wide selection of fabrics both imported and locally woven, browse the shelves at the Graziano Brothers' shop.

In the 1930s Ermenegildo Zegna, the founder of the eponymous company famous for its designer men's fashions, transformed the mountain of Trivero, his birthplace, into a garden and financed the construction of a panoramic road bearing his name. The designer has continued to commit to the refurbishment of his hometown and its surrounding countryside by creating the Zegna Oasis, which encompasses miles of the panoramic road between Trivero and Rosazza and includes places equipped for sports activities, routes for mountain biking and trekking, children's playgrounds, ski slopes and lifts, and a tourist center. The sanctuary of the Madonna Nera di Oropa, near Biella, is one of the most famous pilgrimage spots in Italy. It was founded in AD 369, when Saint Eusebio, bishop of Vercelli, took refuge here to escape persecution, and it was here that he hid a statue of the Madonna that had been brought from Jerusalem.

CANAVESE

MASTER COPPERSMITHS

SINCE THE TIME OF THE ANCIENT SALASSI PEOPLES WHO LIVED HERE in the fifth century BC, metalworking has been a major activity in Piedmont. The guilds of metalworkers and master coppersmiths (the *magnin*) had already established their statutes in the Middle Ages. Even the automobile industry's clever coachbuilders at FIAT, Bertone, and Pininfarina made use of this tradition by recycling the furnaces that had been left inactive at the beginning of the twentieth century. Some diehard workers did not abandon the furnaces and continued to beat copper, pewter, and iron, fashioning objects such as plates, saucepans, fire dogs, lamps, beds, gates, balconies, grilles, and signs. Working with iron is a continued tradition in many of the town centers in the province of Cuneo, such as in Valstrona (Verbania), where copper is beaten. To aid the metalworkers' craft, furnaces were installed in the outskirts of Canavese, in Pont Canavese, Alpette, Cuorgné, Valperga, and Locana; the surrounding Alpette area was even called the land of the master coppersmiths because of the five rich copper mines that existed there. The mineral extracted was first melted in furnaces, adding lead, tin, and charcoal to improve the quality. It was then poured into basins of refractory material to form solid blocks and sheets. Hardened but still hot, these blocks were roughly shaped into various containers with great hammers powered by water paddles. The unformed pieces had to be heated intermittently, and they were ventilated by an ingenious system of hydraulic pumps. Water was driven down into a closed wooden bell chamber after which it would beat onto a flat stone at the bottom creating a mass of air to flow up to the forge, which was thereby ventilated continuously. This process can be witnessed at Castellaro di Ronco Canavese in a factory that dates back to 1675 and where there is a great forge that was used to smelt copper, and a smaller one for beating iron. Beside them is a workspace for the preparation of the charcoal. The rough article, called the *cavato*, was then taken to the village to be honed. Alpette was once teeming with busy workshops that modeled pans for heating milk, cauldrons for polenta, funnels, alembics, and coffee machines. Although it is less common than ever, traditional metalworking continues in some craftsmen's workshops with little change, except for the water-powered hammering, which is now achieved with more modern equipment. In 1983 a school for master coppersmiths was established where the working of copper entirely by hand is taught and practical demonstrations are held. Next door to the school there is a copper museum where hundreds of copper items fashioned by local coppersmiths from the late nineteenth century to the present day are on display.

facing page
An assortment of vases, pots, and utensils in a coppersmith's workshop.

below
Copper articles on display outside a craftsman's shop.

Decorative objects fashioned from beaten copper can be purchased at Ceretto Castigliano in Pont Canavese, where a crafts fair is held every year during the first week of June. Visit the copper museum in Ronco Canavese and shop for locally made instruments, such as lutes, at Bottega Artigiana di Cossato; accordions at Ditta Verde in Leinì, wind instruments at Rampone in Quarna; and organs at Vegezzi in Centallo.

The deep roots of pastoral and religious traditions in Piedmont have encouraged the production of musical instruments that were used during local village festivals and feasts celebrating the harvest or the solstice. The nobles of the House of Savoy contributed to the development of this activity. In fact, during the mid-seventeenth century, the court of Savoy was the first to invite the lute-makers of France to the region, and it is for this reason that Piedmont lute-making differs from that of nearby Lombardy, which remained faithful to the school of Cremona. Excellent traditional lute-makers can be found in the province of Alessandria, in Rosignano nel Monferrato, and Cossato, while organs and harps are made in Centallo and Piasco, accordions in Leinì, and wooden and metal wind instruments are a specialty of Quarna.

SALUZZO

TREASURES OF THE MARQUISATE

ONE OF THE MOST SIGNIFICANT ANCIENT CENTERS IN PIEDMONT, Saluzzo was the capital of a marquisate in the mid-twelfth century. The town's ancient name, Salucula, means "noble residence," and Saluzzo was, in fact, a prosperous medieval center and later the seat of a Renaissance ducal court. Among the historical sites to see is La Castiglia, the town's medieval castle, built in the thirteenth century as a residence for the marquisate and later converted into a prison by King Carlo Alberto of Savoy in the early eighteenth century. Travelers should visit the Casa Cavassa, a fifteenth-century Renaissance structure which today houses the civic museum and whose beautiful interior, once the home of the local nobles, is decorated with a fresco cycle in grisaille and contains an exceptional display of furnishings from the fifteenth to the nineteenth centuries. Churches worthy of interest include the majestic late-Gothic cathedral, which dates to the fifteenth century and was built just outside the city walls on the site of an old parish church, and the Gothic church of San Giovanni, expanded and restructured to include the burial chapel of the marquises of Saluzzo in the apse.

Interior of Casa Cavassa, Saluzzo. Hans Clemer's painting, *Madonna della Misericordia*, hangs on a wall of magnificent wooden inlay.

facing page
An exquisite frame in gold leaf.

From the sixteenth to the eighteenth centuries Saluzzo was the chosen holiday destination for Turin's aristocracy, who built graceful houses and villas throughout the foothills and plains. The influx of the noble classes gave birth to a thriving furniture-making industry that still flourishes today. The so-called "Saluzzo style" is, in fact, one of the two principal lines of furnishings in Piedmont; the other is a rustic style popular mostly in the Alpine valleys. As these holiday homes were being erected they had to be furnished, and the availability of high-quality wood such as walnut, European oak, cherry, and pear encouraged local craftsmen to create furniture characterized by elegant shapes and accents; the effect was often obtained by the simple combination of different woods. Modern production began in the 1930s thanks to Amleto Bertoni from Faenza, who opened a workshop and school in Saluzzo. Bertoni promoted a traditional style founded on a few basic pieces of furniture—the chest of drawers, the glass cabinet, the writing desk—and his taste was inspired by the seventeenth and eighteenth centuries. The furniture makers of Saluzzo consciously re-create pieces using techniques from the period and the same wood as the original, sometimes recovered from older pieces of furniture. Traditional techniques of master furniture artisans have been handed down through generations and firsthand references on display in museums and private houses are ample.

In Piedmont, as in many of the Alpine regions, woodworking is a widespread activity with a long and glorious tradition. Fashioning objects from wood for everyday use, such as sleds and carts, household utensils, musical instruments, and furniture, is an age-old practice. In Val Varaita, Valstrona, and in the Pinerolo valleys rustic furniture is crafted from natural wood and is an important part of local livelihood. Closets, chests, sideboards, and tables in Swiss knotty pine are usually left in their natural color, unstained, preserving the abstract designs of the knots and veins in the wood, and are often decorated with geometrical patterns or figurative engravings. To see some of these masterpieces in wood visit the market in Pinerolo or the museum for traditional arts in the center of town.

Saluzzo hosts a national furniture fair each September, affording local craftsmen the opportunity to exhibit their creations. A popular spot for furniture shoppers is the Centro Liquidazione Mobili at Casalgrasso, which sells pieces from local furniture exhibitions. Scour through the incredible selection of antique furniture at Coccolino Brothers, Rustico, or Castagnole Monferrato da Peschera. Typical Piedmontese furniture can be seen at the palazzina di caccia (hunting lodge) at Stupinigi, one of the residences of the Royal House of Savoy or at the furniture museum in Pinasca in the province of Turin.

TURIN
WRITING WITH STYLE

TURIN IS A CITY OF MAIN THOROUGHFARES AND TREE-LINED BOULEVARDS; its people are rational, hard-working, and proud. Known as the Italian capital of the automobile, Turin is also the city of old-fashioned cafés. Beside the windows of neon-lit fast-food restaurants a strong sense of the past lingers in the city's historical buildings, many of which are redolent of Masonic orders. Turin is known for manufacturing fountain pens that are the least practical, least functional, and most expensive in the world. The fountain pen is often seen casually placed on the desks of those who decide the future of a country; or half-hidden in the top pockets of individuals who move millions of euros on a daily basis; or in the hands of legislators who sign treaties weighing war and peace. The existence of the reservoir pen can be traced as far back as the tenth century, possibly further, but the fountain pen as we know it dates to the seventeenth century and is described in Diderot and d'Alembert's *Encyclopédie* as "a sort of pen designed to contain ink that descends a little at a time, without having to use an inkwell." This stylish writing implement enjoyed its greatest popularity in the late nineteenth century in the United States, when the prestigious Waterman and Parker brands were established. In Italy the first fountain-pen factories were opened in Milan, in 1919, by the Verga Brothers, who produced the Columbus Safety Pen no.1; and in Bologna, in 1919, by Omas and Officina Meccanica Armando Simoni. In the same year the Fabbrica Italiana di Penne a Serbatoio invented the Aurora model, and the company began producing pens that were similar to their American counterparts, made in ebonite and sometimes laminated in gold, with retractable or fixed nibs, and with either an eyedropper or automatic filling method. They were an instant success throughout the social classes, and different styles were developed for specialized shops, newsstands, railway stations, and businesses. At the close of World War II the Aurora company commissioned Marcello Nizzoli (one of the foremost proponents of Italian industrial design) to design a new pen. The result, in 1947, was the Aurora 88, the most successful fountain pen ever to be produced in Italy; its advertisement slogan was "Beautiful and Faithful," and its clever feature was a window on the filler that allowed the ink level to be seen. The Duo Cart, packaged with an extra ink cartridge, was equally successful particularly among students and traveling businesspeople who were guaranteed plenty of ink. Today the most popular models are the Magellano, the most modern; the 1930s-style Optima; and the Gioiello, which is reminiscent of the Aurora 88.

A fountain pen of the Aurora Optima line in variegated blue auroloid with gold finish and a 14-carat gold nib.

facing page
Model of an antique car in the Museum of Contemporary Art in the Rivoli Castle, near Turin.

The world-famous Shroud of Turin, believed to bear the image of Christ's face, is preserved in the royal chapel in the Cathedral of Saint John the Baptist at the center of town. Despite numerous scientific studies and fierce debate among historians, theologians, scientists, and the faithful, the mystery of the Shroud's origin persists. While at the cathedral, stop by the nearby Regia Farmacia, originally the court apothecary, which still specializes in the preparation of medicaments based on ancient prescriptions. Among these are the Elisir di lunga vita (elixir for a long life) and the Balsamo di Gerusalemme (Jerusalem balsam), whose recipe dates back to the early 1700s and whose pungent odor has been described by some as incense and by others as "moldering flowers." Some believe, however, that Jerusalem balsam is a cure-all and it is said to have been widely used by members of parliament during the reign of the House of Savoy in the nineteenth century.

The Aurora fountain pen factory lies on the road leading to the Stura abbey. Fountain pens can be purchased at Torino Penna, Stilografiche Monasterolo, Quill, or Gibus. Just north of Turin at Castellamonte the ancient tradition of ceramic-making is kept alive and some of the finest examples of terra-cotta tiles and ceramic products, including, for those with enough space, stoves made of iron and covered with kiln-fired ceramic, can be found at Castellamonte Crea, Maria Teresa Rosa, or Ceramiche Cielle.

VALENZA

GEMSTONES AND JEWELS

WORKING PRECIOUS METALS HAS BEEN AN IMPORTANT ACTIVITY IN PIEDMONT for a long time; this is primarily due to the presence of the Savoy royal family and the nobles who attended the court. At the end of the eighteenth century, the major production of jewelry and silver work was in Vercelli and Alessandria, where tools and rare hallmarked pieces that date back five hundred years are preserved. Today little of this work is done in Vercelli, but Alessandria is still an important center for the manufacture of silver work. Many workshops create traditional pieces, in addition to exquisite contemporary objects that are sculpture-like.

The fertile countryside around Valenza.

facing page
A precious example of the goldsmith's art.

Since the nineteenth century Valenza has become the jewelry capital, but this ascendancy was a gradual process. At that time Valenza was still a small village on the right bank of the Po River. Fired with enthusiasm and good ideas, some enterprising craftspeople moved to Valenza where they rediscovered an ancient local craft. Legend has it that even in the past there were many craftspeople working the gold from the surrounding mines and that hundreds of slaves were chained along the banks of the Po to dredge the sand in order to extract gold nuggets. This activity took place within the walls of the city, which was named after the Roman consul Valente. Craftsmanship has been passed down from father to son and perfected along the way. It has enabled Valenza to reach unparalleled heights in technology; that along with the creative genius of its craftspeople has transformed this little town on the Po into the world's jewelry capital.

In contrast to others, the goldsmiths of Valenza have turned their trade into an art form. They start with the design of the models; then they work on the fusion of the gold and the cutting of the precious stones. The final setting is an art of which they are masters. In the mid-twentieth century the Fascist government contributed to their craft: it was forbidden to import gold, and goldsmiths were forced to use less precious metals; they had to make elaborate jewelry that would justify their "preciousness" and their cost—the high cost of workmanship had to compensate for the modest cost of the basic material. After the fall of fascism, the craftspeople started to work with more expensive metals and stones. There are now thirteen hundred small workshops in Valenza; the artisans there work with tons of precious metals every year. And at the end of the day's work, the town's sewers are rigorously checked so that there is no loss of gold or silver after the workers have cleaned up.

Alessandria is Italy's major producer of fine silver work. This craft dates back many centuries (some workshops have hallmarks from the sixteenth century) and it is still important. The city is renowned throughout the world for its silver work. Alessandria's silversmiths have been able to preserve their heritage and ancient traditions. Much of their production is faithful to classic pieces—candelabra, ewers, plates, platters, table decorations, jewel boxes, picture frames, and various other decorative objects. But many craftspeople invent original objects, bringing contemporary designs to the market.

Jewelry sellers include Fabbrica dell'Oro, MG Gold, and Orostaff Preziosi. Vincenza, in the Veneto, is also famous for gold jewelry. In Piedmont, Alessandria, Vercelli, and Nizza Monferrato in the Astigiano are famous for silver work. There is a museum of the history of Italian gold in Lerma (in Alessandria).

VARALLO SESIA
LACE FOR THE QUEEN

VARALLO IS THE CAPITAL OF THE VALSESIA. VIEWED FROM THE BELVEDERE of the Sacro Monte, the town looks beautifully designed, mapped out like a mosaic on the left bank of the river. There does not seem to be any separation among the medieval neighborhoods—Mercanti (merchants), il Grano (grain), San Rocco, and San Cristoforo. There is no trace of the city walls that existed or of the covered walkway that led from San Marco Church just outside the village to the great double-arched gateway; the gate was closed at night to protect the city from bandits. Some consider it unforgivable that these historic features were destroyed. The road that led from the stairway of San Gaudenzio to the clock has been demolished. The Franciscan convent was razed to make space for Piazza Gaudenzio Ferrari. The valley road was widened because it was too narrow and twisting to bear the traffic of carts and carriages. The Sacro Monte attracted such a large number of pilgrims to Varallo that a hospital was built in the mid-sixteenth century at a time when larger and more prosperous cities did not have such facilities. In 1584 even San Carlo Borromeo visited. Queen Margaret of Savoy frequently went to Monte Rosa; the observatory-refuge that was built just below the mountain peak in 1893 was dedicated to her. Despite its detractors, Varallo was commended for its careful urban redevelopment during the Architecture Exposition in 1890.

In the Valsesia area, the wool-weaving tradition has been passed down through generations. There are the weaving factories of Borgomanero, as well as work created by residents using handmade winders with which they spin wool for scarves and sweaters. In the tenth century the Saracens arrived in the valley. Although they did many destructive things, documents confirm that they taught the native women the refined art of *puncetto*, a kind of needle lace. This is a cotton lace made in a close-knit web of bridges, called *ragno* or spider, tied with slipknots and intersecting at right angles. For centuries, puncetto was a dowry of young brides; it was also used to decorate the traditional feast-day costumes. This lace work was rediscovered at the end of the nineteenth century by Queen Margaret, and from that time it became the most sought after decoration of ladies of the court. The tradition continues because of the schools throughout the region, particularly in Rossa, that teach young women the craft; today the lace is used mostly for sashes, borders, and decorative elements for bed linens, doilies, and tablecloths. Some small and exquisitely made articles are even framed and displayed in living rooms.

facing page
Delicate handmade lace in white and colored thread.

below
The basilica of Sacro Monte at Varallo.

The Alpàa, a market and exhibition of puncetto lace and local crafts, is held during the second week of July. Textiles can be purchased at the Lanificio Loro Piana of Romagnano Sesia. In Borgomanero, lingerie is sold at the Maglificio di Borgomanero outlet; Tessuti Chic sells fabrics of all types. Knitted cotton and wool goods can be purchased at Filatura in Grignasco.

The painter/sculptor Gaudenzio Ferrari was born in Varallo Sesia. He produced some of the most important works of Renaissance art in northern Italy. They are preserved in Varallo's Pinacoteca, or picture gallery, and are scattered in the churches of the valley—Madonna di Loreto, Santa Maria delle Grazie, and, most important, in Sacro Monte, for which he made a series of remarkably realistic life-size statues. Varallo's Sacro Monte was one of the first of its kind in the western Alps and is still one of the most grandiose: forty-five chapels, one thousand incredibly realistic life-size figures in terracotta, hundreds of frescoes, and works by local artists. A unique representation in one of the chapels, "New Jerusalem," illustrates the holy places; this way the faithful who could not afford to make the pilgrimage themselves could see them.

VERBANIA

REAL AND FAUX MARBLE

MANY STONE AND MARBLE QUARRIES ARE LOCATED ALONG THE WESTERN BANK of Lake Maggiore, in Verbania, Baveno, Mergozzo, Gravellona Toca, and Ornavasso. The quarried stones become building materials or works of art. Baveno has pink granite, Mergozzo has green; there is rose-colored stone at Candoglia, and white at Montorfano. Quarrying has led to specialization by stonecutters and sculptors, who are still involved in the commercial production of granite blocks for building (paving stone, roofing, wall covering and columns, boundary markers, fountains, basins, and fireplaces). Sculptures—statues and religious and civic monuments in classic and contemporary styles—are also created.

A marble quarry at Ossola.

facing page
Jean Nouvel's tea and coffee set is now a famous Alessi product.

The most impressive testimonial of the quality of Verbania's marble quarries is the duomo in Milan, with its surprising wealth of sculpture: there are more than thirty-four hundred statues, in addition to ninety-six gigantic gargoyles, and hundreds of figures sculpted in high relief. Almost all of the original statues are preserved in the Duomo Museum to protect them from the damaging effects of the weather. These have been replaced with reproductions made of Candoglia marble, which comes from the fourteenth-century quarry that was reserved for the building of the duomo. In 1506 the stonecutters of these mountains sculpted the twelve columns for the porch of the Lazzaretto. The columns were transported to Milan on barges that sailed from the Toce River along the shores of Lake Maggiore, the Ticino, and the Naviglio Grande. In 1830 stones were transported to Rome for the construction of the eighty-two columns in the San Paolo Fuori le Mura Basilica. They traveled the entire way by water; it took four years for them to arrive in the capital.

Although nearby Valsesia has a rich supply of marble and granite, in past centuries residents were involved in an unusual activity, given their access to these resources: from the beginning of the nineteenth century, Rima San Giuseppe was the center for the manufacture of faux marble. The artistry involved was revered by all the courts of Europe and brought wealth to this little mountain village. To make faux marble, a paste of white cement is mixed with a base color. Cracks appear once the paste is spread; these are filled in with different colors to imitate the veins in real marble. The panels are then affixed to the surface to be covered and finished by smoothing them with a series of rough stones; the result is lovely. Until the 1960s, craftspeople from Rima San Giuseppe adorned important buildings throughout Europe and overseas with their faux marble. Today the tradition is still alive primarily for restoration purposes.

Various types of stone and marble are available in Verbania at M&SI, or in Cureggio at Granital. Artistic ceramics are also made in Verbania and can be purchased at the PRG Laboratory. In nearby Valstrona, in Fornero and Piana di Fornero, there are many small workshops that make wood crafts.

Gignese is a small village in the Vergante; it is close to Lake Maggiore and can be reached by a private road. There is an unusual building in the village. It is in the form of three open umbrellas placed side by side (there is a good view of the building from the steps of San Maurizio Church). This building houses the Museum of the Umbrella and the Parasol, and there is a collection of more than fifteen hundred umbrellas and parasols from the seventeenth century to the present. One hundred fifty are displayed in glass cases; their ivory and silver handles are particularly interesting. Umbrella and parasol-making has been an activity in the village for a couple of centuries; Gignese is known as "the village of umbrellas." Alongside the few factories that remain, there are craftspeople who make unique umbrellas and parasols with exquisitely carved handles.

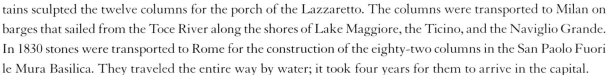

BERGAMO
THE ART OF STAINED GLASS

GLASSMAKING HAS A LONG AND MYSTERIOUS HISTORY, most likely beginning thousands of years ago in Mesopotamia, perhaps invented by the Phoenicians who taught the Egyptians, or the other way around. According to a Phoenician legend handed down by Pliny the Elder, glass was discovered accidentally by some Phoenician merchants who were on their way home from Egypt. During a stop on the sandy banks of a river they used blocks of *natrum* (saltpeter) to contain their fires. The following morning they discovered that the sand and the saltpeter had fused together forming a very hard material that they had never seen before; it was shiny and transparent.

The Phoenicians began to make glass and took it to Egypt, where amulets and other small objects have been found dating to the third millennium BC. The oldest glass object known is Egyptian and is considered the official first use of the material. It is a bottle from the reign of the Pharaoh Thutmose III (1457–1424 BC) and it is preserved in the British Museum in London. Glassmaking spread from Egypt to the Middle East and the Mediterranean. It was already known in Etruria in the center of the Italian peninsula by the ninth century BC; some centuries later it was highly prized by the Romans who encouraged new and different ways of working it to obtain more elegant results. Cicero wrote that "a person should be considered to be poor if he does not possess a house that is hung with sheets of glass." The Romans created extraordinary colors by using metal oxides (an example is the *Vaso con amorini* found in Pompeii), and it is possible that they invented the technique of blowing glass at low temperatures to make decorative molds. Objects include ancient "roman" bottles in geometrical shapes. Among the many forms of glass craftsmanship and art, one of the most creative was certainly the making of stained-glass windows. The technique resembled mosaic or inlay but used lead to hold the glass together. Churches encouraged this work and this led to the development of artisan workshops in every region of Italy, both for making new windows and restoring of old ones. Splendid examples of stained-glass windows made by famous artists can be seen in many Gothic cathedrals, the duomo in Milan in particular. Art nouveau arrived during the twentieth century and spurred the use of the stained-glass technique; windows, doors, screens, lamps, and mirrors were created. Today there are many workshops that make stained glass for private homes and public buildings; many of these works are commissioned. Sometimes they are inspired by religious subjects; sometimes they are based on original ideas. Traditional stained-glass techniques are still in use. Pieces of glass are placed together, painted with a brown opaque enamel, and spliced together with lead.

A crafts show and market is held in the Città Alta on the second and third Sundays of each month, except in July and August. Stained glass is made in many workshops in the area between Milan and Bergamo: Mariano Carrara is in Castelli Calepio, Vecos is in Gorle, Anna Venturi is in Monza, and Grassi Vetrate Artistiche is in Milan. Other stained-glass makers can be found in the Vincenza area (Carion at Creazzo), in Tuscany (Punto Vetro at Cenaia), in Rome (Paolo Corpetto), in Campania (Adam at Telese Terme), and in Vietri a Mare (Perotti).

The valleys of Bergamo were once known for their ironwork. The Nossa River is only one-third of a mile long but has an abundance of water. In addition to two mills and a small power plant on its banks, there are four forges with huge power hammers, one of which was in use until 1987. A foundry-hammer museum at Ponte Nossa contains tools, equipment, and important documents relating to the history of ironwork in the area. Valtrompia, in Brescia, is known for mining and working iron. There is a tour of iron and mines. It begins in Ome, where there is a museum complex in a forge dating to 1155. Then tour groups see the forges and power hammers of Sarezzo, the furnace at Tavernole on the Mella River, the Marzoli mines of Pezzare, and the great factories of Sant'Aloisio.

facing page
A example of leaded glass in the Art Nouveau style.

below
The piazza of the Duomo in Bergamo, and the church of Santa Maria Maggiore in the background.

BRIANZA

INTERIOR DESIGN

SOME OF THE MOST IMPORTANT FURNITURE DESIGNS EVER MADE originated in the area between the Adda and Seveso rivers to the north of Milan. One example: the *Sacco* armchair produced by Zanotta in 1968, which is exhibited at the Museum of Modern Art in New York. Until the beginning of the twentieth century, Brianza was a resort area where residents of Milan spent their weekends. Today it is a leader in the decorative-arts industry, with sixty-five hundred small- to medium-size companies producing 20 percent of the nation's output. But even more important is that the work of the most famous designers of the moment are manufactured in Brianza.

Brianza has been specializing in designing and constructing furniture longer than any other region. Furniture-making in the area started in the mid-nineteenth century, when owners of the new patrician villas needed high-quality pieces to furnish their homes. At first the favored aesthetic was inlay; it became known on the market as the *mobile di Cantù* (Cantù furniture). After World War I, furniture-makers became inspired by more innovative and unconventional models, by the art nouveau movement, by Giò Ponti's "Stile 900," and by the Bauhaus. This created a tight bond between the designer and the producer. It was the basis of the Italian design movement that exploded in the 1950s, when *design* (an English word that was unknown to the Italians at that time) became "the beautiful shape of the useful article." This was not art for art's sake but art applied to functional yet beautiful objects for everyday use.

At the end of World War II mass-produced furniture became popular; millions of apartments that had been destroyed needed to be furnished, and every effort was made to create functional but cheap pieces. This too was a challenge met with creative solutions. In Brianza the domestic landscape became an area for experimentation, the furniture factory a laboratory of ideas. Designers found fertile ground for their visions in the small size of the factories and in the open minds of their owners, characteristics that allowed them to take creative risks in a flexible environment. In this atmosphere revolutionary furniture was made.

Many furniture designs created at that time have reached iconic status: the *Sogno* (Dream) armchair by Giuseppe Terragni in 1934. Today it is manufactured by Zanotta and is called *Follia* (Madness). One of the most emblematic ideas was the *UP* (pouf and armchair) system by Gaetano Pesca. It was designed in 1969 and is still in production. Since the war there has been no limit to the creativity of these designers.

An Arflex shop window.

facing page
The "Libreria Graduate" designed by Jean Nouvel for the Molteni & C. company.

Furniture can be purchased directly at factories, and it is also possible to visit the many expositions such as Area International and Carate Brianza. In Casirate d'Adda there is a market where antiques and restored furniture are sold. Almenno San Bartolomeo has a museum dedicated to wood craftsmanship. It also displays some rare bicycles such as an 1820 Draisina and an 1861 Michandini, and bicycles belonging to famous past champions such as Coppi and Gimondi. Bicycles are sold at Bianchi in Treviglio.

Tour groups fill the streets of Brianza, as do professional cyclists, who train for road races by riding up the steep slope of Brunate in Como or the Ghisallo in the Lariano Triangle. This climb is as hard as anything in the Giro d'Italia. At Ghisallo there is a repository of cycling shirts, trophies, and bicycles belonging to champions and enthusiasts. It is not by chance that bicycles with a capital "B" are built in Brianza: Colnago is located here. The company has been building original bicycles for the last fifty years, and it is the mecca for champions from around the world. The company uses the highest-quality components and carbon-fiber monocoque bodies; their bikes are constructed using research from Ferrari. Other great bicycle-makers—Cinelli and Caleppio in Settala and Bianchi in Treviglio—are farther south.

CANNETO SULL'OGLIO
TOY LAND

LOCATED BETWEEN CREMONA AND MANTUA IN THE COUNTRYSIDE of the lower Po River valley, on the banks of the Oglio River, is Canneto, so-called because of the thick vegetation of reeds or *canne* that cover the banks of the river. Agriculture dominates the economy of the village, which still preserves some remnants of its prosperous medieval past—the massive tower of the San Genesio Castle is one example. The toy museum is housed in a nineteenth-century red brick building within sight of the village. It is dedicated to Giulio Superti Furga, a doll manufacturer, and contains a display of dolls from the nineteenth century to the present. They are dressed in velvets and silks, with ringlets that peek out from caps of ribbons and lace. There are also puppets and various other toys, from rocking horses to miniature furniture. This would be sufficient for Canneto to earn the moniker of "Toy Town," but it is just the tip of the iceberg. Dozens of companies and thousands of people are involved in the manufacture of toys that are exported throughout the world. The first doll-making factory in Italy was founded by Luigi Furga Gornini in Canneto sull'Oglio in 1880. He was a nobleman from Mantua who, by 1870, already had a mask-production workshop in the village. His first dolls were made by hand using molds and papier-mâché; the heads were a composite of stearin and chalk. The eyes were made of blown glass, the hair of mohair, although the most beautiful dolls had wigs made of real hair. Doll-making evolved, and soon heads were made out of bisque (unglazed china) mounted on a body with some parts in wood and others in papier-mâché. Then came felt dolls, stuffed cotton dolls, others in ceramic, polystyrene, and vinyl, with moving eyes, jointed arms and legs, and ceramic teeth. In the 1920s, Furga produced baby dolls in bisque and dolls that looked like real children. But he became world famous for his models in vinyl. They were less elaborate but very popular. Ambrogino was the most famous of them all, Tonino had his high chair, and Bebè took its first steps in a baby walker. In the 1940s, Furga also produced a "Trunk with a Doll" made in wood and divided into compartments to store clothes and accessories, and a "Closet with a Doll" that revealed a folding bed when it was opened. Today, these rare collectors' pieces can be found throughout the world, wherever the company's dolls were exported. The company began exporting in the first decades of the twentieth century, and doll and toy manufacturing in Canneto became a bigger business with many small factories beginning to manufacture dolls and toys of every kind; it became one of the major toy-manufacturing areas in Europe.

The arcade of Piazza delle Erbe in Mantua with stalls selling books and prints.

facing page
An enchanted window of dolls and fairies.

Dolls are sold in Canneto at the Fairplast factory outlet. Many beautiful dolls can also be found nearby, at Andy, in Sotto il Monte, and at Fer Giochi in Mantua. In Cogliate, Giochi Prezioni is an interesting outlet where many toy brands are sold at reasonable prices.

There are many interesting museums in the area. In addition to the museum in Canneto sull'Oglio, there is a museum of dolls in Rocca di Angera (Varese), which is among the most important in Europe. It contains an extraordinary collection of dolls, toys, books, and miniature furniture. The Museum of Toys and the Child, housed in the historic Istituto dei Martinitt in Milan, is one of the largest of its kind in Europe. The Chicco Museum of Toy Horses is in Grandate (Como) and houses the richest private collection of toys in the world. It is located in the Manzoni Stables, where the legendary 1950s thoroughbred Tornese was born. The museum of miniature trains is housed in the former Rivarossi factory in Como. In Bologna there is an impressive national museum of toy soldiers, with a collection of about forty-five thousand pieces, twelve thousand of which are on display.

COMO

SILKS FOR THE BEAUTIFUL PEOPLE

MILANESE NOBLES CHOSE THE SHORES OF SERENE LAKE COMO to build luxury country villas that were later inhabited by English poets and literary personalities. Today, celebrities flock to this area. George Clooney lives in Laglio in Villa Oleandra; Richard Gere is a guest in Blevio and is looking for a home, as are Brad Pitt and car-racer Michael Schumacher. Saadi al Gheddafi owns a villa in Moltrasio; the Rockefeller Foundation is housed in Bellagio; and, in exchange for a publicity campaign, Madonna has asked Donatella Versace for the use of Villa Fontanelle in Moltrasio.

Como also is home to some of the leading silk producers, including Mantero and Ratti. Silk production is one of the world's major industries, and East Asia is Italy's fiercest competition. In the 1970s, 95 percent of the ties sold in New York came from Como; only 5 percent came from China. Today it is the exact opposite.

While weaving is a very old activity in Como, silk production only started in the sixteenth century with the first silkworms imported from the East by Ludovico il Moro. They were fed on the mulberry bushes that he himself had planted in the garden of the castle at Vigevano. The "Moro" name derives from the berry of this bush, called moro. This date is

Soft printed silk from the Ratti silkworks.

facing page
Ties designed by Pierangelo Masciadri are exclusively produced by craftsmen.

very late considering that fragments of silk fabric were found in the tombs of the Yin dynasty in China and dated from the second millennium BC. But the Chinese zealously guarded the secret of silk production. Legend has it that a princess stole the berries by putting them in her braids. An Indian prince kidnapped her, but then she appeared on a Pisan galley and was then purchased by a craftsperson from Lucca.

The true part of this legend is that there were three thousand silk looms in Lucca in the thirteenth century. This silk was considered the most beautiful in the world, and silk production spread throughout Italy. Until the beginning of the nineteenth century, handwoven Como silk was produced solely for the nobles of Milan. Mechanical looms were introduced later and increased productivity, and the city became the largest silk-weaving center in the Western world, known for the quality and originality of its products. It even man-

Very specialized products—colorful blown-glass balls—are made in Bellagio. These balls decorate Christmas trees. The village sits on the land that divides the branch of Lake Como from that of Lecco, and there are many beautiful villas and lush gardens. The Latin writer Pliny the Younger lived near the village, and a castle was later built there. The eighteenth-century Villa Serbelloni can be found here, with its enormous park overlooking the end of the lake and the Alpine mountain range. Villa Melzi d'Eril was built in 1808 by Duke Francesco Melzi d'Eril, an aide to Napoleon. It is a beautiful neoclassical building replete with frescoes and stucco, and has a lovely terrace with a view of the lake. An incredible show of azaleas and rhododendrons in the spring complements the park's splendid statues.

aged to beat competition from France, which had dominated the European market in the eighteenth century. The industry developed even further after World War II, and today there are still eighteen thousand people employed in thousands of factories; the silk threads they weave are mostly imported. Half of the output is exported. The most popular silk items are scarves, shawls, ties, clothing, and furnishings.

The Ratti Museum and the teaching museum of silk are must-sees. Another silk museum is located in Abbadia Lariana. The town's main shopping street is Via Vittorio Emanuele, on the pedestrian mall, but good deals can be found at the company outlets: Diffusione Seta Outlet in Como, Emporio Pinto in Casnate, Frey in Fino Moresco, and B&B Cravatte in the industrial area of Bulgarogrosso. Giovannini in San Fermo sells hand-painted ties. Glass Christmas balls are sold at Mortelmans in Bellagio.

CREMONA

CITY OF MUSIC

CLAUDIO MONTEVERDI, ANDREA AMATI, AND ANTONIO STRADIVARI changed the history of music and that of Cremona, where they all were born. Agriculture could have remained the dominant economic force in the town. Instead, music began to monopolize the economic and social life of Cremona. At the end of the sixteenth century, master lute-maker Amati founded a school for his craft, and he defined the shape and size in which violins would be made until the end of the nineteenth century. A hundred years later, Stradivari perfected the technique for building stringed instruments, elevating it to an art form and making it possible to produce extraordinary sounds from a small box of fir wood. In the seventeenth century, Monteverdi invented opera. Only a little less famous were the nineteenth-century composer Amilcare Ponchielli and Giuseppe Antonio Guarneri, a violin-maker who was as masterful as Amati and Stradivari. Indeed, in 1797, Niccolò Paganini, the greatest violinist of all time, began his career with a violin made by Guarneri; it was nicknamed "the cannon" for the purity and power of its sound.

From the Middle Ages, Lombardy had been a fertile region for music; it was a time when the Church mandated music for voice only and resorted to castration to obtain the delicate male soprano sound. But the palazzos of the nobility indulged in the seductive sounds of the viola and lutes. The best-known composer of the first half of the sixteenth century, Francesco da Milano, was invited to the Gonzaga and the Farnese courts; at the same time, Pellegrino da Montechiaro and Gasparo Bertolotti da Salò were transforming the viola into a smaller and more manageable instrument, capable of incredible virtuosity and a wide range of brilliant and powerful sounds. At first, the violin was used solely by strolling players, because it was easy to carry. In the seventeenth century it was accepted by people in learned music circles; serious scores were written and the violin enjoyed two golden centuries thanks to the art of the Brescia and Cremona instrument-makers. The advent of the harpsichord and later the piano checked the violin's success, but in the twentieth century the violin returned to favor.

Today, more than one hundred workshops in Cremona make musical instruments. They work under the Denomination of Controlled Origin "Cremona Liuteria," which ensures quality. The truly exceptional violins made in Cremona are still called Stradivari, Amati, or Guarneri, heirs of the dynasties that established a high level of craftsmanship more than five hundred years ago.

Sunset in Piazza Duomo, Cremona, with a view of the Duomo and the Baptistery.

facing page
The sinuous curves of a valuable violin.

The construction of the violin reached its epitome of perfection with Antonio Stradivari, but his workshop was active only until 1743, when his son died. Count Cozio di Salabue purchased the contents of the workshop; a lute-maker named Guadagnini continued this work. In 1920 it was purchased by Giuseppe Fiorini, who donated it to the Civic Museum of Cremona; it contains a reconstruction of Stradivari's workshop. The museum presents the history of lute- and violin-making, including hundreds of tools used by the masters, and drawings and shapes of violins. The museum also presents the history of instrument-making in Cremona, from Andrea Amati to Giuseppe Antonio Guarneri. A triennial exhibition of stringed instruments is held in the town, and Cremona Mondo Musica, an exposition of musical instruments and accessories for stringed instruments, takes place during the first half of October.

Musical instruments are sold at the Consorzio Liutai Stradivari or at Brugnini & Beck. Violins also can be purchased at the following places: Bottega Artigiana in Cossato, Piedmont; Liuteria Centro Musica, in Breganse, Veneto; Rossiti in Tolmezzo, Friuli; Eggimann, in Lucca, Tuscany; Cingoli in Borgani, Marche; and Raffaele Calace in Naples, Campania. In the province of Cremona, Casalmaggiore is known for its production of costume jewelry. There is also a gem museum and an interesting museum of prints in Soncino.

GARDONE
VALTROMPIA
THE ARMED VALLEY

VALTROMPIA IS SITUATED IN THE MOUNTAINS BEYOND BRESCIA, and since ancient Roman times it has been known for its iron mines and forges. Documents from the second half of the fourteenth century confirm the presence of armories in forges on the banks of the Mellathe River. These forges were particularly active during the domination of the Venetian Republic. Five centuries ago, armor was made there for Charles V; daggers were made for the Emperor Francis I; and harquebuses were made for almost every European army.

In 1526 Bartolomeo Beretta founded a factory in Gardone Valtrompia, and at the end of the seventeenth century he began to produce firearms that have been used in more than the three thousand wars during the last four hundred years. The company has seen almost five centuries of success in the field of metallurgy and precision mechanics—and more, if one believes that the factory was already active in the fifteenth century. There is a museum of Beretta weapons located in the former armory of the Fabbrica d'Armi Beretta (Beretta Weapons Factory), which was built in 1880. The famous Beretta pistol is standard issue for the Italian army and the police, but it is also standard issue in other countries, including the United States, France, Spain, and Turkey. Beretta supplies the smp/cx4 pistol to NATO; in the near future the company hopes to sell it to China and Russia. This weapon can be used with munitions of four different calibers. But the pistol is not the only reason to be proud. At the 1956 Melbourne Olympics, the Beretta won the gold medal for clay-pigeon shooting, and since then victories have come in quick succession: Rome 1960, Munich 1972, Montreal 1976, Moscow 1980, Los Angeles 1984, Seoul 1988, and Barcelona 2002, not to mention world championships. Today the bulk of the output is used for sports, hunting, and target shooting, among other activities. Automatic weapons, carbines, and semiautomatic pistols are acclaimed around the world for their safety and precision and constitute 98 percent of the production, 70 percent of which is exported. A Beretta Gallery opened in New York; in addition to firearms, it sells clothing and accessories. Beretta also produces weapon components, such as telescopes. The production departments are highly specialized and mechanized. The design is excellent, some of which is the work of the automobile designer Giorgetto Giugiaro, and they are always finished by hand; this makes each of the fifteen hundred pieces produced each day unique.

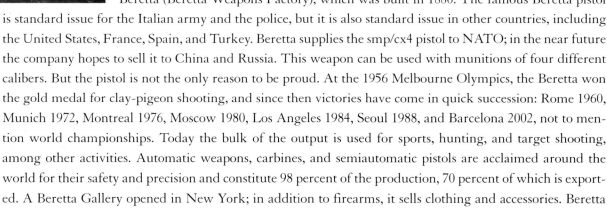

Monte Guglielmo in Valtrompia.

facing page
The elegant engraving on the stock of a Beretta hunting rifle.

Weapons of every kind are sold at the Armeria Brignoli in Gardone Valtrompia. Creative Art and Giovannelli make beautiful engravings on weapons. Some shields and armor are also made, as are weapons which are exported to the United States. The Exa is the most important exhibition of light sporting weapons in Europe. Displayed are items including bulletproof jackets and small pink pistols that can be transported in handbags.

The Luigi Marzoli Museum in Mastio Visconteo di Brescia exhibits weapons and armor. The collection contains more than one thousand pieces made from the fifteenth to the eighteenth century, mostly from Brescia and Lombardy. It constitutes one of the most important international collections of its kind. It details the long tradition and the "warlike genius" of the area. Brescia is also the city of the Mille Miglia, the legendary auto race that was famous until the 1950s; it ended because of traffic and safety problems. Crowds of spectators waited along the Via Emilia and the Apennines, all the way to Rome, to watch the Ferraris and Maseratis, the Mercedes and Aston Martins, applauding Nuvolari, Ascari, Fangio, and Moss. The Mille Miglia has been resurrected, though transformed into a race of antique cars.

MILAN

READY-TO-WEAR

ALTHOUGH IT IS SMALL COMPARATIVELY, THE ONLY REAL METROPOLIS IN ITALY IS MILAN; its population of one and a half million people is less than that in one borough in New York City. The highest skyscraper, the beautiful Pirelli, only has thirty-four floors. Via Montenapoleone is the main street for jewelry and fashion but is nothing compared to the Rue Faubourg Saint-Honoré in Paris. It is also true that Milan can be a step behind: the first underground rail system only opened in 1964. But Milan is in the vanguard in some areas, and fashion is one. It moved into the forefront of fashion in 1979 when the first fashion show was organized at the Fiera. It has captured the haute-couture title from Rome and from Florence, where fashion was born. Milan has become a trendsetter. "Made-in-Italy" was established with extravagant and innovative style and Milan became the capital of ready-to-wear clothing. In the 1980s, it is said that rich American women arrived in Milan without any luggage; they replenished their wardrobes in the boutiques along Via Montenapoleone, but also at Rinascente, the department store under the porticoes of Piazza del Duomo. Young stylists like Armani, Versace, Ferré, and Dolce & Gabbana became as well-known as Krizia, Missoni, and Valentino. In the United States Armani espoused a philosophy of life more than a way of dressing. He made the pages of *Time* and his success skyrocketed with the film *American Gigolo* (Richard Gere lines up his clothes on the bed: Armani jackets, shirts, and ties). Missoni was working for Rinascente before it began showcasing its own label, and now its designs are on display at the Metropolitan Museum of Art in New York. Ferré has been appointed creative director of the house of Dior, something that created a scandal in the world of French fashion. But the French came around and awarded Ferré the *De d'or* (the Golden Thimble), the Oscar of fashion. In 1986 Domenico Dolce, a tailor, and Stefano Gabbana, a designer, presented their first collection of sensual and elegant "shabby chic" clothes. Celebrities such as Madonna were enthralled. It was probably Versace, however, who left the most indelible mark. He "made" the top models, the icons of modern women from the 1980s to the present. Claudia Schiffer, Cindy Crawford, and Naomi Campbell—models for women to imitate and men to fantasize about—are his creations. Today a new "fashion city" is being created in Milan between Piazza della Repubblica and the Garibaldi neighborhood. There will be a museum, professional schools, and a university, and areas for fashion shows.

DMagazine Outlet is on Via Montenapoleone in Milan. It sells high-end clothing, shoes, and accessories at reasonable prices. Emporio Isola on Via Prina is another discounter. Fifteen different clothing and accessory brands can be found at Griffe Diffusion by Mariella Burani on Via Rizzoli or in Arluno. The Dolce & Gabbana outlet is on Legnano; Krizia is on San Giuliano Milanese. Shoes are sold at Visa on Via Jenner. The Fratelli Rossetti outlet is in Parabiago.

The industrial and commercial image of Milan, hardworking and bustling, does not overshadow its tourist attractions. Whatever the reason for visiting the city, no one should pass up on an aperitif in the nineteenth-century Galleria Vittorio Emanuele, or miss the view of the Grigne framed by the forests of spires on the cupola of the magnificent Duomo, or forego the line to see, for a moment, Leonardo da Vinci's *The Last Supper*. The Duomo is the largest and most complex example of Italian Gothic art; its construction began in 1386 by Galeazzo Visconti III, first duke of Milan, and was completed in 1809. The Basilica di Sant'Ambrogio is the most important building of medieval Milan and set a precedent for all Lombard Romanesque churches. The simplicity of line contrasts with the sumptuousness of the basilica's interior—mosaics glitter in the apse and the main altar is decorated in gold and precious stones. Santa Maria delle Grazie, where Leonardo's *The Last Supper* is housed, is the most important Renaissance building in the city. The apse, cloister, and sacristy are the work of the architect Bramante. The oldest church in the city is San Lorenzo Maggiore, dating to the fourth century but renovated many times. It is flanked by a colonnade from a Roman temple from the third century. The Castello Sforzesco, the residence of the Sforza family, was built in 1386 and almost entirely rebuilt in the nineteenth century. Among the famous works of art to be found in the museum housed within the Castello is the unfinished *Rondanini Pietà*, said to be Michelangelo's last work.

facing page
The veiled light in the Vittorio Emanuele Gallery, Milan's sitting room.

below
Milan's Piazza della Scala at night.

The tradition of Italian design was born in the 1930s and exploded in the '50s with the help of postwar reconstruction. In the furniture factories of nearby Brianza research on the part of the most creative designers in the world continues today, producing tables and divans of every kind and style, from neoclassical to postmodern, and with a certain touch that makes them unique. Within the area of the Navigli, between the arches of Porta Nuova and Largo Augusto, are the showrooms of the most important names in furniture design, such as Arflex, for whom Marco Zanuso works; Cassina (from Apslund to Vico Magistretti); De Padova (the Edizioni collection includes furniture designed in the nineteenth century as well as modern pieces; Crespi; Poltrona Frau (the epitome of relaxation); Tanzi Driade (elegantly refined pieces); and Fornasetti (an eclectic artist who designs chairs in the form of musical instruments and disquieting interior decoration in the shape of anatomical parts).

left
Decorative items by Cappellini are made in collaboration with important international designers.

Imagination and creativity characterize Fornasetti style.

below
A glimpse of via Madonnina at Brera.

Milan has been called "the most refined window on international luxury," and not only for the fashion shows that are held in spring and autumn, where the look for the coming season is decided. The most prestigious Italian and international world-famous brands are represented in the shops along the via Manzoni and Napoleone, and the via della Spiga and Sant'Andrea. The best of everything can be found here, from furs to socks, from cashmere to the textiles of the future.

left
Elegant window displays in the center of town.

above
Franco Maria Ricci bookshop, a model of elegance and quality in the world of publishing.

facing page
The most exclusive shops in the city are to be found in via Montenapoleone.

left
The Antiques Market at the Navigli is held every Sunday. It stretches over about two kilometers.

above
Objects of all kinds are to be found on the stalls: lamps, silver, and ceramic objects, glass vases . . .

Cherubs, vases, and plates are just some examples of Fornaci Curti products.

The historic Fornace San Cristoforo is on the outskirts of Milan not far from the church of Santa Rita alla Barona. It is better known as Fornace Curti, a collection of buildings with loggias, stairways, terraces, and courtyards whose walls are encrusted with masks, cherubs, and many other ornaments in bas-relief. It looks like a village criss-crossed by stone-paved alleyways, including an oratory dedicated to Saint John the Baptist. The Curti family founded the first furnace, or kiln, in 1428 next to the Colonne di San Lorenzo. They used clay from the Navigli (canals) and earth from Boffalora.

These were used to decorate most of the monuments in Lombardy, from the terracotta panels adorning the Cà Granda, to those in Santa Maria delle Grazie. Alberto Curti, the last descendant of the family, allows visitors to stroll along the alleyways, visit the workshops, and observe the potters as they work at the wheel and the kilns. There are ceramic and terracotta plates and trays, ornaments, fountains, and statues for sale.

PAVIA

LUXURIOUS FURS

ON THE LEFT BANK OF THE TICINO RIVER RISES THE HISTORIC CENTER OF PAVIA. Its most important monuments are here: the Visconti Castle; the duomo upon which both Leonardo and Bramante worked; and the three remaining towers of the one hundred depicted in the fresco painted in 1552 in San Teodoro Church. The oldest university in Italy is here. It was founded in about 825, when King Lothario I set up a law school. Pavia only became a real university city five hundred years later, in 1361, when Galeazzo Visconti consecrated the school in the name of the Emperor Charles IV. Many famous people studied there. Among them were Alessandro Volta, who became rector, and the playwright Carlo Goldoni, who was thrown out for writing controversial satires. Today the university's buildings, the laboratories, and colleges take up a large part of the city, and the university students play a vital role in creating a youthful atmosphere.

Shop window of the fur store Annabella.

facing page
Aerial view of the Certosa of Pavia.

The fifteenth-century Certosa is nearby. It is one of the most interesting and best-preserved convents in the world. Gian Galeazzo Visconti had the Certosa built on the fringes of the park surrounding his castle, and designated the church as a mausoleum for his family. Rich, cultivated, and agricultural, Pavia rises like an island in the middle of the waters of the lower Po River valley. The ancient Romans chose this strategic place at the confluence of the Po, which is the longest river in Italy, and the Ticino, which has abundant fish and is the bluest of all rivers. As if that were not enough, Duke Galeazzo II Visconti built a canal from Milan—the Naviglio Pavese was begun in 1359 and completed in 1819 by Napoleonic decree—and the monks in the nearby Certosa surrounded it with rice paddy fields. The city is shrouded in mist during the long winter months. The atmosphere is gloomy yet evocative; the weather can be bone chillingly cold.

Maybe it was for this reason that Giuliano Ravizza was such a success: In just a few years he made Pavia the fur capital of the world. In 1960 he founded Pellicceria Annabella in the center of the historic old city, a few steps from the duomo. Now the shop has eleven windows on Corso Cavour and Piazza della Vitto-

Stradella is located in the middle of the vineyards of the Oltrepò Pavese. It is an ancient village that is famous for its wines and accordions; these are exported throughout the world. There is an accordion museum in Palazzo Garibaldi. It is dedicated to Mariano Dellapè, who opened the first workshop for the construction of this instrument in 1876. Festivals would not be the same without it, but it also is played at classical music concerts. The first accordions built by the master are displayed in the museum. Among them is the "liturgica," an extraordinary instrument that was designed specifically to play classical music. There is a complete collection of modern models in the nearby factory, which still carries his name.

ria. The elegant interior contains three showrooms decorated in baroque style, with stucco and mirrors and furnished with antiques. Dozens of saleswomen proffer furs of every kind, from the humble sheepskin to the expensive sable; the store has one of the largest selections in the world. Clients come from Pavia and Milan, but also from other parts of Italy and from Switzerland.

Pellicceria Annabella and Mazzocchi Pellicce are located on Corso Cavour. Dellera and Castelfur are also major furriers in the city. In addition to the famous Dellapè in Stradella are other workshops that make accordions, including that of the Crosio brothers and Lucchini. Another major accordion production center is in Castelfidardo in the Marche region.

PREMANA

IRON-RICH MINES

CLINGING TO THE SIDES OF MONTE LEGNONE IS PREMANA. It disappears between the high Val Marrone and the Valsassina and it is spread across the Lecco side of Lake Como's banks and the Valtellina. It is so steep that the high facades of the houses overlook the valley and the garages are on the top floor. The village is one large machine shop. It is one of the few places in the Alps where the population hasn't declined; this is thanks to the iron industries and crafts workshops that employ half of the twenty-three hundred residents. Many of the workshops and warehouses are located in renovated stables and cellars. The largest companies occupy the entire palazzo, with an unusual vertical expansion for the production departments.

Premana is one of the major producers of scissors and knives; these products are exported throughout the world. Specialization in this area only began in the twentieth century, but metallurgy in the area goes back to ancient times. The iron-rich mines of the Val Varrone were probably used during Roman times, and the first documentation of a forge dates to 1253, when these territories were governed by the Archbishop of Milan. The importance of Premana grew considerably in the following centuries owing to the Sforza family, which, together with the nearby Val Carvargna, was the principal source of iron goods and weapons. A document from 1574 counted 652 souls, among them forty blacksmiths who forged keys, locks, and gratings. The village also counted makers of swords and horseshoes. During the domination of the Venetian Republic and until the twentieth century, these activities continued unabated. However, it was after World War II that Premana became an increasingly important production center. The village took on the dimensions of one large company, even though it was divided into a number of family businesses. The Collinis were merchants from Milan. In the 1920s they founded the Italicus scissor-making factory in the village. Many other companies followed, deciding to specialize in order to compete with businesses that were at an advantage because of their more easily accessible locations. There were only a dozen companies at the beginning of the twentieth century, but this number doubled in the 1950s; today there are 150 large and small businesses. These companies produce two-thirds of the scissors and half the knives manufactured in Italy. Today the bulk of production is automated; it has been protected since 1974 by a consortium. The principal products are scissors of every kind—for the kitchen, office, embroidery and tailoring, manicure, and surgery. There are also some craftspeople who make personalized hunting knives and silk-finished steel scissors that are as beautiful as jewels.

Valsassina's forests contribute to the forges in a number of ways: they are a source of charcoal, and in the past made it possible to develop carpentry and woodworking activities. Craftspeople produced rustic furniture and objects for everyday use. Furniture-making has been a major industry for some time, and many companies have established themselves in more accessible areas such as Brianza. But many villages in the valley still turn and shape wood for kitchen utensils, such as spoons and forks, as well as bowls, cutting boards, honey jars, small decorative objects, and souvenirs. Classic souvenirs are small pastel-colored replicas of the *lucia*, the typical though obsolete Lake Como boat.

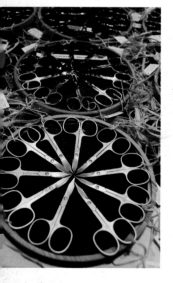

facing page
Wood inlay is another traditional activity of the Valsassina.

below
A selection of scissors that have made the city famous.

The Iron Museum is located in the center of the village. Scissors and knives, including those that are silk finished, are sold at Art or at Pinin. The only iron factory that does not produce scissors or knives is Camp, which also owns the Cassin brand and has specialized, becoming one of the most important manufacturers of mountain equipment, including snap hooks, pitons, nuts, crampons, and ice axes. A museum of *Larian* boats is in Pianello sul Lario.

VALTELLINA
WORKING WITH STONE

OLLARE STONE, A CHLORITE SCHISTLIKE ROCK, IS MINED IN QUARRIES throughout the Valtellina. The rock is formed by a flaky aggregate of chlorite and talc. The color varies from gray to a greenish blue, and it has an extremely fine grain that gives it a compact look. This stone is popular and used because it is light, resistant to fire, and easy to work with a lathe or chisel, particularly when it has just been mined (it starts hardening on contact with the air). Mostly it has been used to create flower and figure decorations that adorn the windows and doors of the many grand houses in the valley, and to make flower pots, holy-water basins for churches, and statues, and various other objects. The skill of the local sculptors is most apparent in the baptismal font in the seventeenth-century San Lorenzo at Chiavenna Church.

In the valleys of Valtournenche and Gressoney (Valle d'Aosta) this stone was also used to seal large blocks of squared stone in order to make large, cylindrical heaters. The Latin *olla*, pot, is mentioned in Pliny the Elder's *Historia Naturalis* as "the green stone of Como," which derives from the fact that it had been used from the time of the ancient Romans to make plates, bowls, soup dishes, and saucepans. But many archaeological finds reveal that use of this stone to make objects was widespread in the Alpine mountains even in the Neolithic era, likely because it could be worked easily with a shard of harder rock such as flint. The production of ollare-stone objects—*lavecc* (saucepans) and *furagn* (vessels used to preserve food)—is probably the oldest documented activity in the Valtellina area.

In the fifteenth century this stone from the Valtellina was transported throughout Italy, and in the eighteenth century the working of ollare stone contributed greatly to the economy of the valley. There were twelve active quarries around Piurno, in Valchiavenna, that employed two hundred people. More than thirty of them were craftspeople who specialized in lathe work. Today the active quarries are found mostly in Val Chiavenna and Val Malenco. The ollare stone extracted from Alpe Pirlo is particularly prized. The color is an intense green, and the texture is almost soft and oily to the touch; other ollare stones contain more talc and are light gray. Although ollare stonework has declined over the centuries, people still use lathes in the workshops of Chiesa Valmalenco and Lanzada in Val Brutta, as well as a few other places. Here various items are produced, including amphoras, jewel boxes, and even necklaces, in addition to the traditional lavecc encircled in copper and with iron handles; these are now used as decorative objects more than as cooking equipment.

facing page
The rustic carpets of the Valtellina were woven with leftover pieces of fabric. Today only the best quality fabric is used.

below
Crockery and pots in earthenware have been made in the Valtellina since ancient times.

Ollare stone is worked by the Gaggi brothers in Chiesa Valmalenco, by Lucchinetti in Piuro, by Palmieri in Sondrio, and by Artistica in Morbegno. Also in Morbegno, Ruffoni makes velvet and linen pezzotti carpets. The Fiera del Bitto is held every October in Morbegno, and area craftspeople give demonstrations. The *frazzate* of Erice (Trapani) are small carpets similar to the pezzotti, but smaller and typically made of cotton.

A special kind of rustic carpet, called *pezzotto*, is still produced in some villages of the Valtellina, including Chiuro, Livigno, Sacco, Arigna, Cettina, and Morbengo. Pezzotto are hand-woven on large looms with threads of hemp and twisted threads of brightly colored strips of fabric scraps; these are usually wool. They are derived from the *pelot*, a small, heavy blanket used by the herders to cover sick animals or by farm workers as mats. They still incorporate traditional designs—simple, decorative geometric patterns, including multicolored stripes (*rigatino*), triangles (*fiamme*), pyramids, and fish tails on a plain white background.

VARESE
ART NOUVEAU WONDERS

LAVENO IS SITUATED ON THE BANKS OF LAKE MAGGIORE, on the Lombardy side and facing Verbania. It is a major producer of decorative ceramics in traditional shapes and colors. The Società Ceramica Italiana di Laveno was established in 1856; in the last years of the century it became an industrial area, producing ceramics that imitated highly decorated floral English designs. The economic tide of the town began to change at the 1906 International Exposition in Milan; eleven pieces, mostly tiles, were presented in "stile Liberty" or art nouveau. Success lasted for decades.

Laveno must thank Varese for this good fortune. The city is located beyond the high Campo dei Fiori. Since the middle of the eighteenth century, Varese was known for its aristocratic residences, and from the end of the nineteenth century the slopes below Sacro Monte and toward the little lake began to fill with luxury villas and hotels. The new art-nouveau style made such an impression on businesspeople and industrialists that a number of new buildings—commercial, factories, company headquarters, kiosks, shops, villas, and hotels—were commissioned. Indeed, the new style made its first appearance in 1898 in the Poretti beer factory of Induno Olona. It was designed by the Bihl & Woltz architectural firm of Stuttgart, Germany, and was replete with decorative lions, shields, and pilasters accentuated by the contrasting colors of yellow and gray. In 1903 the architect Ulisse Stacchini, to whom the Central Station in Milan is attributed, built a villa beside the factory. This is one of his best works. In 1905 an area was created on the Campigli Hill of Varese for well-heeled tourists; it was equipped with a hotel, restaurant, game room, theater, and shooting range. At the end of the nineteenth century, to further establish this as a vacation mecca, the hippodrome of Bettole and the electric tram system were improved.

Dozens of large and small, modest and luxury villas were built, all in the new style that had become symbolic of the flourishing society. The best architects of the time, such as Gaetano Moretti and Giuseppe Sommaruga, were commissioned to design buildings. Sommaruga designed the Campo dei Fori funicular, as well as the great hotel complex, the theater, the Grand Palace Hotel on Campigli Hill, and the tram stations on the Porta Tresa line. Flowers and garlands of wrought-iron adorned gates, signs, balconies, and shop windows. And the walls and floors were covered with increasingly fantastic and colorful ceramics that replicated the same motif from the Ceramiche di Laveno.

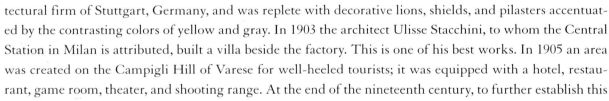

Aerial view of Laveno on Lake Maggiore.

Ceramics are sold in Varese at De Santi or at Arte Ceramiche. In Cerro di Laveno there is a museum of ceramics and in Saronno there is another collection of ceramics and majolicas. Stoves of the Ceramiche Ibis are found in Cunardo; crafted ceramics can be purchased in Camartino. In Gavirate there is a pipe museum. Cantù is known for its pipes, but also is famous for its lacework.

For tobacco cultivators, the towns of Gavirate, on the banks of Varese Lake, and Cantù, in the province of Como, are the two best-known centers for the production of high-quality pipes. The briar root is the underground part of the heather tree, which grows in the arid areas beside the sea in Tuscany, Calabria, Greece, and Spain; however, the best comes from Sardinia. It is a very hard and compact wood that can withstand the high temperatures of burning tobacco, and it does not emit an odor. Almost all the workshops in Gavirate produce pipes mostly by hand, making unique pieces that are highly prized by pipe-smoking connoisseurs. The same craftspeople also make snuff boxes and other quality briar-wood items. They are often inlaid with different colored wood or with silver.

facing page
In Gavirate high-quality pipes are made according to ancient traditions. These are two briar pipes made by the Santambrogio company.

VIGEVANO

SHOES FOR EVERY PURSE

A FEW MILES WEST OF MILAN VIGEVANO RISES ON THE RIGHT BANK of the Ticino River. It is in the middle of the fields and rice paddies of Alta Lomellina, an agricultural area. Beyond the remains of the walls around the Visconti Castle are canals, irrigation ditches, mills, and farms teeming with activity. There is a great surprise in the center of this agricultural village: the historic center around the great Piazza Ducale is one of the most beau-

The Piazza Ducale in Vigevano at night.

facing page
Elegant and scintillating evening shoes by Cesare Martinoli, owner of Caimar, a company that sets a high standard.

tiful Renaissance piazzas in Italy. It is an elegant meeting place for locals and tourists, who linger over their coffee at the outdoor tables, or stroll past the shops under the porticoes.

Piazza Ducale is a lovely rectangle, paved with stones from the Ticino River. It was planned in the fifteenth century by Duke of Milan Ludovico Sforza (il Moro). The existing maze of houses and narrow streets were razed to make space for this urban structure; they continue their meandering course beyond the arched porticoes on the buildings that surround the piazza on three sides. The fourth side of the square is closed by the "artificial" concave façade of the duomo, which is not actually attached to the building. It was built in the seventeenth century by the bishop/architect Lobkowitz, more to adapt it to the composition of the square than to the aesthetics of the church. The Palazzo Ducale is also a surprising building. It is a vast and imposing castle hidden from view by a cluster of houses; it once looked out on the square from a wide stairway. Constructed in 1337 by Luchino Visconti, ruler of Vigevano, buildings were razed and the city plan had to be transformed to make room for it. It was later transformed by the Sforza into an impressive fifteenth-century residence. The stables were designed by Leonardo da Vinci and could house three hundred horses.

Vigevano is famous for the *conzare le scarpe*, first a form of craftsmanship and later a major industry. Shoe cobbling is centuries old and is documented in the Communal Statutes of 1392, in which it was forbidden to cure the leather and work the skins on public streets. In 1866 the first "modern" shoe factory was built. At the beginning of the twentieth century, more than one-third of the footwear produced in Italy came from Vigevano; in 1952, when the first Mostra Mercato Internazionale della Scarpa (International Shoe Exhibition) was held, thirty million pairs of shoes were produced each year. Even though it is no longer the major pro-

The footwear museum in Pietro Bertolini, dedicated to the history and technique of cobblers, opened in 1972; it is one of the few institutions of its kind in Italy. Housed in the former stables of the Ducal Castle, the collection consists of hundreds of models from the fifteenth century to the present. Shoes from around the world are displayed—from Dutch clogs to leggings for Lapps, sandals for African tribes of the Niger valley, wood and mother-of-pearl clogs for Indians, moccasins for Native Americans, Arab *babouches*, Japanese *guetas*, and Balkan *opanke*. There are rare and unique examples belonging to famous people, such as the slippers of Beatrice d'Este, wife of Ludovico il Moro, Benito Mussolini's military boots, and shoes worn by Pope Pius XI. In nearby Novara, the university of cobblers has a museum.

duction center in this area, and there are other important centers in the Marches region, it is the shoes of Vigevano that are important—from the cheap models destined for the outdoor markets, although these are being replaced by the even cheaper Chinese products, to the custom-made shoes that are cut and sewn by hand and commissioned by the rich and famous throughout the world.

There are sixty shoe shops in the Centro Commerciale Ducale. The Calzaturificio di Vigevano produces high-quality shoes. Domenico Asti specializes in shoes for women; Palco produces dance shoes. Parabiago is another important center for shoe cobbling in Lombardy; shoes and clothes can be purchased there at the company outlet of Fratelli Rossetti, Parabiago Collezioni, Riccardo Banfi, or Fashion Point.

M O E N A

THE SMALLEST CREATURES

THE VAL DI FASSA IS IN THE HEART OF THE TRENTINO DOLOMITES. At Moena the valley continues beyond the volcanic chain of the Lagorai and wedges into the ridge of the Sella mountain range; Marmolada is to the east, and Latemar, Catinaccio, and Sassolungo are to the west. It is one of the most beautiful areas in the world, a paradise for trekkers in the summer and skiers in the winter. However, if you go into Fabio Vet-

A view of Moena, in the magical Dolomites.

facing page
Detail of the crowded "Città d'acqua" by Fabio Vettori.

tori's shop you will be confronted with millions of tiny ants that appear everywhere—on posters, puzzles, books, T-shirts, gadgets, and decorative objects. They are hardworking ants that cut trees and build houses, make love and war, play with kites and ride roller coasters, occupy crowded classrooms and frenetic factories, and fill the football stands and tour cities. Thousands of ants make up complex "paintings" with the minutest details. Vettori has a surveyor's diploma and he was a ski instructor, but he was destined to be an artist. When he was in school he began creating detailed drawings of villages inhabited by tiny people and battle scenes with hundreds of soldiers. When he discovered the rapidograph and drawing ink the details that he drew became even more minute, until he began to draw one of the smallest visible living beings—the ant. Since then it is these creatures that animate his landscapes.

At first they were roughly drawn, but gradually they became anthropomorphized, acquiring the virtues and vices of the human race, which are exposed with subtle irony, amusing yet provocative. His imagination is extraordinary; ants crowd the university and the inns of Bologna, they are Romeo and Juliet in Verona, they are merchants on the Ponte Vecchio in Florence. Ants invade the Sant'Antonio Basilica in Padua and try to straighten the Leaning Tower of Pisa with air balloons. Vettori's tiny ants reveal a condemnation of the assault on nature, the problem of pollution and waste, and the absurdity of building complexes, mass tourism, and mass entertainment. But they also evoke poetic images, such as in the *Four Seasons*, which appears on a poster and in a puzzle. It is a tree that divides into four and celebrates the cycle of the

In Ala di Trento, along the Verona-Brenner Highway, there is a museum of the antique pianoforte. It is housed in an elegant seventeenth-century palazzo; Charles III of Spain, Marie Therese of Austria, and Napoleon Bonaparte were guests there, as was Mozart, who likely entertained an audience with some of his compositions. In fact, the museum has a collection of eighteenth- and nineteenth-century grand pianos and upright pianos that belonged to the pianist Temenuschka Vesselinova, who lived in the palazzo. There are many instruments from the Viennese school; Stein, Walter, Böhm, and Graf are some of the craftspeople represented. There are also many from the French school and some from the end of the nineteenth century such as Bechsteins and Steinways. During a visit to this museum you can listen to classical music; periodically concerts are given in the palazzo's reception hall.

changing seasons, with an uninterrupted line of ants that ski in the winter, collect the most beautiful flowers in spring, gather fruit in the summer, end up on the ground between the autumn leaves, then get up again and walk toward the ski slopes.

In Trentino there is a consortium of quality craftspeople who work in specialized workshops making rustic furniture and other objects in wood and iron; there are also textile and ceramics artisan shops. The Ceramica Cicuttin in Trento produces platters, tiles, figures of angels, and other decorative objects. A craft exhibition is held in Tesero in mid-August.

BOLZANO
CULTURAL POTPOURRI

THE BASIN IN WHICH BOLZANO IS SITUATED LOOKS LIKE THE IMPRINT OF A TRIDACTYL, with three fingers that mark the furrows of the Valle dell'Adige, the Val Sarentina, and the Valle dell'Isarco. This plain collected and dispersed the waters of the three rivers, creating a malaria-ridden marsh. But this did not stop it from becoming a natural meeting point for diverse people; although it is surrounded by mountains it is at a manageable 870 feet, and every valley was a connecting road between north and south. The Isarco Valley that rises to the Brenner has always been easy to traverse, even in the winter.

In the Bronze Age Bolzano was a village built on stilts. In Roman times it was partly an inhabited village and partly a military garrison surrounding a bridge—*Pons Drusi*—where Goths, Bavarians, and Lombards mixed. In the Middle Ages it was a famous market town and at the end of the twelfth century a flourishing commercial center developed with the guidance of bishops of Trento and supported by Florentine bankers. In the seventeenth century a mercantile magistrature composed of Italian and German judges was formed; it ensured that the laws governing the many fairs in the city were obeyed. Here caravans of merchants from the Serenissima Republic of Venice brought spices and brocades to exchange for amber and arms.

The area that we see today is a mosaic of avenues of flowering fruit trees, bridges, and castles. Where once there was a marsh and gravel-filled riverbeds, today there are gardens framed by the Rosegarten, an imposing Dolomite peak below which spreads the mythical rose garden of King Laurino. Today, Bolzano is still a frontier town where many different cultures mix; it still has a strong economy as well. The ambiance is Tyrolean. Indeed the city was governed by the Austro-Hungarian Empire until the end of World War I. The old city sits in a triangle between Isarco and Tàlvera. The narrow passageways and little squares are named for many of the town's ancient activities—producing grain, growing herbs, barrel-making, and silversmithing. Arches support the houses, which are full of jutting balconies and pinnacles typical of the Mittel European Gothic architecture, more like theater sets or fairy-tale castles than houses of ordinary people; typical ancient symbols of *Gasthofen*—the eagle, the bear, the lion, the sun, the moon—are a reminder of the close ties with nature. There is no way to avoid shopping in the Via dei Portici or in Piazza Walther; stores sell products from the area, including handwoven Tyrolean loden, felt hats, goose feathers, sweets and Tyrolean cakes, wine, speck, candles, and inlaid wood.

facing page
Fragile and beautiful decorations are on sale in the shops and on the stalls all year round.

below
Via dei Portici, Bolzano. Elegant shops flank the picturesque streets.

Majolica stoves are sold at Kunters in Brunico or at Pernter in Ora. "The original angel of Bolzano" is the praying cherub that was made by the Thun company in the 1950s. This company also produces various other ceramic objects. In December the old city centers of Bolzano, Merano, and Brunico are filled with market stalls selling Christmas products. An international crafts fair is held in Bolzano during the third week of September.

The *stube* stove of Alto Adige is warm and welcoming, placed in the "best room" of a house. It is not the wood-paneled walls but the great brick stove that immediately attracts attention. Some massive stoves are preserved in museums in the valley. They are finished with majolica tiles and decorated with elaborate and elegant designs. Today production is not limited to making a functional heating instrument; instead these stoves become decorative elements that are the centerpieces of homes. Production facilities are concentrated in Bolzena and Brunico, but there are craftspeople throughout the region who custom make them; the popularity of the Kachelofen, a type of popular central European tile stove, recently has spread to the Veneto and Trentino areas—not just in the mountains but even into cities on the plains.

VAL GARDENA

THE COLORS OF WOOD

VAL GARDENA IS SAID TO HAVE MORE WOOD SCULPTORS THAN RESIDENTS. It is true that there is at least one sculptor in each family and that wood sculptures are as much a part of the landscape in the Alto Adige valleys as are the spikes of the Dolomites. Here craftsmanship was born out of necessity; it was not considered an art form. In the past, the farm owners had little opportunity to purchase household tools and utensils. However, winters were long and wood was plentiful. Around the fireplace or by the warmth of the stube stove, these mountain dwellers would sculpt pieces of wood into spoons or ladles, masks for Carnival, toy animals for children, and frames and cases for pendulum clocks. They sculpted utilitarian objects that could be used in the home but that could also be sold during the warmer months in the villages of the valleys down below. There was a time when woodworking was a widespread activity in all the villages, not only those in the mountains. In Alto Adige woodworking was a sort of family business, and entire families would collaborate to produce wood objects. Each family member specialized in a step of the process, from rough-hewing logs to finishing pieces with the bright colors that are still the most typical feature of Val Gardena sculptures. Some of the more gifted craftspeople refined their technique and made inlays of the Madonna and crucifixes for churches or to scatter along the paths that led to the pastures.

Michael Pacher was the greatest of the Alto Adige artists. In the second half of the fifteenth century he produced some important work, such as the sculpted and painted wood altars in the San Lorenzo Church in Brunico; Novacella Abbey; and the parish church in Gries. Pacher's work is still emulated by many, even though today's young people make inlay works with more contemporary themes. Val Gardena natives prefer to use easily worked, soft wood, such as pinewood and the Swiss stone pine that grows at a high altitude, and is scented, compact, and has a lovely ivory color. Craftspeople make saints and Madonnas, Gothic Christs on the Cross, scenes of daily life and animals; they are often brightly colored and very stylized. The Anri company, founded in 1912 and employing ninety craftspeople, specializes in figurines for Nativity scenes, most of which are exported; they are carved and hand painted. Each figure takes from ten to thirty hours to make and they cost upwards of two hundred dollars each. It is also easy to find large figures of peasants and woodcutters at work; Juno-esque Madonnas that are featured in processions on saints' days throughout Italy; gigantic Christ figures, one of which has even turned up in a Protestant church in Honolulu; animals; and various extremely realistic famous people in irreverent poses.

Often real works of art, wooden sculptures of the sacred and the profane, represent a flourishing activity all over the valley.

Many Val Gardena sculptors, including Thomas Moroder and Markus Perathones, display work at the Galleria Unika in Ortisei in the Cësa di Ladins. Thomas Camploi's work can be seen in Santa Cristina Valgardena; Otto Piazza's is found at Selva in Val Gardena. Textiles and embroidery are sold at La Valle/Wengen at the artistic weaving mill of Nagler.

In contrast to the rest of Italy, where precious lace was traditionally made by nuns or by poor people for the rich, in Alto Adige it was the noble women who did this work. They whiled away the time in pleasant conversation and by the warmth of the stube, busy with their *fuselli*, stuffed cushions and pins. It was only later, and following their example, that farm women also began to do this work; it continues today. It has become representative of local craftsmanship, particularly in Merano, in the Valle Aurina, and in Val Sarentina. Beautiful lace is used to decorate the blouses of traditional costumes, and for tablecloths, bed linen, and curtain trims.

facing page
The Castle of Wolkestein in Val Gardena.

VANDOIES

WHERE LODEN IS MADE

LODEN IS A GERMAN WORD MEANING TANGLED WOOL. It is most identified with the jackets of people who live in the Tyrolean Mountains. The jackets are functional and rugged, with buttons made of bone or stag's horn. This fabric can be durable as well as elegant. It is worn by Alto Adige hunters but also members of high society. The fabric also is considered part of the official Tyrolean culture and in Vandoies, a quiet village in the Val Pusteria just north of Bresanone, there is a loden museum. The museum was founded by the Oberrauch family, which has made loden clothing for 150 years. Among the offices and production areas, is an exhibition space that presents the history and techniques of working this fabric. It is a unique homage to handcrafted goods.

Loden is an ancient fabric. The Rhetii people made felt clothing out of wool more than two centuries before the Common Era, as did the Romans, who wanted to make more weather-resistant clothing. In the Middle Ages this type of wool was used by rural people; the pants were so thick and rigid that they stood up by themselves. It was only in the nineteenth century that the aristocracy discovered *lodo*, thanks to Archduke Franz Joseph of Austria, who wore it on hunts. He introduced it to court when he became emperor. The use of this fabric spread from Vienna to Denmark and Greece; it was "officially" anointed in 1927 by the Prince of Wales, who was known for his elegant style. He was imitated by many fashion trendsetters. By the end of the nineteenth century, loden had become the preferred fabric for sports clothing and was the uniform of choice for travelers who went trekking around the world.

It is said that wool has to "suffer" if it wants to become loden, and it *is* really mistreated; wool is fulled, soaked, and beaten until it is reduced to a third of its volume. Before the invention of fulling machines the wool was trampled. The felt is then washed with neutral soap and lye and undergoes teaseling. This can produce two types of fabric: felt with a rough surface; and the shiny, combed fabric that is water repellent. This is the real secret of loden: it becomes waterproof after it is brushed with a machine that uses natural thistles from Corsica and Spain. There are forty different stages in the making of loden. At one time this process took forty days. The factories in the Tyrol and Alto Adige produce three miles' worth of fabric per year. It is exported around the world and is coveted by fashion designers such as Valentino and Yves Saint-Laurent.

A room in the Loden Museum annexed to the Oberrauch outlet.

"Loden Welt" (Loden World) is spread out among buildings that have different functions: on the first floor of a former trouser-making factory there is a manufacturing area and the Oberrauch-Zitt factory outlet. The second floor houses a museum about the history of loden, where visitors can perform almost every part of the process, including sheep shearing. Nearby there is a reconstruction of a fulling mill that was in use in the Alps nine hundred years ago. In addition there is a drying area; a restaurant that serves mutton and lamb specialties; and an organic hotel, with hypoallergenic mattresses and bedding. This complex unites work and play with a philosophy that has led the Institute of Management of the University of Innsbruck to adopt the same interest as they have in the Wattens (Austria) Park of Swarowski and the Ravensburg (Germany) Amusement Park.

Loden clothing can be purchased at the Oberrauch-Zitt factory outlet and the company's shops in Merano and Bolzano. Other reliable loden-clothing sellers include Peter Öhler's boutique in Bressanone and Gerta Runggaldier in Merano, the Mössmer wool factory in Brunico, and Kaufmann in San Genesio.

facing page
In traditional costume—a moment of the Altstadtfest in nearby Bressanone.

AGORDO
FASHIONABLE EYEWEAR

EYEGLASSES HAVE BEEN MADE IN THE BELLUNO AREA SINCE 1878. Even though the industry has seen some downturns, there are still about seventy factories and seven hundred artisan workshops in the province; sunglasses and eyeglasses, underwater glasses, and work glasses are manufactured. Many companies specialize: some may make frames; others may make small eyeglass components.

Leonardo Del Vecchio opened his first factory in Agordo forty years ago; nobody could have foreseen the influence it would have. Today his company, Luxottica, is a giant in the optics field. The media have often played with his initials—the same as Leonardo da Vinci's—describing him as the new Leonardo. While he is among the richest men in the world, he was born in poverty, in a tenement on the Navigli in Milan; he was raised by the Martinitt, a kind of orphanage. But Leonardo studied, and despite his disadvantages he attended the Accademia di Brera; he wanted to find work and to set up his own business. He took advantage of an offer by the government of Agordo: it would give a plot of land free of charge to new businesses that chose to establish there. It was 1961 and Luxottica was little more than an artisan workshop, but it gradually grew, utilizing the most sophisticated machinery and technology. The

View of Monte Agner from Agordo; the statues of the Palazzo Crotta in the foreground.

facing page
A playful eye chart.

company's big break came ten years later, when Luxottica exhibited at the Trade Fair in Milan. At that event eyeglasses were transformed from things people hated to wear to must-have fashion accessories.

At the French and the English courts in the 1700s, eyeglasses were forbidden; two hundred years later they became a symbol of distinction, wisdom, and culture. They suddenly became a status symbol, the use of dark glasses pervasive. Film stars and other famous people wore them everywhere—except when the sun was shining. The frames became more important than the lenses: they were heart shaped; with stars, stripes, or polka dots; with horses' blinkers and aerodynamic lines recalling Formula 1 race cars; or with lenses so small people could read only one line at a time. Thanks to the acquisition of well-known brands such as Rayban, Luxottica has become the most important eyeglass manufacturer in the world. It is listed on the New York Stock Exchange, and has branches in Europe, the Americas—it owns Avant-Garde Optics, the biggest distributor of optical goods in the world, and even in China, where there has been a chain of shops and a factory for many years; there will soon be an office in Shanghai.

Until World War II the primary work of Agordo's residents (apart from working in the mines of Val Imperina), was making chairs. The people migrated among the cities of the Veneto plain to make chairs and weave seats. Among a population of a few thousand at the end of the nineteenth century there were 790 chair-makers. Today, active chair-makers can be counted on one hand; they make custom chairs to furnish rustic inns of the region. The chairs they produce are very special, even though they are simple and made of natural wood. But the component pieces are shaped by hand with an axe, and they are mounted and glued without any other kind of treatment; they are not polished or painted. Seats are made of woven straw.

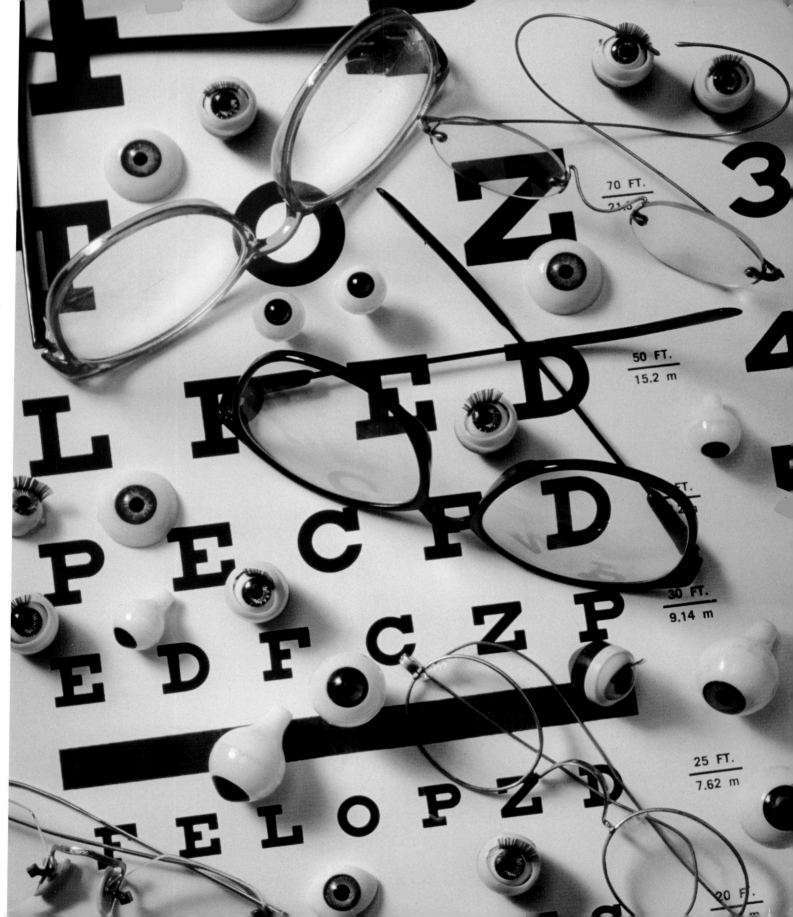

Eyeglasses can be purchased in Agordo at Dieffe Unisex and La Muda, and at Auronzo and G5 in Cadore. There are many eyeglass factories along the Piave River near Longarone and in the Cadore valleys. In Agordo, an exhibition at Palazzo Crotta de Manzoni features an impressive assemblage of optical instruments and eyeglasses from the Ratschüler-Luxottica collection. Another important eyeglass museum is located in Pieve di Cadore.

BASSANO

BRIGHTLY COLORED CERAMICS

THE WOODEN BRIDGE THAT CROSSES THE BRENTA RIVER has been the symbol of Bassano since the twelfth century. At that time, the powerful Ezzelini da Romano family built a castle to control the traffic at the entrance to the Valsugana. Floods and war have destroyed it many times over, but it has always been rebuilt. In 1569 it was redesigned by the architect Andrea Palladio; since then the bridge's unique profile of open wooden arches supported by two lines of nineteen columns has changed very little. The old village rises on the left bank of the Brenta alongside the historic grappa distilleries that have made Bassano famous. Near the bridge on the opposite bank is the Museum of the Alpini (Alpine regiments), indelibly linked to the history of the village during World War I. This leads to the new villages that were built after the war beyond the centuries-old ceramics workshops; these workshops flank the road at the foot of the mountain as far as Marostica and down to Vicenza.

There were many ceramics makers in the Veneto plain in the sixteenth century. They worked with kaolin, locally known as "Venice earth," and made objects of impeccable quality. Bassano was the first place to gain recognition for the high quality of its products; the fine paste, brilliant glaze, and the richness of the decoration characterized this work throughout the seventeenth century. The objects can be seen at the ceramics museum in Palazzo Strum. A wide range of ceramic objects were made, from wine jugs to huge garden pots, bowls, clay pipes, and plates; in addition, workshops made pharmaceutical jars decorated with garlands of flowers and leaves; a space was designated to note the contents.

Nove, a neighboring town, became important in the eighteenth century. There, the civic museum of ceramics houses the Checchetto collection, the most important assemblage of nineteenth-century plates. Nove revived the traditional shapes and decorations, and increased production with more elaborate and expensive objects, such as candelabra, mirror frames, centerpieces, openwork fruit bowls in a white glaze, and even life-size domestic and exotic animals that are still made. Now the two areas are closely linked and share the market with products characterized by precious and refined decorations that recall seventeenth-century designs—scenes of country life, saints, still lifes, and landscapes with ruins. Small ceramic stoves, called *foghere*, are manufactured in Este, another important ceramic-producing area in the Veneto.

The Ponte Vecchio at Bassano del Grappa at night.

Marostica is known for the square where chess is played by people dressed in traditional costumes, and for the imposing castle that overlooks it. The castle was built by Cangrande della Scala, Lord of Verona, on top of a fortification from the High Middle Ages. In addition to ceramics, straw work—woven bags, baskets, and hats—has been a craft here for centuries. It is likely that more than a million hats were made here every year in the mid-nineteenth century. The town has a museum of straw hats, which presents the history of both artisan and mechanized production of this inexpensive material. There is a good collection of hats, as well as documents detailing how the activity was exported, even to the Rio Grande do Sul in Brazil, where emigrants from Vicenza established hat factories. There is another hat museum in Crosara.

An exhibition of ceramics, porcelain, and glass is held every year in Vicenza. Typical ceramics are produced by ABC Ceramiche and Perdomello in Bassano. They can be purchased in Nove in the workshops of Alessi or Rita dal Prà, and in Marostica at Vecia Botega. Each June the international week of ceramics takes place in Este, and in December there is a market featuring Este ceramics.

facing page
Hand made decorations on the artistic ceramics of Bassano make a pleasing show on any dinner table.

THE DOLOMITES OF BELLUNO
IRON SCULPTURE

IRONWORK IN THE BELLUNO AREA HAS DEEP, SOLID ROOTS. Dozens of mines were scattered throughout the region, and there were hundreds of furnaces and forges along the fast-flowing rivers; these produced equipment for woodcutters and farmers. It is said that the ancient Romans also used these mines. Certainly the Republic of Venice greatly increased mining activities and production to supply its arsenal and armies. It industrialized production by making each district specialize in one particular area; for example, Val di Zoldo was known as the "valley of iron"—not for the mines but for the forges. Here the first great forges were established in the twelfth century. The town's blacksmiths made nails until the end of the nineteenth century; they made tiny nails for the soles of shoes and nails that were about three feet long and used to tie pylons. These nails were then transported by mule as far as the Piave River, where they were loaded onto barges and shipped to Venice. There were so many mines in nearby Alta Val Cordevole that they were the subject of fairy tales and myths.

According to legend, there was an underground kingdom called Aurora in the depths of Mount Padòn; it was lit by the glow of gold and precious stones. Some scholars actually maintain that these valleys were the setting for *Snow White and the Seven Dwarfs*, whereas the Brothers Grimm had set it in the Black Forest in Germany. These tales were inspired by history. During their travels, the authors had visited the Belluno valleys and knew the legends of the Monti Palidi (Pale Mountains). The Republic of Venice forced Turkish slaves to work in the mines. They were short and more agile, better able to navigate the subterranean passageways. In a village near Alleghe there is still a palazzo called the "prison of the Turks." There is also the wicked stepmother's castle, called Andràz; its ruins can be seen from the first ramps of the Falzàrego Pass. The following is the basis of the fairy tale: the seven dwarfs (the short Turkish slaves), were cared for by Snow White, a young woman of the village who prepared their food until she met Prince Charming, a noble Venetian who came to visit his mines.

Sottoguda is a little village just above Lake Alleghe, where Val Cordevole divides. Today it produces a lot of wrought iron. Contrary to other centers in the Belluno area, the forges here were established during the twentieth century. A man named Carlo de Biasio opened the first forge in 1923. He manufactured equipment and tools for the woodcutters and farmers, but due to his creativity and skillfulness he began to make decorative objects and furniture. Small souvenirs are made at the Fusina di Biasio, which also makes more elaborate objects that are considered works of art.

In Val di Zoldo, Bruno de Pellegrin works with inlay, while Renzo Lazzarin specializes in stringed musical instruments; he also makes tiny, functional utensils in silver. In Feltre, a regional exhibition of artisanal products takes place during the last week of June. Wrought-iron workshops in Veneto are concentrated in the province of Verona, in Bussolengo, Lazise, and Cogollo di Tragano, and in the province of Trento. The international academy of wrought iron is located in Mogliano Veneto.

These valleys are also known for wood crafts, predominantly objects for everyday use such as carts, sleds, and rustic furniture; in some cases these pieces are works of art. In eastern Cadore, Sappada is famous for its sculpted wood masks worn during ancient pagan celebrations. Similar masks are carved in Val di Zoldo, where the people have also become accomplished artists and have expanded the range of their output with sculptures, stringed musical instruments, and inlay. Moreover, there were real masters of wood carving in the "valley of iron"; such people include Valentino Panciera Besarel, who created altars and choir stalls for many churches in the valley, and Andrea Brustolon, whose famous stalls are in the salon that bears his name in the Quirinale.

MONTEBELLUNA
OUTDOOR SPORTS

THE FORMER TREVISO BRAND IN MONTEBELLUNA IS CALLED SPORTSYSTEM. Caerano San Marco, Cornuda, Volpago, Pedrobba, and Asolo are in an area known for manufacturing top-of-the-line athletic footwear. Almost half of the footwear produced here appears on the feet of athletes around the world. More than 65 percent of the ski boots manufactured worldwide are made in Montebelluna. In addition, manufacturers here make ski footwear and half of all motorcycle boots, football boots, and footwear for cyclists, basketball players, tennis players, and other athletes.

In the 1990s, the industry expanded into new fields, such as manufacturing regular footwear. One example is the phenomenon of Geox, the "shoes that breathe," which have been imitated widely. Some companies manufacture sportswear in collaboration with foreign companies such as Nike, Head, and Lowa, as well as sporting goods such as skis, ice skates, and roller skates. The secret of the area's success is probably its use of cutting-edge technology, research, and impeccable craftsmanship. While low-cost production has been decentralized in Eastern European countries and in Southeast Asia, higher-quality products that are more costly to produce continue to be made in this area.

The manufacture of athletic footwear dates to the nineteenth century when the village cobblers used heavy leather to make mountain boots with studded soles. In the years between the wars, they began to make work shoes and military boots as well as athletic shoes. After World War I, production began to evolve into different areas. Montebelluna reorganized to boost production capabilities and to keep pace with the increased demand in the marketplace, but it became the leader in 1960 when it launched its plastic ski boots. Today the production of generic athletic footwear is also important. This footwear is not for sports but for leisure and influences fashion trends.

Shoes are supposed to protect the feet. In the 1990s it was calculated that thirty million Americans jogged; injuries were numerous. Many of the companies in Montebelluna established research facitilities and began to incorporate biotechnology and ergonomic principles into shoe design. The company inserted a system of cushions in the sole of the shoe to reduce the risk of trauma, and today they produce a system that guides the foot into the best position in the shoe.

The Tecnica Group outlet is in Nervesa della Battaglia; Garmont is in Volpage del Montello. Trekking shoes or mountain boots are also sold at the Flavis or La Reginetta company outlets in Cornuda. Athletic shoes are sold at Lotto in Cornuda, where there is also an interesting exhibit. Scarpa is in Asolo; a school of old embroidery is also located there.

facing page
A characteristic antiques market at Asolo.

below
High-tech sportswear by Tecnica for skiing the Dolomites.

A museum of athletic footwear is located in Villa Zuccareda Benetti at Montebelluna, where the history of footwear is presented and where locally made shoes are displayed. Many models represent important milestones, from the nineteenth-century slipper up to the most modern ski boots. It is likely that shoes were invented in the Americas. The oldest shoes, dating from 9000 to 7000 BC and with soles made of tree bark, were discovered in North America in 1940. Amazon Indians protected their feet with the lymph that oozed from the caucciu tree, which solidified in fire. In America, Wait Webster patented the first rubber-soled shoe in 1832; in 1839 Charles Goodyear discovered vulcanization, a process that made rubber more resistant. The first "modern" athletic shoes were made by the British and called plimsoll; these shoes were exported to the United States and became known as sneakers.

TREVISO

UNITED COLORS

THERE ARE WEAVERS THROUGHOUT THE VENETO AREA. In some places there is a centuries-old tradition of craftsmanship; in others there are new factories that have attained international renown. The brocades made at the Fortuny factory are inspired by ancient Venetian designs. In Asolo there is a school of tapestry where embroidered items include tablecloths, handkerchiefs, and blouses. In the mountain valleys the people work wool and hemp to make blankets, bed linens, curtains, and tablecloths. In many villages between the Piave and Brenta rivers, particularly in Crespano del Tomba and at Cavaso del Grappa on the slopes of Monte Grappa, the wool industry has existed since the end of the seventeenth century. Crespano produces fine fabrics that compete on the European market with those made by England and France; simpler, more generic textiles are made in Cavaso. Mussolente, in the Vicenza area, is still the primary producer in an area known for refined handwoven silk and wool clothing and furnishings.

Villa Pastega, restored by Tadao Ando, is headquarters to Fabrica, the communications research center of Benetton.

Schio and Valdagno continue to be important production centers. Schio has specialized in the art of wool weaving since the fifteenth century, displacing Vicenza. It is the home of Lanerossi, an internationally recognized textile manufacturer. In 1836, Luigi Marzotto founded the wool factory that bears his name in Valdagno. It still makes high-end textiles; Marzotto also owns Valentino's fashion design company. The town of Ponzano Veneto, however, has gained a reputation only in the last forty years. It is a little village at the gates of Treviso. The Benetton Group, one of the best-known brands in clothing, has its headquarters there at Villa Minelli, a sixteenth-century complex that was restored by architect Carlo Scarpa. Unlike the great Italian families that have been in business since the nineteenth century, the Benettons do not have a deep-rooted tradition. The Benettons grew up in a devastated postwar environment, but they had great hopes for the future. They put their passion for clothing to commercial use, aided by faith and the ability to communicate. In the 1960s they invented the colors that wrapped young Italians in optimism; soon the entire world started wearing their sweaters and pullovers. They made the Benetton name synonymous with a youthful outlook on life—

Marbled paper is another craft that is still made in the Veneto area. It is mostly used for binding books and for making desktop accessories. The technique is very old: a sheet of paper is spread on a wooden frame and fairly thick liquid colors are poured over it. The frame is then tilted to spread the colors, creating a pattern of waves. Marbleized paper is still made in Bussolengo, in Verona province, using old wooden forms. This kind of paper and the objects made with it can be found everywhere, even in stationery shops in Venice.

open, multiethnic, multiracial, multicolored. United Colors of Benetton is not a publicity slogan, it is a philosophy of life.

The Benetton Group was founded in 1965 in Ponzano, where it had a modest knitwear workshop. In 1969 it opened its first store abroad. Today there are seven thousand stores in more than one hundred countries. The company also sells Calzaturificio di Varese shoes, Rollerblade and Kästle sporting goods, and cosmetics and watches.

Benetton stores can be found in practically every large and small city in Italy and in the world's major cities. In Treviso stores are located on Corso Indipendenza, Via Crispi, and Via Mazzini. Other nearby cities with shops include Venice, Padua, Mestre, and Castelfranco Veneto. Sartorial Homme, located in Monastier di Treviso, is a company specializing in custom-made clothes for men and women.

facing page
The "Tree of Life" in polished and matte crystal, is one of the artistic products of the Cristalli Varisco company.

VENICE

EXQUISITE FABRICS

IN THE FIRST YEARS OF THE TWENTIETH CENTURY A MAN named Mariano Fortuny y Madrazo, born to a Spanish family transplanted to Venice, was famous for his painting, photography, set design, and, most especially, textile-making. He lived in the Palazzo Pesaro degli Orfei, which today is a museum in his name. He stripped away the romantic, exalted aura of objects from the past, transforming them into "goods" for which the distinction between authentic and fake was meaningless. In the theater he revolutionized the sets and lighting systems of the Fenice Theater stage, transforming it into a diorama of extraordinary illusory effect. He used this technique in other theaters as well. He also oversaw costume design and fabric choices so that these elements were one with the other stage effects. The collection of almost four hundred pieces of fabric and period clothing that he collected during his life constitute an invaluable documentation of the techniques of his textile art. There are ancient Greek costumes, Venetian tapestries, Florentine Renaissance brocades designed by artists such as Pollaiolo and Botticelli, velvets threaded with shining gold and grotesque decorations, vegetable and animal motifs, and damasks with foliage patterns. There was colored baroque, rococo compositions of islands or winding paths, embroidery, Chinese *ke'si* worn by the emperors, and Islamic tunics and robes. For Fortuny, the costumes of the past were not models to be copied but ideas to transform with a Western flavor. He knew that theater and the burgeoning cinema influenced the world of high fashion, and he designed clothes for Sara Bernhardt, Eleonora Duse, and Emma Gramatica. He set up a workshop in Palazzo Pesaro degli Orfei where he first reproduced his designs by printing them onto fabric with wooden dies, or painting them on with the use of masks, such as in the Japanese *katagami* tradition. Later, inspired by photography, he used his own silk-screening technique. He used very fine blocked fabrics soaked in gelatin, and painted on the design with a solution of two-colored alkaline that he imprinted on the fabric photographically. His Knossos scarf and Delphos tunic are timeless. The Delphos tunic was his first style and the most famous. It was inspired by the statue of the Auriga at the Louvre in Paris and made in finely pleated silk. His work has been collected with careful attention paid to this extraordinary artistic heritage. It has even been applied to modern commercial products. The fabrics based on his original designs are now made by Tessuti. Sold in Venice under the label Venetia Studium are printed fabrics, velvet pillows, lamps, and many other items.

The Venetian art of glassmaking has celebrated a thousand shining years. A certain Domenico "fiolarius," or glassmaker (*fiola* was the word used for a glass bottle) is cited in a document dated 982, and since the time of Marco Polo this was where the *conterie* were made (rosaries that were sent to the Holy Land). These beads were so called because they were counted, like coins. In 1291 Venice expelled its glassmakers to prevent the danger of fires in the narrow alleys flanked by wooden houses. They moved to the island of Murano and set up shop along the Rio dei Vetrai, where it is still possible to see the oldest furnaces on the island. In exchange for this move they were accorded certain privileges. They were allowed their own laws, and permitted to mint their own coins. Extraordinarily, they were even allowed to marry into the Venetian noble families. Murano glass has always been a fine example of art and innovation, and since the middle of the fourteenth century it has decorated the courts and noble palaces of Europe: glasses, bottles, chandeliers of the thinnest and purest blown glass can be seen in the Palladian villas of the Venetian plain as well as in the palaces of Vienna and Versailles.

A museum focusing on the history of textiles and costume is housed in Venice's Palazzo Mocenigo; there is a lace museum on Burano. Lacework is sold at Dalla Lidia or at La Casa del Merletto. Venetian masks can be purchased at Laboratorio Artigiano or at Mondonovo. The Consorzio Promovetro consists of sixty-five of the one hundred furnaces in Murano and, under the brand Vetro Artistico Murano, it guarantees the origin and the quality of products. The glass museum is on Fondamenta Giustiniani. La Murrina is one of the largest companies making glass objects and it is located in Marcon, where there is an outlet. The craftspeople of l'Arte Vetraria Muranese, Gambaro & Poggi, and the Vetreria Artistica Ballarin create excellent work.

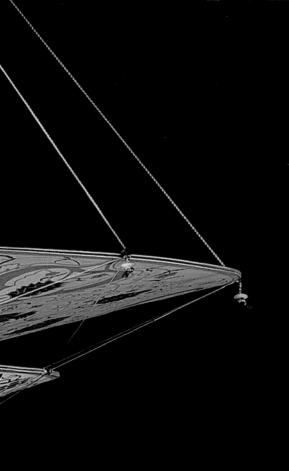

left
The Scheherezade lamp in opaline silk is inspired by Fortuny's designs and is produced exclusively by Venetia Studium.

The Bevilacqua Textile company has been in business in Venice since 1875 and still uses antique frames to create velvets, brocades, and damasks.

Murano glass is made of silicia dioxide, sodium carbonate, potassium, and other minerals that differentiate it from others. *Murrino* glass originated in Alexandria, and it is a mosaic of small pieces of colored glass shaped into flowers. The pieces are then fused carefully to maintain the design. There is also a variation of Roman origin, called *rosette*, obtained with rods of glass rather than pieces. When it is finished it is mounted in gold, and becomes the *murrina*, the typical jewel of Murano. Glass *a ghiaccio* and *craquelé* are characterized by what appears to be a crack in the blown objects. This is obtained by immersing them in water. The silklike finish is obtained by treating the surface with hydrofluoric acid, which creates a translucent effect. If the treatment is irregular it is called *corroso*. Glass that is *incamiciato* or *sommerso* is made of superimposed layers that are sometimes different colors. *Martellato* glass is obtained by lightly tapping the surface.

facing page
"Le Bolle" designed by Tapio Wirkkala for Venini.

above, left
A master glassmaker works with incandescent glass.

above, right
Master glassmakers also create animals as collectors' pieces.

left
Collectors' glasses in various shapes by Carlo Moretti.

Burano is a beautiful island in the lagoon, with houses painted in bright colors. The lace that is made here is the stuff of legend. It seems that a poor fisherman resisted the temptation of the sirens, because of his deep love for his lady, who was waiting for him on the little island. As a gift he received a crown of sea foam to place on his lady's head. Fascinated by the beauty of the veil, the women of Burano tried to imitate it. They fashioned fish scales into needles (they did not know that actual needles existed) and made ever more beautiful embroidery. The real story: lacework has been created on the island since the sixteenth century; originally it was made to supply the Venetian nobles. At the end of the nineteenth century, after a period of decline, lacework flourished again as a result of the efforts of Cencia Scarpaiola. Today it is an important activity on the island.

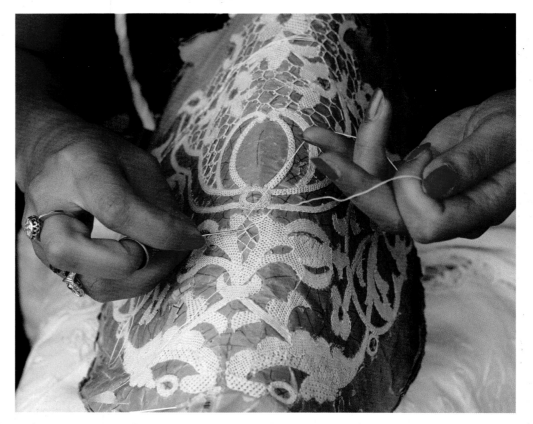

For five centuries, Venetian lace has been distinguished by its originality and quality. At Burano, lace is made with needles (top and facing page), and at Pellestrina, with bobbins (above).

VICENZA

SACRED AND PROFANE GOLD

FEW ARCHITECTS CAN REALIZE THEIR DREAMS OF BUILDING A CITY without the constraints of budget or practicalities. One of those fortunate enough to have been given free reign to his inspirations was Andrea Palladio (1508–1580), one of the most influential figures in the history of Western architecture. In the mid-sixteenth century Palladio built grandiose villas throughout the Veneto plain and left an indelible mark that has greatly

Palladio's Villa "La Rotonda."

influenced the architecture of the succeeding centuries. Vicenza, a small town east of Verona and west of Padua, was virtually rebuilt by the master architect after having suffered damage during the wars waged by the League of Cambrai, a group formed by the papacy, France, the Holy Roman Empire, and other nearby city-states. Palladio designed graceful, exciting villas and palazzos, arches and colonnades, and theaters, and in effect, handed down to posterity a formula for beauty based on "figurative mathematical abstractions," as Goffredo Parise wrote, to satisfy the megalomania of a middle class who were entirely without noble lineage or political ambition, but loaded with money. Originally Vicenza's courthouse or a public gathering place, the Palazzo della Ragione, known as the Basilica, is perhaps Palladio's greatest achievement and the most representative and spectacular example of his architecture. In 1546 Palladio was commissioned to restore the Basilica's two-story loggia, which had collapsed shortly after construction in the mid-fifteenth century, but it wasn't until 1617, nearly forty years after the architect's death, that the project was completed. The Basilica stands on the Piazza dei Signori, the main square at the heart of Vicenza where, in 1352, a goldsmith's guild was founded called the Nobile Fraglia degli Orefici. The art of metalworking had been practiced in the Veneto since ancient times and documents attest to the existence of objects containing gold found in the area dating back to the eighth century BC. Goldsmithing activities continued under the domination of the Romans and the Lombards and flourished during the Republic of Venice from the ninth century until the eighteenth century. Splendid decorative objects and ornaments resulted, including liturgical accessories such as reliquaries, censers and ciboria; beautiful jewelry, earrings, necklaces, bracelets; and clothing and hats, for example the *corno ducale*, a hornlike jewel-encrusted bonnet worn by the doge. Yet another example of goldsmithing activities in the Veneto is the production of *moretti*, literally "little Moors," which are brooches and pendants in ebony and precious stones used as charms thought to prevent invasions by the Saracens.

The twenty-three Palladian buildings in Vicenza's historic center were added to UNESCO's list of World Heritage Sites in 1994 and a proposal is underway to expand the list to include another twenty-four villas in the Vicenza, Padua, and Treviso areas. Andrea Palladio left his mark not only in the Veneto and in Friuli, but also in Western Europe and in America, where the master architect's *Four Books on Architecture* are among the cornerstones of classical architectural study. The great architect combined the poetry of classical form and proportion, executed so gracefully by the ancient Greeks and Romans, with the functionality theorized by the architect and art historian Giorgio Vasari, building works such as the Teatro Olimpico in Vicenza, Palladio's last, and considered one of his most exciting, works. Visitors to Vicenza are encouraged to stop by the sumptuous Palazzo Barbaran da Porto, home to a center dedicated to the life and works of Andrea Palladio.

facing page
The chain made by Pianegonda combines design with high-quality craftsmanship.

Jewelry shops are abundant in Vicenza and noteworthy stores include Cash & Gold and Orobase, GT Erre in Camisano Vicentino, and Ars Oro in Pove del Grappa. Vicenzaoro is an international gold and silver exhibition held in Vicenza during the months of January and June, and in September the Orogemma fair is dedicated to precious gemstones. Beautiful examples of gold work are on display at the civic museum in Padua, at the museum of Castelvecchio in Verona, and at the Tesoro di San Marco in Venice. The Pala di Pellegrino II is an embossed and gilt silver altarpiece in the Duomo at Cividale del Fruili and is one of the masterpieces of medieval goldsmithing.

CIVIDALE

A POPULAR STONE

FRIULI IS KNOWN FOR "POOR" STONE. MODEST HOUSES ARE MADE of untreated stone, as are the paved streets and the grand doorways of the palazzos, the statues, and the mosaic tiles. Stone has always been readily available throughout the province. It is easy to quarry and cut, and it is preferred over wood for construction because it is thought to be indestructible (except through earthquakes). The stone of Cividale, and not precious marble, is the material used for the area's most significant monuments. The Ponte del Diavolo (Devil's Bridge) is made of huge blocks of stone. It spans the Natisone River and is the town symbol. It was built in the fifteenth century to connect Borgo Ponte with the spur that rises before the Roman Forum and later with the medieval village. The Ipogeo, a famous Roman prison, is made of stone and is a complex of artificial caves dating to the Celtic era of the third century BC. A collection of iconic, refined sculptures are preserved in the Museum of the Duomo. They consist of the octagonal and columned niche of the Callisto Baptistery and the stone altar of Istria di Ratchis, one of the greatest examples of artistic expression of the High Middle Ages. The Palazzo dei Provveditori, designed by Andrea Palladio, looks out on the

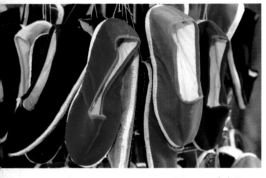

Comfortable and colorful, "Friulane" slippers are sold in many shops and market stalls.

Piazza del Duomo. It houses the archaeological museum, which contains an impressive collection of memorial stones and exquisite objects. This creates one of the most complete pictures of the art of people who have been dismissed by historians as "barbarians." The most precious stone of the region is the *pietra piasentina*, the commercial name for a carbonate rock that is classified among the hard limestone and the calcareous according to its grain. The color is a fairly intense gray-brown—it almost looks black. The origin of its name is not clear; it could come from *piacentina*, since a similar stone is found in abundance near the city of Piacenza. Or it may simply be that "la piase" is lovely to look at and easy to work.

This stone has been admired since ancient Roman times. The patriarchs of Venice used it to beautify their palazzos and to build fountains and porticoes. In the Middle Ages its status was downgraded, and it was used

Friuli, particularly Carnia, is known for the production of *scarpet* (felt slippers). In the past they were made by women during the winter months, when they gathered around the fireplace; they were sold in the cities of the plains by street vendors. These salespeople would travel well beyond the boundaries of the region to places where buyers admired the slippers' softness and durability. Since the twentieth century, slippers have been produced in small factories concentrated in the villages along the foothills. Indeed, making slippers has become an undeniable factor in the region's economy. The slippers are made of a fabric vamp, most often black velvet, and a sole that consists of several layers of felt and sturdy canvas. The slippers are tied together with dense rows of stitching for which durable string is used. *Staféz* are similar; the sole is made of jute, a lighter-weight material, and therefore preferable in the summer.

to pave roads and village squares. It was only used inside the most modest houses to make washing sinks, mortars to pound salt, and drinking holes for animals and troughs. Since the 1960s, *pietra piasentina* has regained some of its previous status. It has been used in elegant buildings and in art and design. It is worked by craftspeople who produce small decorative objects. The pietra piasentina is quarried in the valleys of the Chiarò River, in Torreano, Faedis, San Leonardo, and San Pietro al Natisone; the area's forests and farmland hide the quarries.

In Cividale, Julia Marmi works with stone and marble. Scarpet and traditional costumes are made by Creazioni Wally in Paularo. Unique textiles are sold at Gloria di Martin in Tricesimo. The Nella Fantasia store in Verzegnis specializes in decorative objects.

The great stone bridge, known as the Devil's Bridge, over the Natisone River in Cividale. The central arch rests on natural rock.

MANIAGO

KNIVES AND SWORDS

THE BLACKSMITHS OF MANIAGO COMMEMORATED their one-thousand-year-old heritage with a numbered knife. In the fifteenth century they were famous throughout Europe for the production of sidearms and bayonets, as well as equipment needed for farming. In the eighteenth century they specialized in making cutlery; they dominated this craft. However, the official date of birth of the blacksmiths' workshops in the village is 1453, when Count Nicolò di Maniago obtained permission from the Magistrate of the Waters of Venice to divert the Còlvera River; he built a canal for the irrigation of the fields. This canal was also used by the blacksmiths who set up shop near waterfalls.

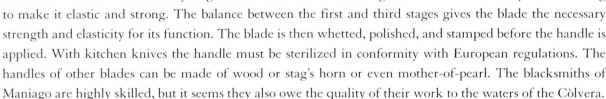

Handmade knives in Luciano Dal Ben's shop.

Making a blade is complex. The steel must have a high percentage of carbon and chrome. It arrives at the rolling mills where the rough shape of the blade is traced, or it arrives at the blacksmith's workshop in the form of rods, where it is forged. When the metal has to be wrought first, it is a more complicated procedure. The most important aspect of determining the characteristics of a blade is its sharpness. The rough blade is first put into the fire at 1,500 degrees Fahrenheit then the temperature is suddenly reduced by immersing the blade in water and oil; an alternative is to put it into nitrogen and inert hydrogen. The blade is then heated again, which is followed by a slow cooling to make it elastic and strong. The balance between the first and third stages gives the blade the necessary strength and elasticity for its function. The blade is then whetted, polished, and stamped before the handle is applied. With kitchen knives the handle must be sterilized in conformity with European regulations. The handles of other blades can be made of wood or stag's horn or even mother-of-pearl. The blacksmiths of Maniago are highly skilled, but it seems they also owe the quality of their work to the waters of the Còlvera.

In Maniago, cutting-edge technology and hand craftsmanship coexist. The town's internationally known companies manufacture knives of every kind—for the table, for work, with traditional shapes or innovative models. Silverware, scissors, bottle openers, surgical instruments, blades for ice skates—even Samurai swords and blades with hafts—are made and sold to silversmiths who mount the handles. The Del Tin workshop has recently become renowned. It specializes in making helmets, maces, armor, and breastplates. This work can be found in the Queen of England's armory museum. The company also made the weapons for the motion picture *Robin Hood, Prince of Thieves* starring Kevin Costner, as well as Mel Gibson's sword in *Braveheart*.

There is a museum of knives in the former Filanda Cadel, which was built in 1922. It will soon move to Via Vittorio Emanuele to the former offices of the Coricama (Coltellerie Riunite Caslino Maniage—the Consortium of Knife Makers of Maniago) which was founded in 1907 by Alberto Marx, who was a knife-maker in Solingen, Germany. The museum displays a comprehensive collection of handmade objects and work tools, and documents the most significant historical moments for the blacksmiths of the village, from the first artisan workshops of six centuries ago to the factories of the twentieth century that resurrected the craft. Intact ancient forges along the banks of the rivers near the village offer knife-forging demonstrations.

The Consortium of Knife Makers of Maniago represents almost all of the craftspeople in the town, and it has a showroom in the central Piazza Italia. One of the best brands is Alexander. There are other important blade-making production areas at Val Varrone in Lombardy's Premana, Scarperia in Tuscany's Mugello, Frosolone in Molise, and Pattada and Arbus in Sardinia.

facing page
The Duomo of San Mauro at Maniago dates back to the Franco-Longobard era.

MANZANO

THE CHAIR TRIANGLE

WOODWORK IS ONE OF THE OLDEST ACTIVITIES AND TODAY it is widespread in Friuli, where a diverse range of objects—from toothpicks to farm carts—are produced. Wooden masks are made in the Tolmezzo area; they are used in processions during Carnival and examples are displayed in the town museum. Craftspeople in Val Cellina carve tools and kitchen utensils that are sold in markets. Furniture is made in the Pordenone province in Brughera, Prata, and Pasiano. There is a deep-rooted woodworking culture in the Alpine areas of the Carnia.

Workshops are scattered throughout all the valleys and supported by a professional school for carpenters. Workshops in Paularo, Sutrio, Paluzza, and Villa Santina make rustic, carved furniture. But workshops in this area also make musical instruments such as violins and organs for churches, as well as toys. The *grop di Salomon* (Solomon's knot) is a curious souvenir. This charm made from hazelnut wood looks like a braid with twelve strands, reminiscent of Solomon's famous knot. Some major woodworking areas in eastern Friuli, almost on the borders with Slovenia, specialize in the production of chairs and other objects such as magazine racks, small tables, and coat stands.

Friuli women husk corn. The dry leaves will be used to create various objects.

Chair making dates back to ancient times, as shown by a detail of the eighth-century *Ara di Ratchis* in Cividale. In the so-called Chair Triangle—Manzano, San Giovanni al Natisone, and Corno di Rosazzo—the generosity of Empress Maria Theresa of Austria gave this craft a boost: In 1756 the empress supposedly gave the residents all the trees of the Ternova Forest so they could build a church. They began to make furniture—especially chairs and coat racks—with the leftover wood. Unlike tables and wardrobes, these pieces were easy to transport, and could be brought to and sold at markets. It is not certain that the empress actually did this, but it is true that around mid-century there were about thirty workshops specializing in the production of chairs. Today, the "Triangle," which covers about thirty-eight square miles, counts twelve

During the winter, in the region north of Udine and Cividale—in Reana, Ronchis di Faedis, and Cortale—the residents crafted corncob leaves into objects such as capacious rustic bags, slippers, placemats, trays, lampshades, and dolls. During the 1930s workshops produced nearly thirty thousand bags a year. In the 1970s the craftsmen's cooperatives supplied the market with a roster of more than four hundred different objects. Today this production has dwindled almost completely, because of Asian competition, but some craftspeople still continue this work. In communities where popular traditions are kept alive, people weave wicker and willow, with or without the bark, into baskets and panniers. The dark and light wood creates contrasting colors.

hundred companies that employ fifteen thousand people; these businesses made more than forty million chairs a year. This is 80 percent of the production in Italy, 50 percent in Europe, and 43 percent in the world. Since the 1950s the "Triangle" has also become one of the industrial centers that is most representative of the Italian style, thanks to the contributions of designers such as Giò Ponti and Carlo de Carli.

Chairs and tables can be purchased at Sedialand, the company outlet of Italsvenka in Manzano. Udine holds an exhibition of chairs. Throughout the region, especially Gorizia, woodwork and musical instruments are sold.

Handmade articles in wood and wicker on display in Manzano.

PORDENONE

AN INDUSTRIAL HISTORY

DURING THE ROMAN EMPIRE A SETTLEMENT WAS FOUNDED ON THE BANKS of the Noncello River near Torre; this was how Pordenone came to be. The ruins of a villa dating from the age of Augustus can still be seen. On the grounds is a large warehouse, proof of the productivity of the area and the natural commercial use of the waters of the Noncello, which was navigable at the time. An agricultural and artisan center developed and has existed for almost two thousand years. Goods and laborers embarked at the river port near Porta Furlana, bound for the Republic of Venice.

The city grew between the fourteenth and eighteenth centuries. During this time the present Contrada Maggiore was completed; it included elegant palazzos for the families of those artisans and merchants who had become wealthy and had purchased aristocratic titles. Warehouses and factories were built along the branches of the river. Ceramics were an important product. This craft had pre-Roman and even prehistoric origins— terracotta vases were found in Palù della Livenza and during other archaeological excavations. Many of the Pordenone craftspeople lived in a village called *la contrada dei bocalari* (the jug-makers' district) across the Noncello River, where the present village of Borgo San Giuliano is located. But even in the city, remains of Roman and medieval furnaces were found.

Shops under a picturesque arcade in Pordenone.

facing page
Ceramic jug made by the Galvani factory and now in the Civic Museum.

"La Fornase" was a village outside the Bossina gateway, beyond the Sant'Antonio irrigation canal. An official document dated 1328 cites a large furnace for the production of platters to be exported to the neighboring towns. The natural evolution that transforms artisan workshops into factories had also arrived at Pordenone. It was also obvious that the dismantling of these factories led to a production crisis. This in turn sowed the seeds for a rebirth of local craftsmanship. One example: the Galvani ceramics factory, founded in Pordenone in 1811 and closed in 1980. During its last years of operation it produced television sets, gas cookers, refrigerators, freezers, washing and dish-washing machines—the basis of industrial production in the area. Galvani supplied the region with vividly decorated earthenware for almost two centuries; the floral-motifed work can still be seen in many homes and local restaurants. Today the tradition continues. The Galvani company was taken over by the workers and the descendants of the family, and in the shops and markets throughout the Triveneto, it is possible to find plates, dishes, bowls, pots reinforced with wire, jugs, soup tureens, and other objects stamped with one of the many cockerel logos of the Galvani brand.

Secluded in the high Val Cellina, the residents of Andreis had to make the tools and clothes they needed. Today there are very few craftspeople who continue these traditions, and they do it more for pleasure than necessity. Their work can be seen in the local museum of farming. Footwear, clothes, and wrought iron and wood objects are displayed. One particularly unique item: combs made from oxen and bull's horns. Until the first years of the twentieth century these combs were sold by peddlers in the cities of the plains below. The horns had to be cut into three- to four-inch-long pieces. These were warmed to straighten them, and closed in a vise for a few days to fix the shape. They were then fashioned with knives and filed to make the teeth.

Flora Zava makes ceramics in Pordenone. In the first half of September, the Artigianato Alpe Adria exhibition, under the umbrella of the Multifiera, is held. At the traditional Christmas market in Pordenone, or at Fiuli Doc, which is held from September to October in Udine, crafts can be found among the stalls. They are also sold at Magia del Legno a crafts show held in September in the courtyards of the houses in Sutrio, Udine, or at the Artistic and Artisan Review of Carnia, organized in July and August in Socchieve, Udine.

SPILIMBERGO

THE STONES OF THE TAGLIAMENTO

FRIULI—VENEZIA GIULIA

THE MOSAICS OF THE ANCIENT AQUILEIA BASILICA ARE A SPLENDID EXAMPLE of the art of mosaic in the Friuli. This is a revered tradition, and it is represented by the works of the School for Mosaics in Spilimbergo. The work of these mosaic artists is appreciated—and on view—around the world: It is found at the Foro Italico in Rome, at the Palazzetto dello Sport in Trieste, in the New York City subway, and even in Japan. In addition to its great commissioned works, the school also makes smaller decorative objects, such as tables, mirrors, and fountains.

The school is housed in the castle, which was built at the beginning of the twelfth century by the counts Spengenberg, originally from Carinzia, to guard an important ford across the Tagliamento River. The town developed around the castle, took the name of the family, and Italian-ized it. The castle was enlarged, rebuilt in the fifteenth century, and renovated again in 1556 by Tadea, the widow of Bernardo di Spilimbergo. Both the castle and the museum within it are worth a visit. Here you can see the teachers and their students at work with little hammers and tongs as they assemble the small, brightly colored stones collected from the gravelly river bed of the Tagliamento. The stones are glued onto different surfaces. They are either placed directly or upside down on paper, which was a method created at the end of the nineteenth century by Friulian Gian Domenico Facchina. Various decorating techniques are used, from the Roman and Byzantine to the most modern, inspired by antique mosaics, frescoes, and famous artists, such as Chagall, Klimt, and Sassu.

The foothills north of Spilimbergo, and particularly Sequals, are home to terrace-makers. They still make terraces "alla veneziana" with a technique that is similar to mosaic. As the famous architect Andrea Palladio explained, these were created using pebbles collected from river beds. The terrace-makers would travel around Europe in the summer doing their work, and spent winters along the Cossa River collecting hard white stones. Yellow stones come from the Meduna River, and black, green, and red from the Tagliamento River. Red stones were called red of the Pyrennees, green stones were called Irish, and the black stones were called Belgium. Friulian terrace-makers worked in all the capitals of Europe by the second half of the nineteenth century. With their stones, they could imitate the most refined patterns of oriental carpets. Their most spectacular work can be seen in many of the palazzos overlooking the Grand Canal in Venice.

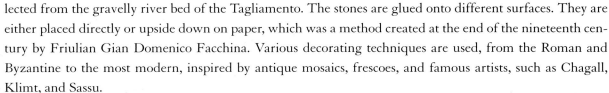

The fourteenth-century Spilimbergo Castle with its lovely three-mullioned windows and frescoes by Andrea Bellunello.

facing page
Detail of a mosaic creation made at Spilimbergo's Mosaic School.

In addition to the School for Mosaics in Spilimbergo, mosaic decorations are made to order by Cristina Cancian. Friul Mosaic in San Martino al Tagliamento and Alverio Savoia in Bertiolo also make mosaics. Gianna Liana in Martignacco makes beautiful flowers and butterflies on fabric, which are used as embellishments on clothing.

A museum of fashion and applied arts is located in the Dornberg-Tasso House at Borgo Castello in Gorizia. The three rooms on the second floor display religious vestments and paraments, and examples of fabrics and textiles made in the region from the eighteenth to the twentieth century. The finely worked silks that were made during Hapsburg rule are particularly beautiful. The Hapsburgs encouraged the cultivation of silkworms and built a large spinning mill in Farra d'Isonzo. There is also a display of rare machines of the period—an ancient throwing machine that was hand operated, not hydraulically driven; and an eighteenth-century sizing and edging machine that appears among the illustrations in the *Encyclopédie* by Diderot and d'Alembert. The other rooms present the work of Gorizia and the makers of the hats, footwear, and embroidery brought by Dutch nuns in 1672.

TRIESTE

DOMESTIC ARTS

IF ITALY CAN BOAST A CENTER FOR SCIENCE RESEARCH comparable to others around the world, Trieste is it. The city already was home to a number of institutions: a historic university, the Observatory of the National Institute of Geophysics, the National Institute of Oceanography and Experimental Geophysics, the CNR Institute of Marine Sciences, and the Laboratory of Marine Biology. Then in 1964 the International Center of Theoretical Physics was established here. It was sponsored by UNESCO and the International Atomic Energy Agency of the United Nations. The director is a Pakistani named Abdus Salam, winner of the Noble Prize for physics in 1979. The International Superior School for Advanced Studies was also established, as was the International Center for Genetic Engineering and Biotechnology (ICGEB). Here 150 scientists from thirty countries research solutions to the major problems afflicting the Third World. The Synchrotron Laboratory was also established in the 1970s. Carlo Rubbia was its first president, and another Nobel laureate in physics. There is now an Area Science Park on the slopes of the Carso Mountains and it is considered to be the most important science center in Italy.

The great park of the Miramare castle, built by Massimiliano of Hapsburg, overlooks the Adriatic.

Research with applications in chemistry and pharmacology, and in the textile, food, and automobile industries is undertaken. But these lofty projects are not particularly interesting to tourists—or to the locals for that matter. They prefer to settle into the velvet armchairs in the old, mirror-lined cafés to sip hot chocolate and eat little cakes. (The Caffé San Marco in Via Battisti is considered a landmark, protected by the Office of Monuments and Landscape and the Historical and Artistic Patrimony and the Ethno-Anthropology of Friuli—Venezia-Giulia.) People sit on the benches of the Buffet dell'Acquedotto in Via XX Settembre eating *porzina* and drinking red wine.

Trieste works hard to protect its old-world ambiance. It was a free port in 1719. In the first half of the nineteenth century it was the most important port of the Austro-Hungarian Empire. Nobles, rich merchants, shipping magnates, and renowned insurance companies, such as Generali and Lloyds, were located in the imposing and luxurious palazzos lined along the seafront or overlooking the Piazza Unità d'Italia.

Trieste's coastline is ideal for enthusiasts of steep rocks and deep waters. The water is so clear that there is a marine park. But there is also plenty for art admirers to enjoy. The lovely Miramare Castle, in Grignano Bay, was built in the second half of the nineteenth century by Archduke Maxillian of Austria, who later became Emperor of Mexico. The Throne Room, in which family portraits glorify the Hapsburgs, is especially interesting. The Navana is a reconstruction of the wardroom of the ship on which the archduke began his career. Farther north, on a spur of rock overlooking the sea, stands the Duino Castle. It was probably built in AD 1000, and has been documented since 1363. It belonged to the princes Thurn und Taxis, and today houses the Collegio del Mondo Unito del Adriatico.

Not very far from there is the Borgo Teresiano, built by Empress Maria Theresa for the workers' families. Here you can wander in the secondhand and antiques shops to search for objects that once filled the wardrobes or decorated the homes of the families of Trieste and Istria; books that once filled the shelves of the studies of intellectuals; and furniture from decommissioned ships. Complete silver cutlery services or ceramic stoves that belonged to the nobles or came from ships' dining rooms are not unusual finds.

Various antiques can be purchased at Lo Scrigno, at Di Pozza, or at the Galleria Antiquaria; Old Arredo specializes in antique furniture, books can be found at the Rigatteria, and prints are sold at Androna degli Orti. The Antiqua is an important antiques exhibition, and all the shops and market stalls in the area participate. It is held from the end of October through the beginning of November.

facing page
The objects in the markets and antiques shops of Trieste reflect the art and culture of both Italy and the Hapsburgs.

ALBISOLA
CERAMIC CREATIONS

SITUATED ALONG THE WESTERN COAST OF LIGURIA IS ALBISOLA *una e trina* (one and three): Albisola Capo is heir to the Roman *Alba Docilia*, but there is also Albissola Marina (with two *s*'s), and beyond it is Albisola Superiore (with one *s*), in the foothills of the Apennines. These three towns create quite a problem for cartographers who sometimes lump them together.

The sea and art have made Albisola famous. Since the Middle Ages, the town has been the home of innovative ceramicists; their genius over the centuries—creating artistic shapes, elegant decorations, and beautiful glazes—has left an indelible mark on high-quality pottery. Thanks to the discovery of lead-based paint, the area around Savona began to produce *protomailoca*, or ancient majolica, in the third century. Blue decorations, obtained with cobalt oxide and applied on a white or blue-gray background, are distinctive features of the so-called "ceramica di Albisola."

In the fifteenth century the workshops in the village produced multicolored tiles, called *laggioni*, as well as cookware for the noble families of Liguria. In the sixteenth century they specialized in pharmacy jars elegantly decorated with figures and ornate blue Arabic script; these were exported throughout Europe. In the second half of the seventeenth century Albisola ceramics attained their highest level of artistry, decorated with multicolored free-form shapes. Much of what was produced went to the noble houses, but the more modest output, called *ingobbiate* (covered with yellow paint) and *grattifi*, were produced for convents or were exported. From the eighteenth century, black pottery—*a taches noires*—came into its own; it was popular though not particularly aristocratic. It was produced in large quantities—output reached twenty-five million pieces a year—and was exported overseas. The decoration included Nativity-scene figures and imitations of ancient styles.

In 1902, at the Turin Exposition, Albisola presented its art nouveau ceramics style. In following years these became well known thanks to the artists who designed them: Lucio Fontana, founder of spatialism; Roberto Crippa, inventor of aeropainting; Piero Manzoni, much discussed for his *Merda d'Artista* in a box, shown at many museums around the world; Dangelo and Baj, founders of nuclearism; and other famous artists, such as Aligi Sassu, Arturo Martini, the Dane Asger Jorn, and the Russian Serge Poliakoff. Today the little ceramics factories continue to thrive and collaborate with artists, such as Treccani, Arroyo, Keizo, and Moncada. However, Albisola is still most famous for its ceramic pharmacy jars, plates, and soup tureens in the "antico Savoia" style, in which a single color, turquoise, is used to depict baroque scenes, biblical subjects, and mythological figures in bucolic landscapes.

The Giuseppe Bausin Mazzotti ceramics factory was founded in 1903 in the ancient village of Pozzo Garitta in Albissola Marina. Mazzotti was an artist/craftsman who played a fundamental role in the history of the art of Albisola ceramics. During the futurist movement at the beginning of the twentieth century, these artists would visit Mazzotti's workshop. In 1988 the factory changed its name to Fabbrica Casa Museo Giuseppe Mazzotti. Here his incomparable artistic and cultural heritage combines with the production of ceramics. Tableware, vases, and handpainted tiles in traditional and modern styles are sold. They are all created by hand using sixteenth-century techniques.

facing page
The "Wall of Artists" created by painters, sculptors, and ceramicists who worked at the furnaces at Albisola.

below
A finely decorated ceramic vase from Albisola.

The Liguria ceramics museum in Albisola Capo has a collection of pieces that span a period from the 1400s to the 1950s. There are other interesting exhibits at the Casa-Museo Jorn and at the Casa dell'Arte in Albisola Superiore. Along the waterfront the Promenade of Artists features mosaic paving, comprised of twenty panels of ceramics with abstract decorations. It was created by followers of the second futurist movement of the 1960s.

GENOA

GLORIOUS TEXTILES

LOCATED ON A STRIP OF LAND WITH NO PLACE TO GROW BUT UPWARD, Genoa has tall houses built one on top of the other like trees growing toward the light in a dense forest. The soul of this maritime city can be seen beyond the port area of the *carrugi*, with its narrow, perpetually dark streets cutting through the houses of the poorer neighborhoods. In this neighborhood are emporiums and artisan workshops of every kind. Some of the neighborhood's little squares have improvised markets where stalls sell unusual items. The atmosphere is more like an Arabian souk than a medieval marketplace in Italy. It is the collection point for goods from the surrounding countryside and the neighboring villages, which supplied the great port with its necessities and the palazzos with their excesses.

Since the Middle Ages, Genoa has produced and sold textiles, and the silk industry was particularly important. At the end of the eighteenth century, Genoa produced the highest-quality velvet on the European market. In the *Grande Encyclopédie* of 1765, this *velour* is described. It was a black velvet of incomparable softness and brilliance. It was used to make garments for gentlemen of the fifteenth century. The ladies preferred fabrics threaded with gold and silver, or the crimson damask from Lorsica. Here multicolored *lampasso* was also made. It was a silky fabric generally used for furnishings, and often threaded with gold or silver. Multicolored velvet was also made.

There are some manufacturers in Zoagli that still make velvet the traditional way on ancient looms; in Lorsica they weave linens and towels that have long fringes mixed with macramé. *Messier*, another antique textile typical of Genoa and cited in inventories of dowries in the third century, is still made by some craftspeople; it consists of seven- to ten-foot squares of cotton or linen decorated with vibrant colors. Examples of this work are preserved in museums in Genoa, Turin, and London. Originally they were silk veils embroidered with gold and worn by the women as shawls. They were then substituted with fabrics imported from the Indies and printed with oriental motifs; the most traditional motif is the flowering tree of life. Often they had sailing ships in the background, minarets, elephants, and monkeys. Rapallo is famous for lacework. It is thought that the women of the village began to make lace to be used by the fishermen and they invented a stitch to mend their nets. The Rapallo stitch was very difficult because of the many spindles required to fashion it.

Jeans, one of the most widespread symbols of American culture, were born in Genoa.

Nothing could be more American than jeans. Yet they were first made in Genoa and one of the most famous witnesses to this "prehistory" was General Giuseppe Garibaldi. His trousers have been preserved among his other mementos. The durable, indigo-colored fabric was known in the European markets as *blue de Genes*, and was used for sails and for cloth coverings for merchandise in the markets. But the fabric was also used to make sailors' clothes. Overseas they were called blue jeans and had a golden age. The first factories—Levis, Lee, and Wrangler—made pants for farmers, manual laborers, and cowboys. Due to the power of cinema, jeans became the epitome of leisure wear and dressed the legs of Hollywood stars such as John Wayne, James Dean, Marlon Brando, and Clint Eastwood. Today jeans are much more than the durable, indigo-colored "American" clothing of years past; they are dirtied, waxed, darned, stone-washed, bleached, and "branded" with the labels of the most famous Italian fashion houses.

In Genoa, furnishings at discount prices can be purchased at Roberto Ferrari and at Lo Scampolo del Negozietto. Clothing is sold at Magazzini del Cotone and knitwear can be found at Maglificio Ferro. In Zoagli, silks and velvets are featured at Cordani; in Lorsica, damasks and *lampassi* are produced by De Martini. The international nautical show is held in Genoa in mid-October and is one of the most important in the world.

facing page
Silk damask from the Zoagli Cordani silk-making factory. In the showroom there is a wide choice of beautiful fabrics and clothes can be made to measure.

LA SPEZIA

THE HOUSE OF SAVOY

IN THE MID-NINETEENTH CENTURY, THE KINGS OF SAVOY started building a great dockyard at La Spezia; since then the city has undergone continual development. "Wide roads and tall yellow houses," is how Ernest Hemingway described it. This nineteenth-century city looks young, and, as is typical of the young, it is untidy, reckless, rebellious, but also intriguing and full of promise. The Ligurian Riviera's most beautiful gulf was called the "Gulf of Poets" and was much beloved by Lawrence and Shelley. Napoleon understood the strategic potential of the area by the first years of the nineteenth century, and he called it "the most beautiful gulf in the universe." His plan was to build a colossal defense system that would reach from his future imperial city all the way to Portofino. Fortunately his great plan was defeated when he himself was defeated.

The idea of the dockyard did not die. It was revived by Camillo Benso, the Count of Cavour and minister of the Savoy kingdom. It began operation in the second half of the nineteenth century. With the opening of the port new residential areas were developed and wide avenues and bathing stations were built. Public gardens designed to equal the beauty of those in Tokyo were created. Space was made from the enormous mass of earth excavated to build the shipyards, and the old city was moved back from the shoreline. Where there was insufficient space extant buildings were demolished, such as Sant'Antonio Church and the Capuchins Convent that had been built on a spur overlooking the sea. Today the military shipyard incorporates significant pieces of naval archaeology. The iron swing bridge is still in operation after 130 years. The dry docks were once enormous and are now better adapted to modern needs. Historic ships are moored here, some dating to World War I. If you are lucky, you can see the *Amerigo Vespucci*, the most famous floating military school of the Italian navy; this is where it is berthed for maintenance.

Many civilian shipyards have developed alongside the military dockyards. They specialize in the production of leisure craft, such as sailboats, motor boats, and yachts. La Spezia's geographical location is desirable not only because it is on the coast, but also because it is in the center of the Mediterranean and close to the Genoa, Milan, and Pisa airports. Boats made by Ferretti, Azimut, Baglietto, Perini, and Sanlorenzo, famous names in Europe, America, and the Far East, are all launched from the Gulf of Poets.

facing page
A Ferretti yacht moored off the Ligurian coast.

below
The Ramba chair, with seat in gold-colored damask, is one of the models produced by Fratelli Levaggi at Chiavari.

La Spezia is home to the Baglietto shipyards, among the world's most important in the leisure-craft industry. Campo Ligure is where lovely filigree jewelry can be found in the workshops of Effe Erre, Pisano, Olivieri, Rizzo, and others. The Museum of Filigree is a must-see, and in August the town hosts a filigree jewelry exhibition. In Chiavari, the town's eponymous chairs are made by Adriano Podestà and Levaggi Alessio & Fratelli.

Campo Ligure is the home of gold and silver filigree, which was imported to Liguria during the Crusades. Creating arabesques and laces from very fine metal threads, the basis of filigree, requires infinite patience. The workshops along the main street of the town make beautiful jewelry, such as earrings, pendants, and brooches, as well as decorative objects. The museum of filigree displays an eighteenth-century aviary in the shape of a noble building, which is considered the greatest example of this technique ever created. Since the nineteenth century, Chiavari has produced "chiavarine" chairs, also known as "Campanino." They are very light, and made from cherry and beech wood; over thirty different models are made. Chairs are engraved, curved, and shaped, have hand-woven rattan seats and bright colors, and even incorporate gold leaf.

LAVAGNA
LANDSCAPES OF BLACK STONE

THE ANCIENT ROMANS CALLED THE INHABITANTS OF THE STRETCH of the Ligurian coast between Rapallo and Sestri Levante (now the Gulf of Tigullio) *Tigulli*, from the Latin *tegula*; these tegula were slate slabs mined from the mountains inland and used as roof coverings. Although the oldest document detailing the tradition of using slate as a roof covering is dated AD 1176, this kind of stone was used in Liguria dating back to periods before the Roman Era. In fact, blocks of slate were used centuries before to build homes and the tombs of the necropolis at Chiavari, from the Iron Age (eighth century BC).

This allotropic rock is formed by fine, dark gray limestone sediment. It is easy to cut, and its extraordinary characteristics prompted its use in all phases of construction. In addition to this traditional use, it was made into decorative objects and sculptures. Many of the buildings in the urban part of Liguria feature this sober and elegant slate: the walls and roofs of palazzos and churches, staircases, entryways, balconies decorated with family crests, fireplaces, and paving. Slate was used as backings for oil and tempera paintings and blackboards, because it can be produced in very thin, large sheets. Sculptures could be made because it is easy to chisel. It is used for billiard tables because it is also elastic and does not change shape. Seen from above, the historic center of Genoa is an expanse of silver-gray rooftops. The oldest churches had columns and capitals sculpted in this stone. The first quarries to be actively mined were in the Promontorio. They were nearest to the city, on the hills of Sampierdarena, but were abandoned in the seventeenth century in favor of the bountiful quarries of Uscio and Recco, and later those of the San Giacomo Mountain beyond Lavagna. Since the nineteenth century, slate has been quarried exclusively in the Fontanabuona valley, behind Chiavari and Lavagna, and the main production center is in Cicagna. This is where the largest number of caves and factories are to be found for cutting and working the stone.

The economy of the Fontanabuona mountain community, consisting of seventeen municipalities, is not solely based on slate. Various crafts are created in the villages: the Picasso foundries in Avegno have been making bells since 1594; the Trebino brothers' foundry in Uscio exports bells throughout the world, as far away as Brazil and Thailand; the first factory that made pendulum clocks was established in Terrile during the ninteenth century; there are four small toy factories and a toy museum in Gattorna.

facing page
A dramatic contrast of black slate and colorful tulips.

below
The Basilica of the Fieschi is one of the most significant medieval monuments in Liguria.

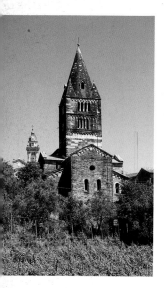

Various slate objects can be found in Val di Fontanabuona at the Consorzio Artigiano Ardesia Fontanabuona, and at Cuneo & C. in Cicagna. The slate museum in Chiapparino is worth a stop. Visitors can go to Isolona di Orero's nineteenth-century quarry, and Tribogna's historic Monte Tuggio caves.

Today Lavagna is equipped with mooring for sixteen hundred leisure craft up to 165 feet long. But in the era of the maritime republics, the village was too small to compete with Genoa. In 1547, the Fieschi family, who had ruled Lavagna for five hundred years, attempted to overthrow the Dorias. The plot failed and put an end to the domination of the family over the small duchy. But the Fieschi family has an honorable place in its history: first, because they gave two popes—Innocent IV and Hadrian V—to the Church, as well as a saint, Caterina Fieschi; second, because Count Opizzo ordered a special cake for his marriage to Bianca de' Bianchi that was large enough to feed all of his subjects. The documents do not say how large the cake was, but the one made today to commemorate this event weighs thirty-three hundred pounds.

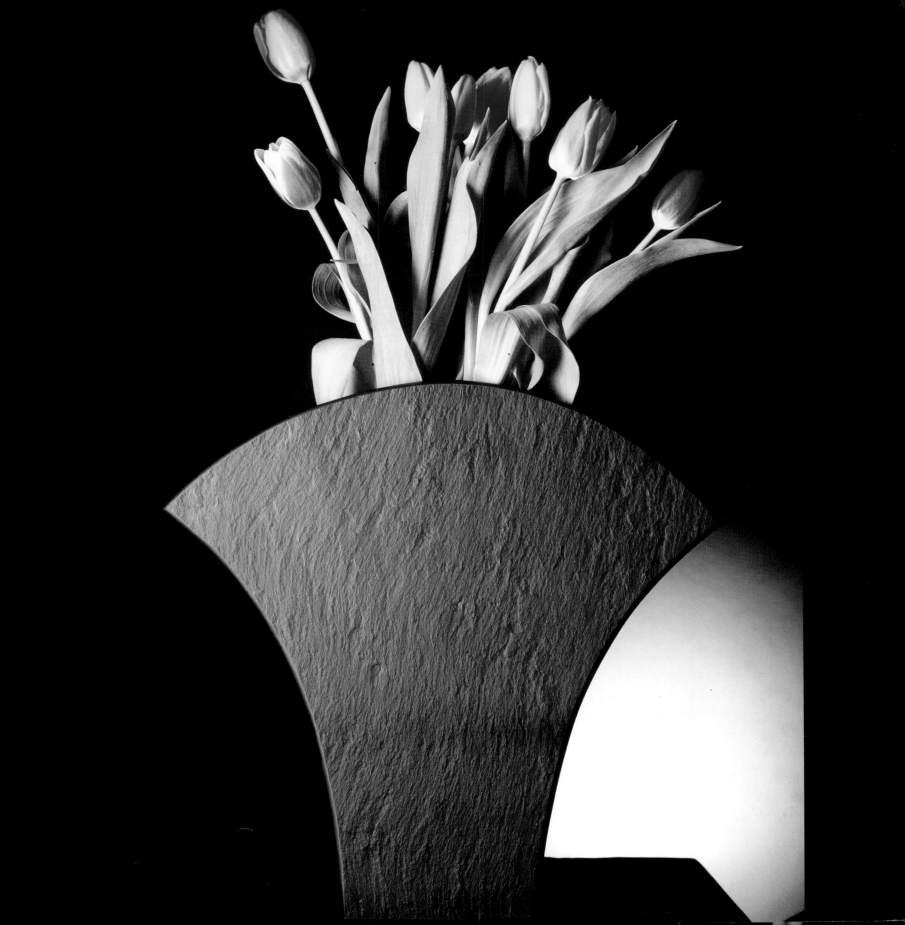

SAN REMO

LIGURIA   RIVIERA   OF   FLOWERS

KENYA MAY BE THE POWERHOUSE OF THE CUT-FLOWER MARKET, with 60 percent of world production, and the country may even export tulips to Holland, thanks to multinationals such as Unilever and Del Monte; however, in Italy, the person who buys carnations, roses, orchids, and lilies prefers to think they come from San Remo, the "city of flowers" and a center for the good life. Some two thousand cultivators, linked in two hundred cooperatives, work in the foothills of the Apennines beyond the city in the glittering-silver greenhouses; inside is an explosion of color.

In January 1951, the first Festival of San Remo, at that time called the Festival of Italian Song and hosted by Nunzio Filogamo, was held at the San Remo Casino. The first prize was awarded to Nilla Pizzi for the song "Grazie dei Fiori" ("Thank You for the Flowers"), in honor of the city's flower-growing tradition. Even the architecture of San Remo is related to flowers: art nouveau characterizes the sumptuous casino, inaugurated in 1905, as well as the hotels and villas, over two hundred of which were built between 1874 and 1906. The entire length of the western Riviera has earned the moniker "Riviera of Flowers." Indeed villages from Cervo to Ventimiglia all feature flowers. The mild climate and the pleasant air, and the seafronts lined with palm trees and gardens with flowers of a thousand shapes and colors, have been a popular tourist attraction.

The first flower market opened in Ospedaletti in the mid-nineteenth century, and the first Italian casino opened in 1911. The spark that created the fortune of these villages was *Il Dottor Antonio* (*Doctor Antonio*), a novel written by Giovanni Ruffini. He was exiled to the British Isles during the Risorgimento, and his book was published in 1855 in Edinburgh. The story takes place on the Riviera and tells the romantic love story of the aristocratic Miss Lucy and the local doctor who looks after her after an accident. The English upper-middle classes fell in love with the story and its setting. They learned about Bordighera, San Remo, Diano Marina, and Alassio, and began to set up residences in these little fishing and farming villages; they built large villas with splendid gardens close to the sea, and organized literary and artistic salons that attracted artists from around the world. In Bordighera the Via Vittorio Veneto is almost an Anglo-Saxon fiefdom in Victorian style, with its beautiful garden in Pallanca. Three thousand cacti and succulents are planted here. Painter Claude Monet was struck by the exotic beauty of the village; during a stay of less than three months in the winter of 1884, he painted more than forty canvases. The gardens at Villa Hanbury in the Mortola, near Ventimiglia, were created in 1867 by wealthy merchant Sir Henry Thomas Hanbury. This incomparable garden features fifty-eight hundred species of ornamental plants from around the world.

facing page
The garden of an artist's studio at Bussana Vecchia.

below
A flower bed in the San Remo park.

Lindita and A&G sell flowers. Bonsai plants can be purchased at the Centro Bonsai on the road to Bussana Vecchia, an ancient village that has been restored and is now an artists' community. The glass museum in Altare, located in an old deconsecrated church, showcases lovely bottles and huge vases.

Altare is a little village beyond Savona, and it has been a glass-work producer since the twelfth century. This type of work was introduced by the Benedictine monks of Bergeggi, who set up the first furnaces here with the help of families from Normandy and Flanders. In 1495, the University of the Art of Glassmaking was founded; the guild protected the master glassmakers and their wares. For centuries the consulate of the university played a fundamental role in the management of its artistic production. Altare specializes in transparent glass in contrast to Murano, where colored glass is preferred. The glass for the Lanterna, the lighthouse of the port of Genoa, was made in Altare. Typical wares of the area—engraved and decorated blown-glass objects, and thin, long-stemmed vases—can be purchased.

BOLOGNA

WILD HORSES

GUGLIELMO MARCONI RETURNED TO BOLOGNA FROM THE UNITED STATES in 1926 to receive an honorary degree for his invention. During that year the young Cavalieri Ducati brothers founded the Società Scientifica Radio Brevetti Ducati for the production of very powerful condensers "as small as a tiny coin." In 1924 the brothers made it possible for a naval unit in the Atlantic Ocean to communicate with five continents by means of a shortwave radio built by Marconi. Ten years later, in Borgo Panigale on the outskirts of Bologna, the Ducati brothers built a modern factory where employees in white coats produced radios, electric razors, cameras, film projectors, and calculators. The machine shops contained such sophisticated equipment that it was requisitioned by the Germans during the war. The equipment was transported to the north, but it was hidden in underground caves and haystacks along the way. At the end of the war the factories geared up to manufacture the Cucciolo (puppy), a small 40-cc engine that reached a speed of twenty-five miles per hour; it could be placed on any kind of bicycle. Mounted on a specially built chassis, the Cucciolo won many competitions and broke many records.

During those first years the motorcycle did not attract much interest among young people and the middle class. It was a means of transport for the poor, used by laborers going to work. During the mid-1950s Ducati upgraded its image when it introduced the Marianna, a Gran Sport 100-cc motorcycle that won every prize from 1954 to 1957. It broke forty-four world records on the Monza circuit in 1956. The Bolognese company built another mythical machine: the Scrambler. It was popular among Americans, already Ducati's best clients, because it represented the rebellious lifestyle that was portrayed in Hollywood films of that era. It was a machine that could go anywhere but was used to go nowhere.

Ducati became the machine to beat, the thoroughbred to tame. The 750 GT Imola was a motorcycle series that also won races. The 851 was impressively powerful and had a cult following in Japan. The shape of the Monster was essential, with all of its parts visible. It is still being imitated but it has never been equaled. The 926 was an extraordinary combination of aesthetics and functionality. In 1998, one hundred motorcycles told the story of The Art of the Motorcycle at the Guggenheim Museum in New York. At the end of the exhibit, at the top of the museum's famous "spiral," the great work of Frank Lloyd Wright, the Ducati 916 and the Monster faced each other.

A brand new Ducati Monster 695.

facing page
An evening under the arcades of the church of the Crucifix on Piazza Santo Stefano.

Artisanal objects are made in many of the villages in and around Bologna: wrought iron in Castenaso, candles and mosaics in Dozza, glass lamps and wood objects in Imola, ceramics in Ozzano dell'Emilia, decorative paper in Sala Bolognese, and glass objects in Sasso Marconi. Bologna hosts a lovely market at Montagnolathere Park every Friday and Saturday. Budrio ocarinas are sold at Menaglio.

Budrio is a village near Bologna, and in 1860, a resident named Giuseppe Donati invented the *ocarina*, a simple wind instrument made of terracotta. The instrument was an immediate success because it was so easy to make and cheap, due to its inexpensive material. It was also simple to use and could make a sound that not even the sophisticated instruments could reproduce. Since that time the ocarina is featured at all the popular fairs in the Emilia where people enjoy ballroom dancing. In Budrio, where the instrument is still made, the local musicians play serious classical music and organize concerts. There is also an ocarina museum in the village, where the terracotta musical instruments are displayed.

THE PO DELTA

D E C O Y S

THE VAST MARSHES AT THE MOUTH OF THE PO RIVER DELTA were considered unhealthy and dangerous. But they have always been used by humans because they were rich in vegetation and animal life. Today the prevailing economy of the region is based on the breeding and fishing of mollusks and eels. Although artisanal crafts once powered the economy, today they are a more marginal, though still important, activity.

One of these crafts is specific to the Bagnacavallo area (Ravenna), and utilizes a seemingly unimpressive but widespread resource found in the shallow waters of the lagoons: marsh reeds.

The stems of these fragile bushes, called *pavere*, are used to weave mats; the leaves are used to make hats and bags. The *bosmarola* seems to be even more useful. This is a very resistant marsh grass used to make brooms and brushes. Reeds are used to make a popular craft related to the numerous migratory birds that stop every year in the Argenta (Ferrara): decoys. These surprisingly life-like decoys—wild ducks, curlews, ducks, and other marsh birds—are made with reeds bound together, modeled, painted, and finished with a sculpted wooden head. They are floated in the pools of water while the hunter is hidden in the reeds with a whistle that reproduces the mating sounds of the different bird species. Flocks of birds are attracted by the sound and become easy targets.

Production of these decoys was particularly active in the nineteenth century when they reached their highest level of artistry. They were made from disparate materials—wood, bone, and reeds—and brass was used for the whistles. Today, this hunting method is rare, and whistles are usually plastic; these whistles are much cheaper and the sound rougher but they are sufficiently effective at deceiving migrating birds. Craftspeople continue to make decoys with reeds because they are popular decorative objects.

Other forms of weaving have developed farther from the delta, where the abundance of poplar and willow replaces the more noble wood. Wicker is used to make furniture and accessories; the branches of the willow are cut into long, thin strips, and woven into hats. They are durable and light and at the end of the nineteenth century they were exported to the other European countries and overseas. Today most of this work has been industrialized and semifinished articles are produced. But some artisans continue their work and produce finished pieces.

Originally used as decoys for duck hunting, this handmade pair now serves a decorative purpose.

facing page
A fishing hut on the Po Delta is an ideal place for bird watching.

Special boats are needed to navigate the narrow canals and low muddy waters of the Po River delta; they are flat-bottomed and easy to row with just the strength of the arms. The *mammalucco* boat, used by hunters, is sixteen feet long. The *batana*, mostly used by fishermen and cane cutters, is longer and wider; these boats are also used to travel throughout the delta. The *velocipede*, used for regattas, is long and tapered. Even though plastic boats are popular, the "masters of the hammer" in the small shipbuilding yards continue to make classic boats by hand using local wood: poplar is used for the bottom and sides, and cherry or walnut wood is used for the ribs.

Many woven products are made by Grazia del Pozzo in Argenta. Cane furniture is sold at Arredamenti Cavallini in Forlì, at Arredamenti de Angeli in San Polo d'Enza, in the Emilia-Romagna region, and at Giovanni Ferrari in Roccabianca, in the province of Parma. Villanova di Bagnacavallo has an interesting museum of wetland vegetation.

FAENZA

MAJOLICA MASTERPIECES

CERAMICS ARE AN IMPORTANT PART OF THE ECONOMY OF EMILIA–ROMAGNA. The region is also known for textiles, motors, and fine food. But tiles from Sassuolo, in the Modena area; bricks from Casalgrande, in the Reggio area; and the artistic ceramics of Faenza and Imola all are world renowned. Excellent, nutrient-rich clay in the area lends itself to manipulation and is resistant when fired. But the merit of this earthenware is also due to the manual dexterity of the craftspeople and the lively entrepreneurial spirit that characterizes the region.

It all began more than eight centuries ago in Faenza. The city was already famous for its ceramics, even though there was competition from the older Tuscan tradition that had roots in the Etruscan civilization. Since that time, the city has kept the ovens lit and its fame alive and has created followers everywhere. It is a difficult record to equal.

During the first centuries Faenza produced a ceramic of good quality but similar to others in its Gothic and Arabic decorations. During the second half of the sixteenth century, the people of Faenza began to cover the terracotta with a white lead-oxide glaze; this embellishment was an important innovation, because it increased the value of the objects. But the glaze was so beautiful in and of itself that soon artists made objects in white glaze without any decoration. Throughout Europe the "white" ceramic of Faenza became synonymous with excellence; the shapes were often extravagant. It is still the most appreciated kind of ceramic work in the world.

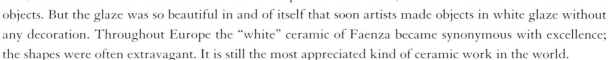

Piazza del Popolo at night.

"Faenza" has been translated into almost every language: *fayence*, *faïence*, *fajans*, *fajansas*, and even into Arabic and Chinese. Even to those who make it, the word has come to mean white-glazed ceramics that are decorated minimally or not at all. A visit to the city's international museum of ceramics relates the history and techniques of Faenza ceramic, and details the styles used, including archaic, floral, *berettino*, and others. The museum has a rich assemblage of ceramic work from all periods and countries; objects from Roman amphoras to the modern works of Chagall are in the collection. Creative vase-makers and decorators work in the town's many workshops and factories, and in specialized schools that date back to the Middle Ages and the Renaissance. Contemporary artists have also contributed modern shapes and colors to this output.

Ceramic, from the Greek *keramòs*, or clay, is a fairly porous and compact clay paste. It is baked in special ovens at high temperatures and then covered with paint or glaze. The resulting types of earthenware—these differ depending on the minerals contained in the paste, the density, and the length of time and temperature at which they are baked in the oven—are terracotta, faenza, majolica, or porcelain. After it has been treated in the oven the terracotta remains porous and takes on a color that ranges from yellow to red (after the first firing it is called bisque). Once the terracotta is painted and returned to the oven, the result is faenza, which is used for glazed, artistic ceramics. Majolica—the name possibly derives from the Spanish island of Majorca—is similar to faenza and is obtained from clay that is covered with glaze or glass. Porcelain is a translucent and compact ceramic, a white paste that is used for high-quality work.

Among the many ceramics workshops and factories in Faenza, the most important are Gatti, Vignoli, and the Maestri Maiolicari Faentini. A biennale of antique ceramics is held every other year in September. Each year from mid-June to mid-October Estate Ceramica, a market and exhibition of Faenza's ceramic tradition, takes place.

facing page
Some Faenza ceramics with decorations inspired by classical medieval and Renaissance styles.

GAMBETTOLA

ELEGANT LINENS

A STRONG ODOR OF VINEGAR PERVADES OLD PRINTWORK FACTORIES in Gambettola, and that's because vinegar is used to prepare color to be printed on fabric. This tradition is unique to the region of southern Romagna, where it began at the end of the eighteenth century. It is called "rust printing" because the principal ingredient of the color is soft lead. It is rusted with wine vinegar and treated with nitric acid; this sets off the fermentation that gives the mixture a glue-like consistency. There is no precise rule about the amount and the method of preparation; there is no handbook. The only thing that counts is experience acquired after years of experimenting. The printing is done solely by hand. Pear wood is used because it is easy to engrave and is resistant to hammering. Xylographs, or wooden dies, are engraved to a depth of up to one-quarter inch, which is sufficient to collect the color and not smudge the fabric.

Every printwork factory has its own collection of dies. They are often made by the same craftspeople and are zealously guarded. After the paste and the dies are prepared, the fabric is stretched on a padded bench. The die is pressed onto a wad of absorbent material soaked in the color and then placed on the fabric. It is beaten with a hammer that weighs about nine pounds; this makes it stick to the surface and imprints the design. The fabric is hung up and allowed to dry; after this it is treated with caustic soda to fix the color. *Ranno* was used in the past: boiling water was poured over wood ashes and then filtered through a sieve. These lengths of fabric are used as tablecloths, napkins, bed coverlets, and curtains. In the past they were made for modest houses and were made of rough canvas printed with simple designs with just a few homemade colors; the rust was made with old pieces of iron. It seems the resulting fabric was first used to cover oxen; it was decorated with the image of Sant'Antonio Abate. They imitated the rich fabrics that were embroidered or printed with more refined techniques. And it is indeed the imitation of these rich fabrics that later led to copying the elaborate designs of carpets and brocades. A recurring example is the thistle, which was often found on fifteenth-century fabrics (note the gold-brocaded cloak of Sigismondo Pandolfo Malatesta). To evaluate the authenticity of a fabric printed with this technique, all one needs to do is turn it over; the back is where the design and the color can be seen and the imperfections are more evident. In fact, as opposed to silk-screened fabrics, where the colors look flat, the design on the fabrics that are hand-printed with wooden dies is blurred, and the repetition of a die is never the same.

Inside the Pascucci printworks at Gambettola

facing page
Prints, antique instruments, and examples of designs that are still in use to create hand-printed textiles.

Gambettola is a paradise for lovers of scrap iron. There is a market for old and antique automobiles, and a "Militaria" market that sells military equipment and other old objects. Gambettola's Mostrascambio (exchange market) is held on the second weekend of May and the first weekend of September. There are eight hundred to one thousand stalls and incredible items can be found: original replacement pieces that are impossible to find anywhere else—even airplanes and tanks are sold or exchanged. The tradition dates back to the nineteenth century, when Gambettola's "rag-and-bone" men went around to farmhouses collecting everything they could, from used clothing to rabbit skins. This activity was more important after the end of World War II. In the village there is even a monument to the *Strazzer del Bosch* (the rag-and-bone man of the forest).

Pascucci have been printers and dyers for five generations. Theirs is the oldest workshop in Gambettola; it still contains a circa 1820s mangle, which was used to iron fabric before it was decorated. Bertozzi is another print work company. Similar companies also can be found in Cesenatico, Sant'Arcangelo di Romagna, and Rimini.

GRAZZANO
VISCONTI
URBAN PLANNING

AN ENIGMATIC PAINTING OFTEN APPEARS ON THE WALLS of Grazzano Visconti, a lovely village in the plains of Piacenza. The painting shows a carnation and in Gothic letters is the phrase *Otla.ni.adraug.e.enetapipmi.* Read from right to left it states "impipatene e guarda in alto," which means "Don't give a damn and look upward." According to experts on the work, it is the village creator's answer to his critics and detractors. In fact, Grazzano Visconti is a "medieval" village that is less than one hundred years old; it is a beautiful but "artificial" creation.

To understand the origins of the village one must know the real history of the Viscontis of Milan, who gave governmental control over the village of Grazani to the Anguissola in the fourteenth century; the Anguissola family was one of the most powerful in the Piacenza area. This family built a castle that survived, withstanding much inept restoration, until the end of the nineteenth century. At the beginning of the twentieth century, Grazzano was a modest hamlet of farms and stables surrounding the ruins of a country residence. The owner, Count Giuseppe Visconti di Modrone, took it upon himself to have two of the cas-

The blacksmith Luciano Savi's workshop at Grazzano Visconti.

facing page
A characteristic building in the medieval village.

tle's towers rebuilt. The Ghibelline battlements and the communication passages were restored as well. He restored the walls and the red brick facade; these were then decorated. A park of tall trees, avenues, fountains, and allegorical statues was created. He even built a village in the style of those from the centuries just after AD 1000, with porticoes, arched windows, columns, family crests, wrought-iron signs, wells, fountains, and even a little Gothic church. Walking around the village is like being transported back in time, even if the oldest building is only about one hundred years old. Wrought iron, wood, textile, and ceramics workshops were established. In 1915 the village looked as it still does and this is the way it has been preserved. It looks so authentic that it provides a natural background for historical reenactments, such as Caterina di Anguissola's farewell feast, when she left to become the bride of Louis d'Orleans, brother of the King of France. It has been the setting of many historical films. It is also said that a ghost, Eloisa, resides in the castle. According to lore, she died of jealousy because of her husband's repeated betrayals. Her statue stands near the Piazza del Biscione; it was

The typical wood furniture of Grazzano Visconti is featured at the Istituzione Giuseppe Visconti di Modrone in Piazza Galeazzo Visconti. It also sells furniture and beautifully restored antiques. The Visconti "reptile" is among the wrought-iron objects made. The shops in the tiny village sell ceramics, textiles, and souvenirs.

Tourism is the primary source of income for Grazzano and local crafts abound as a result. In the past there was real craftsmanship; for example, until the mid-nineteenth century a man named Giuseppe Savi worked as an all-purpose blacksmith and head of a group that thrives to this day. His workshop faced the castle gate. Grazzano's souvenirs are not mass-produced or "made in China." Under the porticoes there is a blacksmith's forge, and the workshops of a ceramicist, a carpenter, and a maker of ironworks, as well as silversmiths, and makers of vases and plates, and "Grazzano style" furniture, such as chests, beds, cupboards, and cabinets characterized by very deep bas-relief. For those with the talent there is also a school of craftsmanship.

made to match a description she gave of herself during a séance. In honor of its creator, and by royal decree, Grazzano added the name Visconti. The originality of this business lies in the fact that Grazzano is not a "fake" village at all, nor a reconstruction to be locked in a museum. It is alive and inhabited by people who live and work there and is visited by thousands of tourists.

MODENA

EMILIA— ROMAGNA CRADLE OF MYTH

Maranello is a little town south of Modena. It is a place of pilgrimage, as important as Fatima or Lourdes—only the religion is different. The devotional object is not the Madonna—it is engines. This little town has given birth to great machines, automobiles, and motorcycles as well as famous drivers. Ferrari, more a legend than an automobile, has its headquarters in Maranello. The name gives rise to great feelings and passions. These cars are beyond the means of many, who must content themselves with admiring their physical beauty. Ferraris have been designed by famous technicians such as Pininfarina, Bertone, and Vignale.

The first Rossa was officially introduced in 1946, but the young Enzo Ferrari had been a frequent visitor to the autodromes as of the 1920s. In 1929 he founded a racing team in Modena; it sponsored drivers and prepared Alfa Romeo cars for competitions. He was then hired by Alfa Romeo as manager of the new racing department, but soon left to found another company that he called Auto Avio Costruzioni; this company apparently produced airplane components, because Alfa prevented him from taking part in motor racing for four years. He built the Auto Avio Tipo 815—definitely the first Ferrari, even if it did not have his name. This car was used in only a few races before the start of the war. In 1943 the factory moved from Modena to Maranello, where it still has its headquarters. In 1946 he started to build his first racing car, the 125 S, which began to win races; it quickly became famous.

As a result of this car's success, and to finance the races, Enzo Ferrari manufactured a small line of sports cars. These cars were popular, even though they had unreliable and unstable engines—at least until the introduction of electronic injection in the 1980s. For enthusiasts, this was a part of the "character" of the cars and they defended the fallibilities of their beloved. Scuderia Ferrari (Ferrari Stable), as in horse stable, referred to the prancing horse logo that was the symbol of Count Francesco Baracca, a legendary Italian ace fighter pilot of World War I. The first world championship of Formula 1 racing was held in 1950. José Gonzales won in 1951; Alberto Ascari achieved the title of world champion in 1952. He was followed by many others: Nuvolari, Fangio, Hill, Lauda, Villeneuve, and Schumacher. Ferrari is the only automobile manufacturer that has not abandoned Formula 1 racing. And Ferrari is the company that has achieved the greatest success: fourteen championship titles, fourteen champion drivers, and 182 victories in the Gran Premio.

Bordered by the Duomo, the Ghirlandina tower, and the airy portico of the Palazzo Comunale, the Piazza Grande was once an ancient gathering place. The piazza is a UNESCO World Heritage site.

Carpi is a large agricultural town in the Modena area. Since World War II it has become one of the most famous knitwear districts in the world. About thirteen thousand employees work in twenty-five hundred small but highly specialized factories. The few large companies that sell and export all over Europe, and to the United States and Asia, subcontract to small family-run businesses that specialize in only one aspect of the work. Carpi manufactures most of the knitwear, shirts, and women's clothes that are designed but not made by the important fashion houses.

The Galleria Ferrari is near the car factory in Maranello, and it is here that the history of the Rossa and its founder are celebrated. Each year 175,000 people visit. Clothing, gadgets, books, and scale models are sold in the shopping center. Tourists can rent Ferraris in Italy; see www.redtravel.com. Carpi has many clothing shops, and among them Frarica-Fino Erre sells shirts, Italo Confezioni sells knitwear, and Lepel sells lingerie.

facing page
An antique model of the popular red Ferrari.

RAVENNA

MOSAICS OF LIGHT

GALLA PLACIDIA, DAUGHTER OF EMPEROR THEODOSIUS and regent of the Empire, chose Ravenna as her capital in the name of her son, Valentinian. She built her mausoleum here, and it was innovative for the period: simple in form but decorated with the mosaics that are the signature art of Ravenna. These mosaics are unusual because the tiny tiles of glass paste are not placed on the supporting mortar to make a surface that is smooth and uniform; instead, they are placed at different angles. The result of this positioning is that light is reflected in the eyes of the viewer no matter where the direction of the light comes from. This is analogous to the system "invented" by the divisionist painters fourteen centuries later. A mosaic made in this manner always produces splendid colors and seems to emit its own luminosity, irrespective of the direction or quality of the light, or the time of day. These are striking works. They light up the decorations on the mausoleum. The windows are closed with thin sheets of alabaster; this provides a much more effective diffused light for the figures on the wall mosaics and the vault than the direct light of the sun. Emperor Theodosius recreated these conditions for his own mausoleum, and with the same simple exterior of plain bricks and sumptuous interior the Byzantines built Sant'Apollinare in Classe Church and San Vitale Church, the monuments that best represent Ravenna.

Sant'Apollinare was built near the ancient gateway of Classe, which had already begun to sink into the sand. It is lavishly decorated with mosaics representing scenes from the Old and New Testaments, landscapes, and processions. San Vitale is more like a Byzantine church. The presbytery is decorated with beautiful mosaics of processions that accompany Emperor Justinian and his wife Theodora.

Today, the art of mosaic is kept alive in Ravenna at the mosaic schools, the most important one being the State Institute of the Art of Mosaic, housed in the gallery of the Accademia. This school teaches techniques needed to faithfully reproduce antique mosaics. Students reproduce the design on a piece of paper and apply the tiles onto this with glass paste similar to that used in Roman and Byzantine times. They also experiment with new techniques—famous artists such as Chagall, Guttuso, Cagli, and others have made contributions. There are also many workshops in the town where the art of mosaic is passed down in the traditional way—from father to son. These workshops make decorative mosaics of any size.

The Ravenna Cooperative of Mosaic Workers at plying their trade.

facing page
Glorious Byzantine mosaics decorate the mausoleum of Galla Placidia.

Various mosaic works, decorative objects, and panels can be purchased in the town's workshops, including Artemosaico, Cooperativa Mosaicisti, Belkis, and Mosaici Antichi e Moderni. Dimensione Mosaico are sold in Fornace Zarattini and Arredomosaic in Sant'Alberto. In addition, mosaic work can be commissioned.

Ravenna's monuments provide evidence of the three important civilizations that have left their mark here over four centuries: the Roman, with Galla Placidia (fourth to fifth century AD), the Gothic, with King Theodoric (fifth century), and Byzantine (fifth to eighth century).The mosaics in Galla Placidia's mausoleum should be visited, as should the Arian Baptistery (the *Baptism of Jesus* in the cupola). Sant'Apollinare Nuovo's interior is completely covered in mosaic. Visit the Neon Baptistery (*Baptism of Christ* and the *Apostles*), which is called the Orthodox Baptistery to distinguish it from the Arian Baptistery; Sant'Apollinare in Classe, where in the basin of the apse St. Apollinare is surmounted by a great cross, which appears for the first time in the history of art; and the presbytery of San Vitale.

SASSUOLO

THE KINGDOM OF TILES

EIGHTY PERCENT OF ITALIAN TILE IS MANUFACTURED IN THE MUNICIPALITIES between the provinces of Modena and Reggio Emilia—that's 230-square-miles' worth; 70 percent of this output is exported. Until ten years ago this constituted half the European production and 30 percent of production worldwide. Output has not declined and Sassuolo still is the leader in this area. Even though countries such as Mexico, Brazil, and China have made inroads, the most important tile-making center is this "district of ceramics."

The name Sassuolo could derive from "olio di sasso," the petroleum that is found in small quantities in the area and that sometimes gushes from the earth. Most likely, the name comes from a primitive settlement on a rocky spur surrounded by clay that covered the vast bed of the Secchia River; this is where the name *saxum solum*—isolated rock—originated. Certainly, the little town that grew from this modest elevation has had a long and prosperous history; above all under the dukes of Este, who transformed the pre-existing fortified castle into a grand palazzo. They chose this as their summer residence, because of the good climate and the nearby Salvarola thermal baths, which have existed since Roman times.

The arches of the Baroque facade of the ducal palace.

facing page
A room decorated with tiles from the Ottagono series, one of the lines of the Ceramiche Provenza.

The first "mezzamaiolica" (half-ceramic) factory was established in 1741; the presence of clay in the area and an exclusive concession from the duchy helped propel this work. Other small pottery industries developed; these produced number plates for the city and even modern tiles for pavements and walls. Companies began to export their wares to the Mediterranean area and even to South America. Until World War II Sassuolo was a small village surrounding a park and the castle, which was falling into disrepair. After the war there was an increased demand for tiles and a new Sassuolo was born, with a surge in the number of furnaces and warehouses. This sudden development was undoubtedly due to reconstruction demands after the war, but it was also due to a revolutionary concept: building tiles did not have to be white. As a result the ceramicists of Sassuolo took to heart the proverb "the house is a beautiful woman to be dressed," and created tiles of different shapes and sizes, and in thousands of shades and colors. They entrusted their designs to famous artists and transformed what was a product reserved for sanitary fixtures into an important element of interior decoration.

Assopiastrelle, a center that documents the history of ceramic tiles, is housed in the sixteenth-century *palazzina*, or little palace of Casiglia. The organization has just celebrated its fortieth anniversary. A collection of more than one thousand pieces showcases the evolution of the production of Sassuolo from World War II to the present, and provides a history from the first prototype to the industrial production of the present. Displayed are models made throughout history at the different factories. They document the use of the material—terracotta, monocottura (once-fired), porcelain, and grés—as well as the decorative techniques, such as stencil, decal, silk-screening, hand painting, and bas-relief. Particular focus is on contemporary techniques and models.

Today there is a vast range of choices—different shapes and sizes; in red, porous fired brick; once-baked unglazed and glazed ceramics; twice-baked glazed majolica (the first firing for the shape, the second for the glaze); and *grès* or clinker, produced in large quantities but also designed by hand.

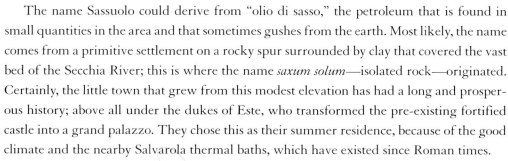

One of the principal
world producers of
tiles is the Marazzi
Group, which has a
major presence in
the United States.
Tiles can be
purchased from
Enrico Brandoli;
Manzani produces
handmade bricks;
and there is a
ceramics museum in
Fiorano Modenese.

SAN MARINO
FREE TRADE

WHILE VACATIONING ON THE ADRIATIC RIVIERA MANY PEOPLE spend a day in the Republic of San Marino. They go there to visit the ancient village and the castle on Mount Titano, as well as to shop—one can get better deals here than in Italy.

Even though San Marino is completely integrated into Italy and the Italian way of life, it is an independent state with its own constitution; its constitution has remained substantially unchanged for fourteen centuries. It is governed by a sixty-member council, one-third of whom are nobles, one-third of whom are middle class, and one-third of whom are rural people. An independent judge serves for three years and administers justice; its army of forty men defends the rock. San Marino is the oldest, smallest, and one of the richest and best politically and commercially organized republics in the world.

A tenth-century manuscript dates the birth of the village to the fourth century. This was when Marino, a stonecutter from Dalmatia, was working on the restoration of the walls of Rimini. He was persecuted for his Christian faith and took refuge on Mount Titano's cliffs, where he founded a large religious community. The village developed around this community, and the first form of independent government dates to about the year AD 1000. At this time the power of the community passed from the abbot to the Arengo, an assembly of heads of families who wrote the first statutes. In the fifteenth century, governmental powers were entrusted to the Consiglio Grande (Grand Council); since then, San Marino has enjoyed complete independence. The republic has watched the battles between municipalities and duchies, maintaining its freedom in a difficult balance between the Papal States and the several armies that in turn threatened them.

The republic covers only twenty-four square miles, and it is possible that it was too small or lacking in interesting resources to attract the attention of the powerful duchies that surrounded it. Moreover, the republic itself had no ambitions of expansion; Napoleon offered to extend the republic's power over the territory of Montefeltro in 1797 but the people refused. In exchange, they received one thousand quintals (about 220,000 pounds) of grain and four cannons from the general; the grain arrived, the cannons did not.

This little state attracts much curiosity for its thousand-year history of freedom, for its natural and artistic beauty, and for its shopping. After a tour of the castle towers, take time to walk through the village streets to shop or relax at a bar. Rather than buying souvenirs, it is advisable to look for sunglasses, clothing, tobacco, or local crafts, because the prices are considerably cheaper than in Italy proper.

facing page
Local craftsmanship on display in a shop in San Marino.

below
Aerial view of the Rocca, known as the Prima Torre (First Tower), which looms over the cliff precipice.

Visit San Marino after the summer high season if you want to avoid the influx of tourists. Leave the car at Borgo Maggiore, at the foot of Mount Titano, and take the cable car to the center of the town. Reasonably priced objects and souvenirs can be purchased at the stalls, and good-quality clothing and accessories can be found in the shops along Borgo Castello. Angel Shop is a clothing and accessories outlet; the prices are very reasonable. Fecit, on the road to Rimini, sells stone sculptures.

Stucco decorations are prevalent in the churches and noble houses of the Emilia-Romagna—they were easy to execute and much cheaper than those in stone (there is a dearth of stone in the region). *Scagliola* is a material that is very similar to stucco, and it was also widely used in the region from the seventeenth to the end of the nineteenth century. Carpi was the most important production center. Altar fronts were made, in addition to tables and small pictures; all were painted in faux marble or decorated in pale colors with architectural scenes, landscapes, human figures, animals, and still lifes. Scagliola manufacturing has declined, but in Rimini there are still craftspeople who restore or preserve existing pieces and who still produce scagliola objects according to eighteenth-century tradition. Most of these pieces are exported.

Autumnal view of the road from Norcia to Savelli in Umbria.

CENTRAL *Italy*

AREZZO

ARISTOCRATIC ANTIQUES

ON AN OLD MAP OF TUSCANY DRAWN BY LEONARDO DA VINCI (preserved in the British Museum in London), the city of Arezzo sits atop a steep hill enclosed within ramparts such as those painted by Piero della Francesca in his monumental fresco cycle *The Legend of the True Cross*, which visitors can see here at the Church of San Francesco. Today it is an important center for handicrafts and the clothing industry, as well as for footwear, railroad carriages, and, above all, objects of gold. Goldsmithing activities in Arezzo date back to the Etruscans, who mastered the art of micro-fusion by way of a process called granulation. Throughout the ages this technique has enabled artists to produce exquisite jewelry designs and engravings for the noble classes, as well as liturgical objects for the church. Uno A Erre, the largest company specializing in the manufacture, export, and distribution of gold worldwide, was founded in Arezzo in the 1920s. The factory grounds were located on a large industrial complex dedicated to working with precious metal and the company was nicknamed "The Temple" because the workers had to abide by certain rules worthy of a sacred society, such as washing their hands in specific basins, dusting their shoes with care before leaving, and wearing special clothes while working. The Temple is closed now, but goldsmiths continue to ply their trade in the thousands of small workshops sprinkled throughout town. On the first weekend of every month Arezzo hosts a thriving antiques fair on the Piazza Grande. On designated weekends Arezzo's historic center is transformed into an attic of old-world delights and the streets are strewn with historic pieces such as convent tables and nineteenth-century plate racks, and decorative objects exhibiting a range of periods and tastes from rustic furniture to Chinese porcelain—items that once belonged to the local aristocracy—are brought out of storage closets from nearly every province in Italy. Today the antiques fair is one of the most highly regarded in Italy, with nearly one thousand exhibitors, and with a selection of some of the finest antique furniture for sale. The best time to attend the fair is September, when it is moved to Prato and when the largest number of exhibitors is present. The Giostra del Saracino (Joust of the Saracen), a costumed medieval festival, also takes place in September (and in June) and is one of the oldest and most popular events in Tuscany. On the morning of the joust, four men dressed as knights representing the four quarters, or neighborhoods, of the city attend church for a benediction before

mounting their horses, lances to the ready, to ride against an effigy of King Saladin, the ancient Saracen enemy who steals the harvest, defiles the townswomen, and kidnaps Christians to make slaves of them. The "knights" must avoid the deadly blows from the mock enemy's murderous mace, a spiked iron ball swinging from a chain.

facing page
An antiques shop on via di Seteria. In the Middle Ages this street was lined with silk merchants' storefronts.

below
The area surrounding Arezzo is known for the production of objects in terracotta, such as vases, oil jars, statues, garden pots.

Both fine and costume jewelry can be bought at Uno a Erre's company outlet store at Carniani. The Mecenate Archeological Museum, housed in the ex-convent of San Bernardo is worthy of a visit to see its important collection of red-painted Roman ceramics, with decorations in relief, made in Arezzo in the first century BC. Terracotta objects can be purchased at Chini in Impruneta.

In Tuscany, as in other regions of Italy, terracotta (literally, "baked earth") objects have evolved from primitive forms into honed ceramic works of art. Arezzo and its surrounding area is particularly well known for its many terracotta workshops, such as those in Cortona, Anghiari, and Monte San Savino, as well as Montelupo and Sesto Fiorentino. Simple terracotta tiles, however, are still widely prized all over the region. Indeed, the trademark *cotto toscano* is widely exported as a popular floor covering produced by almost all Italian tile manufacturers. Impruneta is home to the largest center for the production of terracotta tiles baked in furnaces that have been active since the Renaissance, and are noted for the aesthetic and functional quality of their product. They produce floor tiles, as well as pitchers for oil, vessels for sauces and brine, tubs and vases for the garden, and terracotta cooking dishes and bowls.

COLLE VAL D'ELSA

C R Y S T A L C I T Y

NINETY-FIVE PERCENT OF THE GLASS AND CRYSTAL PRODUCED IN ITALY comes from Colle Val d'Elsa, and more than half of it is exported to European countries and the United States. This Tuscan town has become one of the most important glass and lead crystal producing centers in Italy. Glassmaking activities in Colle were first documented in the fourteenth century. In the Grand Duchy of Tuscany, it was forbidden to possess glass made outside the municipality of Colle Val d'Elsa or its surrounding area. Not until the nineteenth century, however, did Colle achieve recognition in the European market. In 1820 a Frenchman by the name of Francesco Mathis established the first crystal and glass factory on the site of a former Augustinian monastery, which today is home to Colle's Museum of Lead-Crystal Glass. Mathis was attracted by the area's ample supply of minerals needed to produce crystal and the abundance of wood for firing up the kilns. After Mathis's death in 1832 the factory was run by the Bavarian Giovan Battista Schmidt, a master of production techniques and glass engraving whose work was awarded several prizes at Universal Expositions. Furnaces were undergoing improvements at the time and many modern glass-firing techniques derive from this period. It should be noted, however, that this era in the factory's existence did not produce actual crystal but crystal glassware, and it was only from 1963 on that real crystal (i.e., glass containing at least 24 percent lead oxide) was produced in Colle by using high-quality lead oxides, resulting in stunning pieces with an index of refraction equal to that of a diamond. Both glass and crystal are obtained by the fusion of silica (sand) mixed with substances that determine the point of fusion and its characteristics. Crystal is obtained by fusing an amalgam of sand with sodium carbonate, potassium nitrate, calcium, boric acid, arsenious dioxide, and antimony oxide in a furnace heated to 1,400 degrees. To introduce color, a little selenium is added for pink, cadmium for red, cobalt for blue, copper oxide for green, manganese oxide for purple, gold for ruby red, and sulfur and cadmium for amber tones. Producing crystal was, however, not a simple game of alchemy but a series of carefully choreographed steps based on traditional methods. A so-called "first maestro" oversaw a group of five to ten glassblowers, each with a precise job and each who had to take great care to ensure the right amount of molten glass had been scooped from the furnace in order to be transformed into a drinking glass, vase, sculpture, or other object of decorative use. The *portantino* carried the equipment to the artisans, or he brought the finished work to the warehouses; the *serraforme* sealed the molds; the *passagambi* took the stems of glasses with a pincer and passed them to the *attaccagambi*, who attached the stems to the bowls of the glasses; and the *levapiedi* was most likely the person who removed the drips from the glass.

Country houses and vineyards in Val d'Elsa.

facing page
Detail of an engraved glass vase from Boreno Cigni.

San Gimignano is one of Italy's best-preserved medieval towns. Set atop a hill, this spellbinding village dominates the Val d'Elsa with its tall towers, well visible to the pilgrims who once traveled along the Via Francigena on their way to Rome. Beside the Palazzo del Popolo (today the Civic Museum), stands the thirteenth-century Torre Grossa, the tallest tower in town—over 1,780 feet—with spectacular views well worth the climb. The Torre Grossa once served an important military and social function as a defense post. Traitors and renegades were once executed at the foot of tower, and its water well was guarded day and night to prevent the water supply from being poisoned. The three bell towers on top summoned the townspeople to meetings or warned them of fire or of the enemy's approach.

The best places to shop for locally made fine crystal are Colle Cristallo, Vilca, Compagnia del Cristallo, Calp, and Compagnia Italiana del Cristallo. For custom-made engraved glasses and vases contact Mario Belli. Attend the crystal fair, which takes place every weekend in September at Il Castello di Piticciano. Take home a souvenir horse's head, symbol of the Val d'Elsa, or a set of crystal drinking glasses and a vase to remember your trip.

FLORENCE

ITALIAN HAUTE COUTURE

COMMONLY IDENTIFIED BY A FLEUR-DE-LIS, BOTANISTS HAVE SUGGESTED that Florence's coat of arms is actually the *Iris fiorentina*, called the "spadone" or "broadsword" iris for its wide, flat, sword-shaped leaves. It was between wars and duels in the centuries after the year 1000 that Florence prospered on the banks of the Arno River, becoming a powerful and influential mercantile center. The city imposed its common language (the vulgate) on an Italy that was still fragmented by a thousand city-states, and founded, in 1583, the Accademia della Crusca, an institution that brought together Italian philosophers and linguists to maintain the purity of the original Italian language, as well as to mint coins, increase trade, and establish local guilds.

In the 1950s the marquis Gian Battista Giorgini initiated haute couture fever in Florence. During the 1920s Giorgini had been a buyer for some of the most important American companies, supplying them with shoes, ceramics, crystal, and antiques, but fashion stubbornly remained the preserve of France. He tried to persuade the most exclusive fashion houses in Milan and Rome to design an original line that would distinguish Italian fashion from Dior and Balenciaga. The answer, however, was always the same: the Americans bought their clothes in Paris. Along with several other associates passionate about fashion, Giorgini ambitiously organized a fashion show at his own home, the Villa Torrigiani, in Florence with participating designers such as Emilio Pucci. The date was February 12, 1951, and fashion journalists and selected retailers from the United States and Canada were in attendance. The show went over so well that the following year it was necessary to hold it at the Grand Hotel to accommodate the crowds. Photographers from *Time* and *Life* magazines called in advance to make sure the electrical system in the hotel would support their equipment. Then, in 1952, Giorgini received permission to organize a show in the historic Sala Bianca of the Palazzo Pitti, an honor never before bestowed upon a private organization. It was here that Italians witnessed their first catwalk in Italy. The runway was shaped like a T, was 100 feet long, and covered with beige carpeting, and for years it was the symbol of Italian fashion. The fashion editors were seated at one end with places assigned according to a precise hierarchy, at the other end sat the fashion elite, and on either side of the catwalk were the potential buyers, also seated according to their prominence in the fashion world. For example, the last 33 feet separated the significant buyers from California from the less well-known Texans. The following year initially skeptical public institutions came forward with support and Florence was declared the capital of Italian fashion.

facing page
Hanks of embroidery thread, printed fabrics, and damasks—the best Florentine silk.

below
Original wedge-heeled sandals on exhibit at the Ferragamo Museum.

Shop for designer apparel at Il Guardaroba, in the heart of Florence. For the big names in fashion browse the shelves at Lori or Clara e Lorenzo. Raffaelle Buccioni, a small factory in the outskirts of Florence, creates beautiful shoe designs, a selection of which are for sale in the shop above the factory; for classic footwear shop at Beltrami. For designer fashions, including Ferragamo shoes, walk down via Tornabuoni, Florence's Rodeo Drive, where Prada, Gucci, Roberto Cavalli, and Giorgio Armani all have boutiques.

The Italian luxury shoe brand Ferragamo has become synonymous with style and can be seen in luxury shop windows all over the world. The story of its founder, Salvatore Ferragamo, is worthy of a television miniseries. Born in 1899 in Bonito, not far from Naples, to a family of little means, Ferragamo became an assistant cobbler at the age of ten, displaying a passionate interest in his craft and a talent for shoemaking. At age eleven he worked for a cobbler in Naples, at fourteen he opened his own workshop, and at sixteen he emigrated to the United States, first settling in Boston with his brother. Eventually the brothers headed west and opened a store in Santa Barbara, then Hollywood, where Ferragamo's designs quickly became prized possessions among celebrities. Among Ferragamo's first clients were Mary Pickford, Jean Harlow, Rudolph Valentino, and John Barrymore. Among his many creations was the wedge shoe, of which a particularly colorful pair were designed for Judy Garland in 1938. After the war Ferragamo's international success increased with his "invisible" sandal made of transparent nylon.

The traditional Mercato del Porcellino is held on the left bank of the Arno River, near the Ponte Vecchio, under the sixteenth-century loggias of the Mercato Nuovo. The market takes its name from the statue of a little boar that adorns the fountain in the square. Traditional Florentine crafts are found here, such as objects in straw, embroidered linens, laces, ceramics and porcelains, and articles in wood and cast iron.

left
Stalls of the San Lorenzo Market.

top
Reproduction of the wild boar—the symbol of the Porcellino Market.

above
Detail of a terracotta vase, an example of the production of Impruneta

facing page
The market at Piazza dei Ciompi

The picturesque Ponte Vecchio is the oldest bridge in the city and one of the classic symbols of Florence, second to its charming shops characterized by wooden shutters. When the bridge was built in 1345, at the narrowest part of the Arno River, these shops were entrusted to the Arte dei Beccai (Butchers' Guild), and their owners were given to discarding their refuse into the river. In the sixteenth century, Cosimo de' Medici passed the shops on to the gold and silversmiths guilds that continue to occupy them, keeping alive their traditional craftsmanship in gold and precious stones, which Florence has been famous for since the fifteenth century.

above
The Ponte Vecchio at night.

right
The shop founded by Ubaldo Baldini at the end of the 1920s produces handmade objects in bronze and brass.

facing page
Detail of chasing work on silver in the Brandimarte workshop.

left
Florentine marbled paper. Each sheet is a unique creation.

Shoes, bags, gloves: Leatherwork is the height of Florentine craftsmanship.

FIRENZUOLA

SACRED STONE

PIETRA SERENA, COMMONLY CALLED FIRENZUOLA STONE, HAS FUELED THE ECONOMY of this small town in the Tuscan Appennines ever since it was founded in 1332. Once a fortified outpost built by the Grand Duchy of Florence as a refuge from the threat of the Ubaldini people of Romagna, the city of Firenzuola is strewn with the remains of the medieval fortress and the Palazzo del Popolo, having been repeatedly besieged and almost completely destroyed during World War II.

Pietra serena is not as valuable as the white or blue-gray marble quarried in Carrara, so beloved by Michelangelo and prized since Roman times, nor is it as hard or compact, noble or durable over time. Marble is extracted from the Apuan Alps by sheer brute force, often using explosives to detach the blocks from the mountainside, after which it is cut by a handsaw and then a water saw sprayed with water and abrasive sand from nearby Massaciuccoli Lake. The block is then lowered to the valley on wooden rollers waxed with soap, called *lizze*, and braked with handheld ropes.

Firenzuola stone is softer and easier to work; less muscle is needed for its excavation and processing and it is similar in color and texture to the pietra serena of the Fiesole hills prized by Renaissance sculptors. In the past it was simply cut into blocks for building palazzos or into slats for roofs. The fourteenth-century walls of Firenzuola are built in part from pietra serena and seventeenth-century engravings illustrate hundreds of years of stone-mining activity in the quarries outside the village. Today stonecutters continue a trade that has been passed down through generations, working the stone by hand, producing ornamental objects and sculptures for gardens and interior decoration. Firenzuola is home to a professional stonecutters' school and a museum dedicated to Firenzuola stone, which outlines the history of the quarries and explores the intrinsic relationship between the townspeople and the region's natural resources. The museum also possesses a collection of antiques from local farmhouses, including fireplaces, washbowls, troughs, fountains, doors, and floor coverings. A large part of the museum exhibits the work of craftsmen and artists of various periods and displays a range of objects, such as Renaissance capitals, bas-relief, and sculpture. The entrance to the museum is through the old moat of the fortress and is decorated with sculptures by contemporary artists.

Handmade inlay in *pietra serena*.

facing page
A majestic view of the valleys and mountains of the Garfagnana.

Local crafts, including objects made from pietra serena, are for sale at the Cooperative Scalpellini in Firenzuola, in Alberaccio, and at La Pietra Toscana, and semiprecious stones are available at Coman, in the hamlet of Santerno. The Museum of Pietra Serena can be found at the fortress of Firenzuola, and a museum of gesso figurines in Coreglia Antelminelli.

In northwest Tuscany, in Garfagnana, a less precious yet widely used material called *gesso*, or chalk, is excavated from the mountains. Gesso, which is soft, white, and malleable was traditionally mixed with glue to create a primer coat for panel painting and has been employed for centuries by painters throughout the Renaissance. The craftsmen of Lucca, particularly in Bagno di Lucca and Coreglia Antelminelli, paint their white gesso sculptures with bright colors and create plaster busts of famous individuals and figurines of saints, and have achieved such a great level of artistry that their work is exported. Today gesso is combined with other materials, such as papier-mâché and synthetic resins, to create religiously inspired objects and figurines for nativity scenes, among other decorative ornaments.

ISOLA D'ELBA

MINING MINERALS

BETWEEN RIO MARINA AND PORTO AZZURRO, THE WESTERN COAST of the island of Elba plunges into the sea, its sharp, rocky cliffs the result of years of erosion by water and wind. As black as pitch or pastel-colored reds and yellows, Elba's craggy coastline is made up of ferrous minerals that have been quarried for centuries. At one time there was such an abundance of minerals on the island that Elba was known as the "mine of Italy."

The Demidoff Gallery in the annex of the Villa San Martino, Napoleon's summer residence. Today the villa is a museum.

The Etruscans were aware of these rich deposits and frequently extracted iron, which would be transported to foundries in Populonia, just north of Piombino. Today almost all the island's mines have been abandoned because they were thought to be unprofitable. The mines are presently inactive but can be reactivated if necessary. Most of the retired mines are located around Rio Marina; others are at the foot of Mount Calamita, near Porto Azzurro (Terranera), and in the north at San Piero in Campo, as well as on the slopes of Mount Capanne. Some of the mines are underground, and guided tours are available for the curious. In other open-face mines, deposits can be found of natrocalcite, humboldtina, minguzzite, goethite, epistilbite, and andalusite—abstruse names for the uninitiated, but well known to passionate mineralogists and collectors. Some of these minerals have legendary origins. Hematite, for example, is a reddish colored ferrous oxide found in crystallized rhombohedral prisms whose name derives from the Greek word for "blood," *aima*. It was the ancient Greeks and Romans who believed that hematite was coagulated blood and had the ability to heal wounds. The dominant mineral found in Rio Marina, hematite is associated with pyrites and is found in clusters of splendid crystallizations that are much sought after by collectors and museums. Magnetite, on the other hand, is thus called as it was believed to have been discovered by the Greek shepherd Magnes, who noted that it attracted the iron point of his staff. Mount Calamita rises out of the sea at the south point of the island and contains rich stores of magnetite. The Etruscans avoided the southern tip of the island because they believed that its magnetism was so strong it could pull out the nails from their boats. The Calamita mine is also known for its secondary minerals, above all the sub-products from minerals of copper; quartz, epidote, and chlorite can be found in the Ginepro mine on the other side of the mountain. The mines of San Pietro in Campo are rich in quartz and orthoclase. With a bit of luck small crystals of malachite or azurite can be found on these sites. These minerals are exceptionally beautiful and are used as precious stones.

An hour-long ferry ride takes visitors from Piombino to Portoferraio, the capital of Elba. The fortress of Falcone and La Stella (so called because of its five-pointed star shape), rise here. The walls of the Linguetta close off the bay and the sturdy octagonal tower at the entrance to the port, both of these structures were built in 1548 by Cosimo I de'Medici, first Grand Duke of Tuscany. After his forced abdication, Emperor Napoleon Bonaparte was imprisoned here, and from May 1814 to February 1815 he lived in the Palazzina dei Mulini, which today is a museum dedicated to the exiled French King. The museum stands beside the Falcone fortress and its grounds include a manicured Italian garden overlooking the sea. Just outside the town, a couple of miles down the road to Marciana, is Napoleon's summer residence, the Villa San Martino, which is open to the public. The rather modest building was bought in 1851 by a Russian prince who expanded the villa with a neoclassical building that was later transformed into a museum committed to preserving Napoleon's possessions.

Minerals from Elba can be purchased at Cose Belle in Portoferraio or Giannini in Porto Azzurro. A small museum in the municipality of Rio Marina houses a collection of minerals found on the island. The Ricci collection, which comprises more than 700 minerals, is on display at the Elba Mineral Museum, in Rio dell'Elba, and organized excursions are recommended. After this incredible assortment of minerals, visit the Museum of Iron and Cast Iron in Follonica, which offers a detailed history of the local iron and steel industry.

facing page
Prismatic barite crystals.

LUCCA
TUSCANY
THE REAL TOSCANO

THE TOSCANO, OR TUSCAN, IS A DRY-CURED, THICK CIGAR WHOSE HEAVY AROMA and intense flavor is a favorite among serious cigar smokers. There are many variations on the traditional Sigaro Toscano, such as the Millennium, Original Selected, Antica Riserva, Antico (considered the best), Extra Aged, Garibaldi (the mildest), Moro (the longest), and the Toscanello (half the length of a Toscano). The Extra Aged is DOC stamped, listed in the Italian Slow Food regulations, and made with tobacco from the Chianti and Tiber valleys in a former monastery in Lucca, where the curing of tobacco was established in the first half of the sixteenth century. The birth of the Toscano was pure accident: In August of 1815 a bale of tobacco leaves, intended as a tax payment to the Grand Duke of Tuscany, was left out in the rain. The water, combined with the amount of time the bale sat out in the heat, caused the tobacco to ferment. Instead of throwing it out, the manager of a nearby workshop decided to use the fermented tobacco as fill for lower-quality cigars called "Toscani." The outcome was an immediate success, resulting in strong, well-balanced cigars at a low cost. Today, after almost two hundred years, cigars are still handmade and the process repeats the original "accident." Dried tobacco leaves are fermented and cured for a period of time that ranges from twenty-five to forty-five days. The tobacco leaves destined for the outer wrapper are separated from the filler leaves and moistened with water. The ribs of the leaves to be used for the wrapper are then removed, while the tobacco for the filler is put into a cycle of aging, then dried, pressed, and placed in bales where a second aging takes place before it is broken up into pieces. The outer leaves are then wrapped in a spiral around the fill and the finished cigars are placed in wooden forms to dry. Cigar rollers have perfected the irregular shape of the Toscani: thick in the middle and tapered at the ends. The finished cigars undergo two phases of maturation over a period of at least nine months under the proper conditions. There is a precise ritual to smoking a Toscano, beginning with the cutting. Generally one half is smoked at a time. The cigar must be cut clean, without rough pieces at its end, and is lit with a sulfur-free, wooden match (no waxed matches, or gas-filled or petrol-filled lighters), turning the cigar over the flame in an oblique position at a distance of about two centimeters, slowly warming it without turning it black. The first match is used for this preheating. Inhaling the cigar comes only with the second match, with deliberation, to savor all its intensity.

Lucca is a hub for shoppers and the townspeople celebrate their enthusiasm for this age-old pastime with an exhibition of shop windows that takes place every year on the last Sunday of October; the best window display is awarded a prize. Lucca's main street, the via Fillungo, is also the best place to shop. Browse the weekly market on Wednesdays in via dei Bacchettoni for fresh produce, flowers, and household items.

For centuries Lucca has been the political, commercial and cultural center of the Garfagnana area. The jewelers in the old town still maintain their centuries-old traditions. In fact, they have carefully preserved the shop windows in carved wood or stone that were once commonplace. The Antica Farmacia Massagli still prepares teas and ointments from medicinal herbs and their famous digestive liqueur, China Massagli. Lucca is so renowned as a shopping center that the city organizes an annual "Shop Window Show". A prize is awarded to the most sumptuous and imaginative display in the city. Believe it or not, there is a shop for every four inhabitants, and a stroll down via Fillungo, the main shopping street, will confirm this. This narrow street is flanked by the beautiful as Barletti and Samminiati palazzos, the 2nd century church of S. Cristoforo, and the "Tor dell'ore" (the tower of hours), whose ancient clock chimes the quarters. The 18th century Caffé Caselli, now called De Simo, is also on this street. It was a meeting place for poets and musicians such Pascoli , Puccini and Mascagni. The street is lined with hundreds of shops, the most important being the jewelers, herbalists and the hand-woven textiles. "Filaticcio" fabric was once made from silk waste and has been much appreciated since the 17th century.

MAREMMA

COWBOY CHIC

INLAND THERE WAS A VAST GULF OF THE SEA FROM THE PROMONTORY of Piombino on the Argentario and as far as the foothills of Mount Amiata. It was an unpleasant, marshy area and, until the beginning of the last century, it was unhealthy and inhabited only by charcoal burners and bandits. Some believed it was a wonderful area for meditation, but a popular song described it as "Maremma Maledetta" (cursed Maremma). The city of Grosseto was plagued by mosquitoes. Indeed, in past centuries, civil and religious leaders of the city relocated to the hills from May to September to escape the tormenting insects. This is the land of the *butteri*, the cowboys of the Maremma; they were skilled horsemen long before the fabled cowboys of the American Far West. There was actually a face-to-face meeting between Italian and American cowboys in 1890. The legendary Colonel William Cody, better known as Buffalo Bill, arrived in Rome with his circus; they were on a tour of Italy. He said he could tame horses better than the butteri. No one knows the outcome of the bet, but it is certain that Buffalo Bill left with the one-thousand-lire wager amid heated debate.

The *butteri* way of life preserves the traditions of horse-breeding and wrangling.

facing page
Butteri, or cowboys, at work at the Azienda Regionale Agricola in Alberese.

The butteri herd the white cows of the Maremma, which have distinctive long, lyre-shaped horns. These cows originated in the northern steppes and arrived with the Barbarian invasions. They were stocky and strong and able to survive in the wild both in summer and in winter. The horses of the Maremma, a cross between the northern horse breeds, Arabian stallions, and English pure-bloods, are also hardy and can survive in the marshes. Nor are they afraid of any wild animals they come across. The butteri wear the *maremmana* to protect themselves from the inclement weather. This is a wide jacket in durable rough canvas, with sturdy stitching and large pockets; they are oiled with linseed to make them waterproof. Actor Marcello Mastroianni wore one of these jackets. Though it was not oiled, he wore it so much that it turned from brown to a reddish color. The butteri give the same treatment to the narrow-brimmed hats they wear, ignoring the pungent smell to uphold tradition. They wear leather boots, often without spurs; if they do have spurs they are with-

In Pancole find the Antica Sartoria di Maremma, which sells sports jackets and pants in velvet and fustian, a strong cotton and linen fabric. The clothes have names that remind one of the Maremma: Tiburzi, the infamous Maremma bandit; *trapelo*, a draft horse; *lonca*, a stick used by the butteri; *macchiaiola*, the breed of black pig; *centone*, a typical wild plant; and so on. Riccio in Grosseto sells leather goods.

Today the Maremma is a very hospitable area. Land reclamation has paved the way for a controversial form of tourism among the forest and sea; people are interested in seeing the many medieval villages and the remains of an ancient civilization. Before it belonged to the butteri, the area was inhabited by the Etruscans. There are many remains of this civilization, and one of the most important is at Roselle. Roselle is on a hill a few miles from Grosseto. Luckily, it is an archaeological site that has not been overrun by urban sprawl. Scholars work there, and it is possible to see the many types of buildings in Etruscan and Roman cities. The city covers eighty-six acres and dates to the seventh century BC. It was inhabited until the Middle Ages, enclosed by a ring of massive walls in the sixth century BC that were more than 1.8 miles in length; most are still intact.

out the barb and the wheel. The saddle is the Del Frate *scafarda*, named for the colonel who invented it in the first years of the twentieth century. It enables the weight of the body to be distributed on either side of the horse's withers, allowing freedom for the backbone. The "uniform" of the butteri is seen beyond the Maremma; people on the cosmopolitan streets of Florence and Rome, or along the beaches of fashionable resorts, wear the getup.

PIETRASANTA

FROM AN IDEA TO A WORK OF ART

PIETRASANTA'S MARBLE TRADITION DATES BACK TO THE FOURTEENTH CENTURY; in the sixteenth century, Michelangelo himself enlisted the help of the workers there. Today there are more than 150 workshops in the town, 40 of which specialize in sculpture and decoration. Thousands of craftspeople work here, and they are easy to spot: they have white marble dust around their eyes and on their faces, and they wear hats made of newspaper. Most of them make objects that, at first glance, may seem ordinary. But they confirm one of the many definitions of art: "the beautiful representation of something and not the representation of something beautiful." Marble-work includes fruit and vegetables painted to look real; fruit baskets and columns; statues and fountains.

Some of these craftspeople are also able to reproduce copies of great works of art that are so close to the originals they can make even the experts wonder. These replicas are executed with the well-known Tuscan spirit of irreverence. Tuscans think of themselves as the intellectuals of the compass and the chisel, even if today's chisel is electric and the compass has been replaced by an electronic calculator. Theirs is the difficult task of turning a master's idea into a work of art, and there are many great artists who entrust the great unformed blocks to the minds and hands of the marble workers of Pietrasanta. They are given a model in *gesso* and from it make their interpretation of the artist's work. Many of these models can be seen at a gallery of plaster casts near the Sant'Agostino Church at the end of the Piazza del Duomo. The sculpture is not always made in this manner, with "finishing touches." Rather, it is carved directly from the stone by the artist. In terms of the great sculptures, this method, the "direct chisel"—or the artist working the stone directly—is becoming rarer. For complicated works, such as religious figures, work may be divided: the block of marble is roughly shaped by one worker; the primary lines are put in by the modeler; the drapery is made by a specialized worker; the floral motifs by another; the details by yet another; the chiseler creates the architectural parts; and the final details of rasping and polishing are done by others.

Since the last century Pietrasanta has also become an important area for the art of founding bronze, and since the 1960s the town has seen the arrival of the most important contemporary artists who work on their pieces here. In the summer, the urban landscape of the Piazza del Duomo changes; it is transformed into an art gallery, as is the deconsecrated Sant'Agostino Church. The works of some of the most celebrated artists in the world, including Botero, Cascella, Dalì, Mirò, Moore, Folon, Giò, and Arnaldo Pomodoro, among others, are displayed here.

There are many workshops that produce decorative objects, such as Fratelli Galeotti, Bacci Marmi, and Pelletti & Simonetti. The realistic marble fruit is particularly interesting. Stone and marble from the caves of Carrara are also worked by Dino Felici in Avenza and Marco Bedini in Marina di Carrara.

There is a museum of marble in Carrara. Exhibits provide information about the evolution of this valuable stone over time and the ways it has been used in architecture and sculpture. The first exhibit presents the history of Carrara's quarries, from the Roman period to the present day; the extraction techniques used throughout history; and the processing of the blocks of stone to extract slabs or statues. Other exhibits reveal the range of possible uses of marble—for columns and monuments; in the architecture of interiors with facings and staircases; in the craftsmanship of furnishings such as vases and small columns; and in the art of sculpture itself. The Marble Gallery has a collection of more than three hundred examples of rare marble from all over the world, one hundred of which are quarried from the Apuan Alps.

facing page
Franco Cervietti's marble creations.

below
Quarries of white Carrara marble.

PISTOIA
TUSCANY
FLOWERS AND IRONWORK

PISTOIA, LOCATED HALFWAY BETWEEN PISA AND FLORENCE, was at a remove from the great events of history, enclosed in its circle of walls from the eighth to the eleventh centuries. But there was a vegetable market and there were craftsmen's workshops. In 1851 the Maria Antonia railroad opened, linking the town to Florence. The railroad station was inaugurated in the same year, and the town changed from an agricultural area to an important railroad junction and prosperous industrial center.

Today, all that remains of the station are two elegant cast-iron street lamps in front of the entrance. They were made in 1896 by the Officine Giuseppe Michelucci. For more than a century this company has been at the center of industry in Pistoia, specializing in works of bronze and cast iron, as well as decorative ironwork. The workshops produced pieces for home interiors, conservatories, and pavilions—including railings, banisters, and gates—for the aristocracy and many sovereigns in Europe. Indeed, many of these gates still stand proudly in front of the luxury homes for which they were created. Many examples of the work of the Michelucci Company, and of others that followed in their footsteps, can still be seen in Pistoia. These are scattered around town and most are not as highly regarded; examples remain at the Appennino Hotel in Via XX Settembre, or the headquarters of the Cassa di Risparmio on Via Roma, a splendid example of art deco architecture for which an entire medieval neighborhood was demolished. Other important examples of art deco that were contributed by Michelucci are the Vittorio Emanuele Gallery and the villas of the so-called Pistoia Nuova, almost entirely built in the first decades of the twentieth century.

Today, the economy of Pistoia relies on two completely different activities: the railroad and nurseries where flowers are cultivated. The Società Autoferrotramviaria San Giorgio had its offices in Via Pacinotti, which then became Via Breda. The company is still active in its new offices outside the historic old city. Pistoia is also considered to be Italy's flower-cultivation capital; the nurseries are the pride of the city. They are to the flower market what San Remo is to cut flowers; the town is known as the "cradle of gardens." The growers cultivate flowers on areas as large as 7.5 to 9.5 acres, and all kinds of plants can be found here—plants for apartments, gardens, and large parks. Plants grown include antique roses, dwarf palms, great pines, and Himalayan rhododendrons. Many of the nurseries specialize; for example, Barni cultivates roses only: creeping tree roses, miniature varieties, and climbers. The company creates new varieties that are sometimes dedicated to famous people, such as the stylist Rosita Missoni and Nobel Prize–winner Rita Levi Montalcino.

facing page
An antique wrought-iron shop.

below
Aerial view of the market on the Piazza Duomo in Pistoia.

Any type of plant can be purchased at the nurseries of Capecchi, Magni, Tesi, and Angori. Metal is manufactured at the workshop of Re.Bi or at Arte del Ferro. Classic knives of the area are sold at the Coltellerie Berti in Scarperia, at Conaz Coltellerie, and at Saladini. Every September 1 there is a fair in the village with an exhibition celebrating the handmade knife.

The manufacturing of iron products has always been important in Scarperia, in the province of Florence, particularly the production of the knives for which the town is famous. The Museum of Cutting Tools at Palazzo Vicari displays about five hundred pieces from various periods; it is housed in what originally was a cutlery shop and displays antique equipment for the handcrafted blades and handles. Occasionally craftspeople give demonstrations in which they make knives using traditional techniques. The workshop, which is managed by the craftspeople, is very interesting. Provided is information about the structure of knives with fixed blades or folding blades; also identified are knives typical of different regions in Italy.

PONTEDERA

ETERNAL YOUTH

THERE ARE VERY FEW MODES OF TRANSPORTATION THAT CAN BOAST the youthfulness of the Vespa. When it debuted at the end of World War II, this scooter was said to be "modern, with the popularity of the bicycle, the power of a motorcycle, and the elegance and comfort of the automobile." The design of the Vespa hasn't changed since then, frozen as if it were an immortal work of art; it is an ideal synthesis of form and function. Comparable designs include the chair by Michael Thonet, the Arco lamp by the Castiglioni brothers, and the 1911 Colt pistol. When the patent for the Vespa's design was granted on April 23, 1946, the Piaggio company, located in Sesto Ponente on the Ligurian Riviera, had existed for sixty years; it manufactured airplanes, trains, and motorboats. And for some decades at Pontedera, the company was involved in heavy industry and other machinery, making everything from ovens to cigarette lighters. By the early forties, the factory at Pontedera had already produced some Vespa prototypes. They were completely different from motor-scooter models found in other countries, which were little more than small scooters; these included the 1904 Auto-Fauteil, with its padded bamboo seat, the 1921 Skootamoto, used on cricket fields, and the 1938 Cushman, re-named the milking stool. The Vespa prototype was an ugly and awkward little thing. It was uncomfortable and slow, and was nicknamed *Paperino* (Donald Duck) in the factory. At the end of 1945, it became a real motor scooter—versatile and practical and ideal for a "quick getaway." The Piaggio company had come up with some innovative changes: the body was made of light and sturdy molded metal with platforms and ample leg guards. The box at the back contained all the motor mechanics, which were separated from the driver; the saddle was atop this. Best of all, the controls were on the handlebars. It was Enrico Piaggio who gave the scooter its name. When he saw it he said, laconically, "It looks like a wasp," referring to its line—its rounded sides and narrow center. The first models, which were not immediately popular, had a 98-cc engine. When the Vespa debuted, journalists in Italy and abroad were puzzled by the small wheels, the controls on the handlebars, and the rounded shape painted in an improbable pastel green color. But after

they took it for a ride, they admitted that it did not require any acrobatics to mount, and that it was easy to balance even in city traffic. It also enabled a person to arrive at an appointment unruffled, as though he had just come from his car. In 1956 the one-millionth Vespa came off the production line, and in 1988 ten million had sold. Today there are about sixteen million Vespas on the road; thirty thousand are used daily in the United States, where they are known as "urban insects."

facing page
The thermal baths of nearby Montecatini.

below
The classic Vespa.

Ceramic objects can be purchased at Arte in Ceramica in Pontedera and at the Studio Chironi in Monsummano Terme. Monsummano is famous for its leatherwork and, above all, for footwear. Charming desktop objects can be found at the Bino book-bindery in Montecatini; artificial flowers are sold in Larciano; and worked copper objects are the specialty in Pescia.

Montecatini is a few dozen miles north of Pontedera. The thermal baths that have made the area a mecca for today's spa-goers were used by the ancient Romans and became famous again in the eighteenth century after the turmoil caused by centuries of war. In the eleventh century, Montecatini Alto was at the center of a conflict between the lords of Maona and the monks of Pantane. It was then invaded by the people of Lucca and Florence and sacked by Cosimo de'Medici. The thermal baths returned to some prominence in the fourteenth century when the Bagno Tettuccio was built. But the definitive development of the baths was due to the Grand Duke Leopold I, who, from 1773 to 1782, created the "city of baths" and built the great Bagno Regio, the Terme Leopoldine, and restored the Tettuccio. Montecatini became a thermal spa resort at the beginning of the twentieth century, patronized by the nobility and the upper-middle classes of Europe, thanks to the sumptuous grandeur of the Excelsior thermal baths.

PRATO

TEXTILES OF THE FUTURE

THE CITY OF PRATO, ABOUT SIX MILES FROM FLORENCE, is one of the most important textile centers in Europe. The province as a whole has been innovative in the production of textiles for cotton, wool, linen, silk, and synthetic clothing. Many types of fabrics, synthetic leather, and fur are produced for the clothing, footwear, and home-furnishings industries, among others.

A rainbow of fabrics produced by the textile industry of Prato.

facing page
The cathedral of Santo Stefano in Prato at night.

There are also beautiful places to visit. The historic medieval city center has excellent monuments and sites that house valuable works of art. The castle of Emperor Frederick II is a must-see, as is the Romanesque duomo, which has a notable cycle of well-preserved frescoes by Filippo Lippi. The Museo dell'Opera del Duomo houses one of Donatello's most important works, the *Danza dei Putti*, on seven panels. In addition, the following are also recommended: The Museum of Wall Painting, which contains the sinopia, or preliminary drawings, by Paolo Uccello; the Museum of Contemporary Art, which is one of the most important in Italy; and the Palazzo degli Alberti, which contains works by Filippo Lippi, Caravaggio, and Giovanni Bellini. The important Palazzo Datini was the residence of banker Francesco Marco Datini, a patron of the city. He promoted the city's textiles throughout Italy and around the world, filling the warehouses of Florence, Milan, Genoa, Venice, Paris, and Barcelona with the products of Prato.

The city has always been a force in the marketplace, inspiring new trends in fashion and clothing, and innovating cutting-edge textile technologies. The fairs held there—for the spring and summer seasons and the autumn and winter seasons—present thousands of new types of thread and showcase future design trends. This was the birthplace of washed silk, non-woven fabric, sound-absorbing fabric for cars, and elasticized fabric for athletic clothing, which now are used for everyday clothing as well.

Today people want fashionable clothing that is comfortable, wrinkle-resistant, soft to the touch, and easy to care for. Prato meets the demand with laboratory-engineered fabrics that are antibacterial, waterproof and breathable, soft and resistant, and that have anti-stress properties and protect against ultraviolet rays and electromagnetic waves. Other recent innovations include fabrics that control the temperature of clothing; cosmeto-fibers with bio-stimulation qualities (hydrating, relaxing, slimming); medicated fabrics made of spongy biomaterial that can contain and release anti-inflammatory, antiseptic, depilatory, and self-tanning substances.

Prato and the surrounding towns are packed with clothing shops featuring a range of items. Osvaldo Bruni specializes in knitted goods and cashmere; Machattie, Nieri, and Monteferrato offer a variety of clothing; Geronimo specializes in casual clothing; Futura Trade sells work clothes; Alexander features many types of fabrics; and stock clothing can be found at Fabric Stock House.

The Museum of Fabrics is located in a restored nineteenth-century textile factory building, the Cimatoria Campolmi. It now contains six thousand samples, including a wonderful collection donated by Loriano Bertini, and fabrics found from archaeological excavations. The collection of fabrics from the fifteenth to the nineteenth centuries, such as velvets and damasks, is particularly valuable. It contains embroidered fabrics, fabrics from India, and Central and South America, and fabrics from the Industrial Revolution to the present day. It displays the fashion trends featured at the Prato Expos from 1982 to the present day. There is also a collection of antique textile machines and tools; one is an unusual rag machine dating from 1850, which was used to recover textile fibers from rags.

VIAREGGIO
FLOATING PALACES

SAILING ENTHUSIASTS AROUND THE WORLD KNOW VIAREGGIO as the place where the most renowned builders of sailboats and motor yachts—and the most experienced restorers of historic boats—are located. Luxury floating palaces and small, fast racing boats are launched from the many shipyards along the coast. These shipyards are the European leaders in the building of fiberglass boats. Master carpenters and designers produce futuristic boats, and craftspeople fashion their interiors with impeccable attention to detail. There is such a great concentration of shipyards and dry docks here that Viareggio has become the meeting place for international and Italian high society.

At the beginning of the last century, the coast of Versilia was still wild, and Viareggio was only a hint of what it would become; here a young boy named Giovanni played on the beach in front of his house (he was the scion of the Agnelli family and would make the Fiat company great). Regina Margherita Avenue, the meeting place of the townspeople, was flanked with cafés and shops and the entrance to the beaches. These were built as temporary wooden pavilions that changed every season. In 1917, they were completely destroyed in a fire and the town had to modernize.

This is still exemplified by Galileo Chini, a ceramics artist who built a luxurious villa at the Lido of Camaiore; it overflows with decorative tiles. (He decorated the Royal Palace at Bangkok with his ceramics.) The season of art nouveau seemed unstoppable. The Viareggio style of art nouveau can be seen from Regina Margherita as far as the docks: the Supercinema, built in 1927 and decorated with ceramics from the Chini factory; the Magazzini Duilio 48 general store, built in 1930 and one of the most whimsical and representative of this style, with the curved lines of the windows on the second floor and the signs in colored ceramics on the facade; the Asian influence of the Gran Caffé Margherita—the most exclusive meeting place after a walk; and, next door, the Galleria del Libro, once the Chalet Balena boutique, which was decorated by the architect Gae Aulenti after its latest restoration. Farther along the promenade is the entrance to the Bagni Balena bath house. Along the avenues behind the beach stand the great Viareggio resort hotels: the Hotel Palza & de Russie; the Bristol; the Bretagna (known today as the London); the Liberty (ex-Castaldi villa) on viale Manin; and the Royal, the Regina, and Imperiale on viale Carducci. And last but not least, the Select, built to resemble the great hotels of the French Riviera and still has many of its original furnishings.

The Gran Café Margherita in Viareggio was built in the 1920s in the Art Nouveau style.

facing page
A glimpse of the Perini Navi Cup, an annual regatta reserved for Perini Navi yachts.

Tecnomar, Perini, and Codecasa are all famous builders of yachts and pleasure craft. Effebì is the most well-known maker of fiberglass boats. Euro Sailer makes and restores wooden hulls. Other important builders of pleasure craft can be found at La Spezia, Naples, Forlì, and Pesaro. Enthusiasts of outdoor markets should not miss the one held each Wednesday in Forte dei Marmi. Brand-name clothes and cashmere sweaters are available there.

The park of the Versiliana was described by the poet Gabriele d'Annunzio as "the most beautiful place in the universe," but perhaps this was because of the passionate nights he spent there with Eleonora Duse and the fact that he could gallop noiselessly along the wide swaths of sand that cross the heath. At that time, the nineteenth-century villa and the farm, with two hundred acres of coastal woodland of oaks and pines, was the property of the count Digerini Nuti. Since 1980 it has become a public park with a network of paths for pedestrians and bicycle riders. The La Versiliana Festival takes place in the park every July and August. The festival, which started twenty years ago, has become a big event, with theater, music, ballet, and art exhibitions in the villa; and the Fabbrica dei Pinoli is a meeting place for people from the worlds of culture, politics, sports, and entertainment.

VOLTERRA

CITY OF ARTISANS

VOLTERRA IS BUILT ON TOP OF A HILL THAT DOMINATES a lonely and austere landscape; it is far off the beaten track. In the thirteenth century, Volterra was described by the poet Fazio degli Uberti as "strong and ancient, as much in Tuscany as anywhere else." It is a city built by craftspeople and has always been a warren of small workshops. These workshops have been, and still are, a source of employment for the inhabitants; they are also meeting places, where values of tolerance and respect for others, and real democracy, are instilled. Without craftspeople, Volterra would be like an empty museum, a body without a soul, and it would lose a great deal of its fascinating qualities.

The primary goal of the workshops—even more important than producing goods—is maintaining the efficiency of tools and keeping alive the traditions that might otherwise be lost forever. As one strolls around the beautiful squares and the narrow streets, it seems that the stones themselves are breathing. There are quaint little ceramics and glass workshops, and stores where fabrics are handwoven on wooden looms, where maps and books are restored, and where small masterpieces in gold are created. Volterra is a city of stone: the palazzos, the towers, the streets, and the walls are all made of a gray stone called *il panchino*; the stone resembles sea shells, almost as though it were a living material rather than an inert one. Alabaster dust hangs in the air and whitens the shops. This stone has predominated in the area since Etruscan times, many centuries before the Christian era. Alabaster was considered the stone of the gods and Etruscans used it for urns and sarcophagi, decorating them with the figure of the deceased and scenes from everyday life. Many of these are preserved at the Museo Guarnacci at Volterra, but also at the Vatican Museum in Rome, the British Museum in London, and the Louvre in Paris.

Alabaster is a remarkable material: it is as white as snow; it is so soft that it can be sculpted to look like lace; and it is so transparent and translucent that it can be made into lamps that create a unique, beautiful light. The word alabaster is probably Egyptian, possibly derived from the city of Alabastron, which was famous thousands of years ago for the production of small vases and perfume jars. There are two types of alabaster: oriental alabaster is composed of calcium carbonate; chalky sulphate alabaster is made of calcium hydrate. The chalky stone is worked in Volterra. There are quarries at Castellina Marittima, where it is found in its purest form, with an incomparable beauty and transparency. There are many shops and workshops on Via Matteotti and Via dell'Arco where this stone is sculpted. All types of objects—statues, fruit dishes, plates, and bowls—are created and look as if they were made of wax.

facing page
An alabaster workshop in Volterra

below
An alabaster sculpture in a shop in via del Mandorlo.

Alab'arte, near the Museo Guarnacci, sells sculpture and other objects, as does the Cooperativa Artieri. Gloria Giannelli makes beautiful plates and vases. There are also many small workshops in Volterra, such as Fabula Etrusca and Paolo Colvicchi, which create unique works in gold. Vegetable-tanned leather accessories are sold at the MT in Pisa.

Many tourists flock to the curious Leaning Tower of Pisa, which belies the words of Henry James after he visited Piazza dei Miracoli: "really enchanting, and very slightly spoiled by the famous inclination of its tower." It is said that miracles also occurred there in the world of science, when Galileo Galilei threw his wooden balls from the tower and observed the oscillations of the great bronze lamp of the duomo, thereby revolutionizing the laws of physics. Today the former maritime republic is called the "widow of the sea." It is far from Porto Pisano and is connected to the sea by the Navicelli canal, where a fisherman's catch may consist of *ce'e* (tiny blind eels) and mullet. The shipyards of Porto a Mare are well-known around the world for their production of small boats.

DERUTA
SINGULAR STYLE

IN UMBRIA, THE CERAMIC-MAKING TRADITION DATES BACK THOUSANDS OF YEARS. It has developed in many parts of the region; each area has a different technique for baking and decorating it. Giorgio Andreoli was the greatest Umbrian ceramicist of the sixteenth century. He put Gubbio on the map thanks to his gold-flecked majolica (earthenware) made with an ancient Arabic technique. Some workshops in Gualdo Tadini still produce these ceramics, called *a terzo fuoco* (a third firing); even with modern production methods, medieval styles and decorations prevail. Orvieto also has an ancient ceramics tradition—it is one thousand years old—and the objects made there are characterized by a style that is partly Etruscan and partly Romanesque, with unmistakable decorative motifs of plants and animals. In Umbertide, ceramics became big business in the 1930s; these objects have a distinctive metallic sheen obtained from the *nero Fratta* technique. In Città di Castello it is the heraldic decorations and reliefs that are unique to these pieces. In other towns, including Ripabianca, Ficulle, and Castel Viscardo, the terracotta is made into bricks, which are then left to dry in the sun. Vases and amphoras are also made. Deruta is the most renowned for this work and has the oldest tradition; a document dated August 12, 1290, provides a record of a barter agreement in exchange for vases. This was known as the archaic period in Deruta's ceramics history. During this time, everyday objects such as bowls and basins were made; decorations were simple—geometric lines or animal forms in a copper-green or brown. In the following centuries this work developed and was perfected; it reached its peak of beauty in the sixteenth century and was in demand at the most important European markets. It was distinctive because of its very white enamel, decorated with original and unique details (floral, animal, and grotesques) in orange, blue, and yellow, and with a metallic sheen and golden highlights. Style and decorations were produced with quick, short brushstrokes and Moorish-inspired "calligraphy" replete with flowers, and birds and other animals. The "Grazia" ceramic was celebrated in the 1920s with its return to traditional motifs. Today the little town is alive with more than a hundred workshops and factories that produce earthenware of various kinds. Shops and showrooms feature the best locally made pieces. The Regional Ceramics Museum in the former San Francesco Convent is worth a visit. The museum was established in 1898 as a repository of historical materials and, more importantly, as a "library" of the styles of majolica-makers throughout the centuries; it also promotes local production. Today the museum contains more than six thousand pieces displayed in chronological order, going from ancient times to the first years of the twentieth century; there are an additional five thousand pieces by contemporary artists.

There are also non-commercial forms of ceramic craftsmanship in the region. One of the richest collections of votive majolica plaques in the world is housed in the seventeenth-century sanctuary of the Madonna del Bagno. The sanctuary is near Deruta, just off Via Tiberina. The oldest of these votive objects is a Madonna painted in red and blue on a fragment of a majolica cup; it is mounted on the central wall of the sanctuary. In 1657 it was placed in the hollow of an oak by a haberdasher from Casalina whose wife was dying; suddenly she recovered. Thus began the tradition of votive offerings, or *ex-voto*, that are now collected in the sanctuary in their thousands, one on top of the other, all on majolica bricks that are painted and decorated with simple designs.

facing page
Hand-painted ceramic crockery in the artisan shop of Marina Montanari.

below
Traditional ceramics on display under an ancient arch.

A variety of terracotta and majolica jars, vases, and other vessels can be found in Bettini. The Bottega del Vasaio makes majolica inspired by styles from the sixteenth century. Plates, salt shakers, jars, tea service, and other items—both traditional and modern—can be found at Ubaldo Grazia. It is worthwhile to visit the regional ceramic museum. Antique majolica can be purchased at the exhibition and fair held each year in May.

GUBBIO

ELEGANT EARTHENWARE

BOCCARO IS A VERY FINE GRAY OR REDDISH CLAY, RICH IN FERROUS OXIDE. It has a unique smell; in fact, it was once used to make disks to scent homes and vases to keep water fresh and scented. The word is from the Spanish *bucaro*, a type of earthenware imported from South America and made with colored and scented earth. But this type of ceramic was known in ancient Greece, in Asia Minor, and in North Africa. In Italy, boccaro first was used in the seventeenth century, but it was around for a long time before that; in fact, traces have been found in the Villanova civilization of the first millennium BC, and many excavations in the necropolis prove its widespread use by the Etruscans. Beginning in the seventh century BC, they made objects of incomparable beauty, particularly shiny black vases. Boccaro was introduced to Gubbio in the second half of the nineteenth century; it imitated the Etruscan product. Elegant, beautifully colored objects were produced. The decorative work on some of these objects can be overdone, and sometimes they reveal experiments with innovative techniques, such as silver coating, that detract from their quality.

Palazzo dei Consoli in Gubbio, seen from the Piazza Grande.

Boccaro clay is extracted near the workshops. It is purified and mixed with an organic material that produces a more elastic clay; this elasticity makes it possible to create extremely thin plates and vases. Objects are actually classified as "thin" or "heavy" depending on their thickness. The ceramics are generally made on a potter's wheel. They are then cleaned and rubbed with a wet sponge. Next, they are left to dry, which takes about twenty days. Once dry, they are rubbed with straw and sandpaper to remove markings from the wheel and then smoothed with sticks of boxwood; this gives objects their shiny color. A soft cloth also can be used to obtain an opaque effect. Decorations are made by carving into the objects. In addition, objects may be decorated in relief with terracotta figures molded and then applied to the surface. Sometimes they are engraved and brushed with gold or ruby red.

A special technique is used to bake the clay; it is not done in a traditional furnace. Instead, objects are placed in a metal basin filled with wood covered with reflective material. The wood is placed on top of the object as well (the wood and object are separated by metal netting). The container is closed with a metal lid, sealed with sand and clay, and put into the furnace; it is heated to 1,650 degrees Fahrenheit. The oxygen-free baking process gives the clay its black color. After baking, objects are polished with wire wool and sandpaper, and then polished to a shine with sticks of boss wood.

Gubbio provides one of the most typical examples of what medieval communal life was like. The Palazzo dei Consoli houses the town's picture gallery, with paintings from the fourteenth and fifteenth centuries. The *Tabulæ Eugubinæ*, seven bronze tablets from the third to first centuries BC, are preserved in the chapel. Inscriptions are in Umbrian, in Etruscan, and in Latin, and the tablets are one of the most important Italian antiquities. Gubbio is also the town of the Confraternity of the Matti di Agobbio. In order to become a member, a person must undergo a "purification" ritual. The person runs around the fountain of the Bargello reciting magical incantations while being sprinkled with water by an officiant. Occasionally, tourists will reenact this ritual.

Ceramics are sold at Fornace del Bucchero, Aldo Ajo, and Mastro Giorgio Ceramics. The municipal museum displays a collection of ceramics. Gubbio has hosted a biennial of ceramics and metalwork since 1956. In addition to boccaro, Gubbio also makes decorated majolica *a fiore*, with flowers on a white or glossy background, and with the medieval-inspired *zaffera*, a cobalt blue relief.

facing page
Elegant imitations of Etruscan vases from the Fornace del Bucchero.

ORVIETO

LACE AND EMBROIDERY

LOOKING OUT FROM THE WINDING ROADS THAT EXTEND OFF THE VIA CASSIA, it appears that Orvieto is flat. On approach, the tall spire and bell towers appear. The popes of Rome arrived from this direction and saw the dramatic view. The people of Orvieto allied with the popes during the turbulent struggles against the emperors. During the twelfth and thirteenth centuries, in exchange for Orvieto's hospitality, the popes and prelates built churches and palazzos. Powerful religious orders also were established, including the Premostratensians (the Norbertines) of the Santi Severo e Martirio Abbey (it is now a luxury hotel), the Dominicans, the Franciscans, the Servants of Mary, and the Augustinians.

It is possible these orders were responsible for a great deal of the fine crafts, such as lace-making, of the town. Lace-making is such an ingrained tradition that there is a beatified lady by the name of Vanna da Cannaiola who protects all lace-makers and watches over the places where this flourishing activity takes place. Lace-making is a recent activity in Orvieto; it started at the beginning of the twentieth century under an initiative of Count Eugenio Faina, who wanted to provide poor women with a means to make money. He started a society for Orvieto's noble women, who financed the production of "trina d'Irlanda," or Irish lace. This kind of embroidery was chosen for its beauty and also for its modular structure; work could be subdivided among many people. The lace was then embellished with Renaissance motifs inspired by the bas-relief on the façade of the city's duomo, and original patterns of extraordinary symbolism and beauty were created. This distinguishes *merletti di Orvieto*—Orvieto lace—which is still produced and admired. The "Assisi" stitch is much older. It was made in the convents and is particularly complicated, a mixture of cross-stitch and stem stitch, with dense geometric embroidery depicting fantastic animals. It dates to the fourteenth century and was an adaptation of an original Coptic technique; today it is widespread.

The school of the Giglio Monastery was famous. It was founded in 1702 by Angela del Giglio and has preserved the art of smocking or pleating. Pieces were pleated by hand and decorated with embroidery; they are often seen on religious vestments. Around Lake Trasimeno and on Maggiore Island, where there is a permanent lace exhibition, a different type of lace-making was introduced in 1904 by Elena Guglielmi. A very delicate lace called "irlandesi" was made; it got its name because it was originally made by Guglielmi's Irish servants. In Panicale, the tradition of embroidering on tulle is still popular. This method utilizes ancient techniques and was adapted at the beginning of the twentieth century by a school founded by Anita Belleschi Grifoni. The production of this embroidery rivals that of the work done in Brianza and in Florence.

No less finely executed is the craft of working wrought iron. It is pervasive in Umbria: in Assisi, Città della Pieve, the area of Spoleto, and around Lake Trasimeno. The little workshops in the historic center of the town generally produce small objects such as andirons and other fireplace pieces, clothes stands, lamps, and decorative objects for the home. Some areas have specialties: Gubbio reproduces antique weaponry, Villamagina makes files and rasps, and Norcia has made surgical instruments since the sixteenth century. Concentrated in Magione, on Lake Trasimeno, are master craftspeople who fashion copper objects, such as jugs, pots, decorated vats and plates; the copper is hammered, etched, or worked in relief.

facing page
Orvieto lace—placemats and coasters—to decorate the table.

below
Orvieto in the evening: a mysterious, ancient street in the center of town.

Embroidery can be purchased in Orvieto at Albero on Corso Cavour. In the region of Perugia, wrought-iron objects are sold at Arte Ferro or in Emiliani at Città di Castello, Forgia di Giano dell'Umbria, Artigianato Ferro Artistico, or Medioevo di Gubbio; in the region of Terni, wrought iron can be purchased at the Bottega del Ferro in Guardea.

PERUGIA

TAPESTRIES AND ALTAR CLOTHS

UMBRIA IS THE REGION OF ITALY WHERE CRAFTSMANSHIP HAS BEEN PERFECTED. Traditional crafts have been regulated and protected for thousands of years by guilds. In fact, while the first standards were introduced in the Middle Ages, in Umbria the *Tabulæ Eugubinæ* (seven bronze tablets that date back to the third and first centuries BC and are preserved in the Palazzo dei Consoli in Gubbio), describe the disposition of the craftsmen's guilds according to their activities. Craftsmanship is still recognized today in the regional statutes: "The Region recognizes the value and the important function of craft activities, and promotes their development. It safeguards artistic craftsmanship and keeps its tradition alive. It adopts the measures necessary to encourage professional training for artisans." Textile-making began in Umbria in the eleventh century, and the craftsmen who worked with wool and cotton belonged to the same guild. The Guild or Confraternity of Merchandise was a prolific producer of textiles, and the Bergières, who came from Lille in France, set up a workshop to make tapestries that would compete with French products. Perugian tablecloths were in demand from the thirteenth century to the sixteenth century, and remain popular today. Typical colors used are turquoise, brown, or red and many examples feature geometric patterns or animals such as eagles and griffins. Many paintings of the period depict these tablecloths, which were used to cover church altars; examples include the frescoes of Pietro Lorenzetti and Simone Martini in Assisi, and the frescoes of Ghirlandaio in the San Marco Church at the Ognissanti Convent in Florence. Although production slowed in past centuries, work continued in the convents. Textiles were used for liturgical purposes and in households as dowries for marriage-age girls. This type of work had a resurgence at the turn of the century. At the 1906 exposition of the "Industrie femminili italiane" (Italian women's industries) organized in Rome, the Ars Umbra showcased antique tapestries to great acclaim, thanks to an audience of cultured and progressive aristocrats in the region. At the end of the 1950s, Alessandrina Torelli Faini was still making meticulously precise tapestries in flame stitch. During the early 1900s, the Umbrian Workshop of Handwoven Textiles was founded at Città del Castello by Baroness Alice Franchetti Halgarten in an effort to promote the craft of weaving among rural women. The workshop is still active today, selling tablecloths, bed covers, and woven carpets in the traditional *occhio di pernice* triangular design. Decorative motifs recall the griffin, a symbol of Perugia, and the geometric patterns of the Renaissance and are produced in the classic colors of gold-yellow, blue, and red.

Via Antonio Fratti, in the medieval quarter of Perugia.

Maridiana, a farm in Umbertide in the Upper Valley of the Tiber, is unique in Italy. It breeds herds of alpacas, and a selection of sheep and angora goats. The alpaca is a camel-like animal native to South America, and it is bred for its precious coat, which is hypoallergenic, lanolin-free, and can be found in more than twenty different natural colors. At this farm, the wool from these animals, each of which produces about nine pounds a year—enough for eight sweaters—is made into fine fibers that are handwoven by small companies located nearby. The companies produce high-quality scarves, pullovers, gloves, and hats in unique designs and natural colors. Maridiana also receives paying guests and, upon request, organizes courses in spinning, weaving, and textile-dyeing.

Clothes are sold at the Luisa Spagnoli outlet or at Confezioni Ikebana. Knitted clothes and cashmere are sold at Sterne International, which is owned by Lorena Antoniazzi, or at Piazza Pitti in Ponte San Giovanni. Textiles typical of the Umbrian region can be found at Sposini in San Valentino della Collina.

facing page
Fabrics on display in Giuditta Brozzetti's workshop in the ex-church and convent of San Francesco delle Donne in Perugia.

SOLOMEO

ITALIAN CASHMERE

BETWEEN LAKE TRASIMENO AND PERUGIA IS A TINY MEDIEVAL HAMLET called Solomeo; it is so small it does not appear on road maps. Brunello Cucinelli, known as "mister Cashmere" and the "Benetton of cashmere," is a major player in Italian fashion, and he has set up a "humanistic factory" there. He is the creator of made-in-Italy cashmere products, including sweaters, pullovers, cardigans, and accessories in classic col-

Bags from the autumn 2006 collection by Brunello Cucinelli.

facing page
Piazza Carlo Alberto Dalla Chiesa in the restored medieval village of Solomeo.

ors of white and beige, as well as warm pastels. In 1978, at a time when industries were globalizing, Cucinelli chose to go against the tide and brought Italian cashmere to the fashion world, challenging the English, who had been the undisputed leaders in the market; this choice was indicative of his character.

Cashmere is the long, fine hair that grows under the fleece of the Tibetan goat. Each animal can produce no more than fourteen ounces a year, so it is a very rare material and therefore synonymous with luxury. It also requires very careful workmanship. Thanks to the inventiveness of its clothes and its well-run organization, today the firm of Brunello Cucinelli has become the leading cashmere-maker on the market—in Europe, America, and Asia. But this is not the reason this company is so unusual. In the 1980s, Brunello Cucinelli combined his entrepreneurial skills and his personal values and dreams; "the man who changed matter into style" took to heart the message of Friedrich von Hayek (Nobel Laureate in economics in 1974), and the lesson in solidarity of St. Francis of Assisi. The charismatic Cucinelli bought a small hamlet, complete with a thirteenth-century church and castle. He restored it and transformed it into a village/factory, where work and play mix together, where there are no time cards to punch, where people feel free to express their creativity, and where there is no distinction between manager and worker. He chose to use this type of model rather than those of Werner von Siemens and Adriano Olivetti, who had founded working cities. In Solomeo, as in the small Renaissance workshops, the emphasis is on craftsmanship, pride in one's own work, and perfection.

Solomeo was almost in ruins and uninhabited. It was necessary to research how to reconstruct the original village and return it to its former glory, transforming buildings into workshops and warehouses, the Renaissance rooms into dining areas, and the town squares into outdoor theaters. People work in a relaxed atmosphere that stimulates creativity. Solomeo is a town where people want to live and work; it is not a place to run from in search of a factory job in the suburbs of the big cities.

Crafts of Assisi are connected to the religiosity of the place, including rosaries, both simple and ornate; crucifixes made from wood or wrought iron; Byzantine-type icons; and decorated ceramics. Even the fabric and lace are inspired by sacred motifs. Particularly lovely objects are the plates and vases with scenes from the lives of St. Francis and St. Claire; copies of the relics of the saint and of Christ on the cross in the San Damiano Church, where Jesus spoke to Francis; reproductions of the Giotto frescoes; and books about the saint and the history and art of the town. The best bookshop is in the cloister of San Francesco. Shops are full of souvenirs and there is a permanent exhibition of the town's crafts.

In newer sections of Solomeo other knitwear and clothing companies, including Gunex and Rivamonti, have set up shop. Their outlets offer good prices. In Assisi, keepsakes can be purchased at Angelucci in via San Francesco or at Bolletta in Piazza San Pietro.

ASCOLI PICENO

ACCESSORIZE FROM HEAD TO TOE

FOR CENTURIES ONE OF THE MOST IMPORTANT PRODUCTS MADE IN THE MARCHE region has been shoes. Indeed, the rules regulating the shoemakers' guild date back to the Middle Ages. Leather was imported from Albania and the Balkans. In the nineteenth century the major production centers were in Piceno, where mono-form *chiochiere* and *pianelle* (slippers) were sold mostly in Rome and in Tuscany. Until the end of the nineteenth century shoes were made entirely by hand. The industry automated in the 1950s, and shoes were produced in factories with advanced machines. This automation primarily occurred in the provinces of Ascoli Piceno and Macerata, where to this day high-quality shoes are made at very competitive prices.

Less well-known is the fact that 70 percent of hats manufactured in Italy, almost half of those made in Europe, come from Montappone, a small village of only eighteen hundred inhabitants in the Marche. Montappone is tucked away in the hills of the Apennines in the region of Fermo. Since 1860, the village has been the European capital of hat manufacturing; hats of every kind are produced here, from straw hats to those made of felt, wool, and leather. Eventually, hat-making spread to the nearby villages of Massa Fermana, Loro Piceno, and Mogliano; more than fifteen hundred of the area's residents were employed by about a hundred small companies. The companies carved niches for themselves in order to diversify the hats made. Montappone is still the center of production and more than half of the hat-making companies are concentrated here. Sixty million hats a year are produced there. Even the mayor produces beautiful hats and exports almost all of them to Japan and the United States.

Hat-making tools and the finished products are found everywhere in the village: fabrics and completed hats can be seen in the garages of small houses, they appear behind the windows of apartment blocks, and they are piled up in basements. Indeed, under the only tree in the village, beside the museum and facing the International Exposition of Hats, there is a molding press for hats of every kind, from baseball caps to bowlers. There is a factory neighborhood in Montappone, but it is usually deserted; people prefer to stay at home and work rather than waste precious time commuting to the factory to clock in. Much of the work is commissioned by top fashion houses—Fendi, Benetton, and Diesel, to name a few—but some companies promote their own brands, and they have expanded the range of products made, including accessories such as shoes and gloves.

The elegant Piazza del Popolo at night.

facing page
Every kind of hat from the workshops of Montappone.

The Montalto Nannerini Palazzo at Sant'Elpidio a Mare is near the walls surrounding the historic city center. It houses the Museum of Footwear, where one can learn about the evolution of shoe production—from handcrafted to machine-made—in the Marche region. Displayed are shoemaking tools and machines used over the centuries, as well as models of Italian and foreign shoes from the eighteenth century made out of various materials—even silk and velvet—when shoes for the left and right foot were the same. Also displayed are the shoes of famous people; those in unusual shapes, such as Chinese shoes for bound feet; platform sandals of the Ottomans; elasticized boots; hobnailed shoes; shoes made during the war when leather was not used; shoes with stiletto heels; and the platform-soled shoes, or "rafts," worn by young people in the 1970s.

There are also many shoemaking companies in Montegranaro and Casette d'Ete, and good company outlets offer competitive prices. In Casette d'Ete you can find Della Valle Tod's, and Ikam, a small company that produces good-quality shoes. Kid's Heaven specializes in children's shoes. Zintala produces custom-made shoes. Amaranti offers shoes and bags; bags and luggage can be purchased at Torresi. The footwear factories of Marilungo and RDB, and the bag-maker Lara by Lara San Paul, can be found in Montegranaro. Hats by Chaday Complit are sold at Montappone.

CASTELFIDARDO

ACCORDION CONCERTS

THE SOPRANI FACTORY AT CASTELFIDARDO IS FAMOUS FOR ITS ACCORDIONS. The factory opened in 1863 to produce the *accordèon* that Paolo Soprani, then a young farmer, saw and heard played by an Austrian pilgrim who was on his way to the sanctuary of Loreto. Soprani was the first accordion-making workshop in Italy, followed soon after by others; accordions were also made in the distant town of Stradella, in the province of Pavia, and at Vercelli in Piedmont. Castelfidardo is a charming village overlooking the Musone River Valley in the province of Ancona; the skill of the craftsmen of the village was so great that at the beginning of the twentieth century many were already exporting their instruments around the world. The first *Akkordions* in Germany and Austria, precursors of the accordion, were built at the beginning of the nineteenth century. From there they spread to Eastern Europe and to France and Switzerland, where they are called *Physahar-monika*, which means a harmonica with bellows. This name, along with "organetto," was adopted in Italy. But it was a rather rudimentary instrument in looks as well as sound. Mariano Dellapè perfected the instrument at his workshop in Stradella; he created the wonderful polyphonic instrument that we know today.

The accordion is an integral part of village festivals, and it is a typical accompaniment for ballroom dancing. It is an extraordinary instrument, aesthetically intriguing, and both simple and complex. These instruments have a range of sounds and can be used to perform classical music repertoire. Accordions are decorated with inlaid wood and mother-of-pearl or with colored celluloid. Each instrument is made of one thousand pieces. The sound is produced by metallic reeds that vibrate by the flow of air produced by the bellows. There are three primary parts of the instrument: the sound box, called the "canto," the bellows in the center, and the harmonica sound box called "bassi" on the left. They can come with a keyboard like a piano or chromatic keys like buttons. The first can have 120 "bassi" and 41 keys (there are 45 in the classical accordion); the second can have more than 52 buttons, each one corresponding to a different sound. Sound is produced by the vibration of several reeds at the same time. It is thus possible to obtain different kinds of sound, some similar to the organ or the violin. The quality of the instrument is determined by the "voices," the heart of the accordion, composed of an aluminum plate on which two reeds are placed in opposite directions; they make a sound only if the amount of air comes from the right direction.

Briar pipes.

facing page
An accordion featuring inlay work from the Victoria company.

In Castelfidardo and Recanati the large-scale production of smoking pipes began during the first years of the twentieth century. It was initiated by French entrepreneurs, who seized the opportunity since pipes were already being made by craftspeople in small workshops. In 1903 a pipe factory was built at Castelfidardo (it was then transferred to Loreto); the pipes had an unusual name—"The frog doesn't sing"—and could be found in markets all over the world for many years. The name comes from a design in which two small holes were made in the stem of the pipe to prevent the gurgling noise caused by excess saliva; the sound resembled the croak of a frog. There are well-regarded pipe factories in Recanati and Pesaro. They use quality briar for the bowl and bone for the mouthpiece. Cigarette holders, combs, and gambling chips are also made with bone.

In Castelfidardo, accordions can be found at Nello Negascini or D&D; in Castagnari at Recanati. The International Museum of the Accordion at Castelfidardo is worth a visit, and there is a collection of antique accordions at Camerano. Accordions, pianolas, and barrel organs are also made in Camerano, Osimo, Numana, and Loreto. Lutes are made in Ascoli Piceno, San Benedetto del Tronto, and Pesaro. Handmade briar pipes can be purchased at Moretti in Recanati.

FABRIANO

A PAPERMAKING TRADITION

FABRIANO IS LOCATED IN A VALLEY OF THE CENTRAL APENNINES. It has an ancient history that began with the Piceni and was followed by the Romans (from whom they took the name *Faberianus*, or the farm of *Faberius*). It became a medieval feudal town with the arrival of nobles during the Renaissance. Together with Camerino and Urbino, Fabriano was the center of painting in the Marche region; this art form reached its highest level here in the first half of the fifteenth century with Gentile da Fabriano. Today, there are lovely monuments to see—the duomo, founded a thousand years ago; the Palazzo del Podestà, which dates from 1255; and the sixteenth-century Bishop's Palace—even though the town has lost a great deal of its old-world charm.

Papermaking in Fabriano dates back to the thirteenth century and the craft made the town famous. In his book *Il Milione*, Marco Polo writes that the Chinese invented paper, and even though the Chinese emperors zealously guarded the secrets of papermaking, knowledge of the craft began to spread in the seventh century; the Arabs brought this knowledge to the Mediterranean. It appears that the Arabs were the first master paper artisans in Fabriano; they used linen and hemp for their product. They made sheets of very high-quality paper; this product soon established a place on the market, replacing the expensive parchment that had been used until that time. With the invention of moveable type in the fifteenth century, paper became an indispensable way to disseminate ideas and information. During the fourteenth and fifteenth centuries in Fabriano, the production of paper was strictly regulated. Paper factories were not allowed to be built within a fifty-mile radius of the town. The penalty for disobeying this law was the confiscation of goods and property and exile from the city. In a document from 1445, signed by the priors of the commune, it was stated that a craftsman named Piero di Stefano, the only person who constructed frames for papermaking in the Marche region, was required to teach his art to his son or to an apprentice of his workshop; and he was not allowed to build or repair frames outside the district of Fabriano. In the eighteenth century, high taxes forced many papermaking factories to close. From a high of forty soon only three remained; at the same time, there was growing competition from factories in northern Europe, which were able to make whiter paper with a more delicate sizing more suitable for drawing and printing. But paper production was on the rise by the end of the century, thanks to Pietro Miliani, who made papers for printing, writing, drawing, and etching. Miliani also invented the watermark and was the sole producer of "French paper," tracing paper that was particularly adapted for drawing and etching; he also made fine paper for money, also used abroad.

A paper factory in Fabriano where paper is made by hand.

facing page
A monk from the San Silvestro monastery at Monte Fano studies a sheet of watermarked paper.

There are many stationery shops around Fabriano where special paper can be purchased. Papermakers Cartiere Miliani-Fabriano and Artem also sell stationery. Other paper production centers in the region are Pioraco, Esanatoglia, and San Severino. Prints of important works of art on Fabriano paper can be purchased at the Antica Bottega Amanuense. There is a museum of paper and watermarks at Pioraco. There is also an interesting museum of natural colors at Lamoli di Borgo Pace (Pesaro and Urbino).

The Museum of Paper and Watermarks provides guided tours in many languages. Here all the steps of the papermaking process are presented, from the arrival of rags to the dispatch of packaged reams to the Port of Fano. There are also demonstrations of handmade papermaking. A reconstructed medieval Fabriano fulling mill—the laboratory where the master papermakers worked centuries ago—is also on site. Visitors can make a sheet of watermarked paper as well. It takes about an hour, from the pulp stage to the rolling out of the sheet. The museum displays examples of every kind of paper, as well as artistic watermarks from the thirteenth century to the present day, and molds for making watermarks.

R O M E

S T A R S T R U C K

ROME IS THE CAPITAL OF ITALIAN FILM AND POLITICS, and the place where the most famous stylists and jewelers in the world have studios. After all, movie stars and politicians must be well-dressed! Anybody who wants to know about the newest trends must visit the area between Piazza di Spagna and Piazza Barberini, and along the Via Condotti and Via Veneto; this is where top designers have their boutiques. The Fontana studio, founded by sisters Zoe, Micol, and Giovanna, opened in Parma in 1907; in the 1930s, the Fontana sisters moved the family studio to Rome (it closed in the 1980s). At that time, they were enormously popular with the city's elite. In 1949 they made the wedding dress Linda Christian wore when she married Tyrone Power; the press could talk of nothing else for weeks. This got them noticed in Hollywood; soon the stars flocked to their studio on Via Liguria. Elizabeth Taylor, Jane Mansfield, Ingrid Bergman, Jean Collins, Kim Novak, Ursula Andress, Raquel Welch, and Ava Gardner were all dressed by the Fontana sisters; the sisters even began to design costumes for movies. Another famous designer is Valentino Garavani, who immodestly described himself as a "creator," something that probably no one else—not even Picasso—has said of himself. Valentino was born in Voghera, learned French, and worked in Paris for many years. In 1959 he opened a small studio on Via Condotti, an enclave of designer boutiques. At that time, he had to pay newspapers to write about him. In 1962, at the fashion show at Palazzo Pitti in Florence, he attracted the attention of some important American buyers, and since then he has dressed some of the most famous women in the world: Christina Ford, Paola of Liege, and Jacqueline Kennedy. Today, Valentino is based in Paris. In addition to his clothes, he produces fragrances and accessories and he has opened boutiques all over the world. Another fashion legend was Roberto Capucci. He was a twenty-year-old student at the Accademia di Belle Arti when a friend persuaded him to open a studio on Via Sistina in Rome. With a cutter and two workers, he made clothes for his sister's friends. In 1951 he went to Florence and sold the fifteen designs he brought with him. In 1957 he began making sculptured clothes and became famous for his "box" line. He still designs unique, colorful pieces; some wrap the body like pieces of geometrical architecture. His designs have been exhibited at Vienna's Kunsthistorisches Museum. At Villa Litta in Biumo in the Varese, his clothes were shown next to works by artists such as Max Cole and Allan Graham; at the Hôtel de la Monnaie in Paris his creations appeared with those of Picasso, Moore, and Giacometti.

The Forum, center of ancient Roman political and spiritual life.

facing page
The stairway of Trinità dei Monte, leading to the church.

The Fendi sisters' boutique is on Via Borgognona. (At their shop on New York's Fifth Avenue, the entrance to the boutique in Rome is reproduced.) A Bulgari outlet is on Via Aurelia, and at the Discount delle Firme, clothes and accessories by top designers can be purchased at good prices. In the Romanina area, the Marzotto outlet sells clothes and fabric. The Porta Portese market takes place every Sunday.

Rome was a great city since its foundation on that fateful day, April 21, 754 BC. In the first century AD Rome was home to one million inhabitants and dominated the known world. After the fall of the Empire it became the heart and mind of Christianity, seat of the Papacy and a place of pilgrimage. The glory of Rome contains so many testimonies that a summary is unthinkable. It would take a lifetime to know it all, and neither is a long stay enough to inspect the monuments and the works of art of a brief period of its history. Apart from the small and immensely large Vatican Museum, there are many, imposing ruins of Ancient Rome: the Roman Forum, the Colosseum, and the Baths of Caracalla to name just a few. The Renaissance and Baroque monuments of the city are its luxurious palazzos, Piazza di Spagna and the Spanish Steps, its beautiful fountains, and glorious museums. The two sides of the coin of Rome to visit today are the "Dolce Vita" of the historic center and Trastevere, a popular area where merchants sell their wares and, historically, pilgrims flocked.

left
Prints and frames in
via dei Capellari.

Window shopping
for modern art,
kitchen designs,
lifelike marble fruit,
and more.

Since the nineteenth century, Porta Portese has been the largest and most famous market in Rome—probably in all of Europe. On Sunday mornings, thousands of stalls overflow with everything from precious antiques to ordinary replicas of high-fashion labels. Most of the customers seek the latter and the market has turned into an obvious example of globalization, however, there are still good deals to be had at the stalls selling antiques and more contemporary designs; to find them, head toward Porta Portese and Viale di Trastevere.

left
Relaxing in a bookshop's cafè.

below and right
Bric-a-brac, objects of all kinds and ages at the regular Sunday market in Porta Portese.

For decades, during the most productive years of Cinecittà, the via Veneto was the most famous street in Rome. Wide and tree-lined, the via Veneto rises from piazza Barberini to Porta Pinciana, flanked by hotels and elegant cafés. This was the stage for starlets and movie stars, consenting prey to paparazzi in search of gossip. Today, the center of attention has moved to via Condotti, looking up from Largo Goldoni to the scenic Spanish Steps rising to Trinità dei Monti. Famous jewelry shops, elegant boutiques, and leather shops providing made-to-measure shoes reside along the via Condotti and in a few of the surrounding meandering streets.

High fashion in the center of town.

Via Condotti, the most fashionable street in Rome, and the famous jeweler, Bulgari.

TARQUINIA
LAZIO
AUTHENTIC ETRUSCAN—OR NOT?

ON THE MONTEROZZI HILL, NOT FAR FROM TARQUINIA, a vast necropolis dating back to the sixth century BC has been unearthed. Since the discovery and classification of roughly six thousand tombs on this gentle hill it has become the most significant site for the study of the ancient Etruscans. The first tombs, discovered in the fifteenth and sixteenth centuries, were plundered. Other tombs were found in the nineteenth century and seem to be the most important and the richest. In 1958 an official excavation of the area began, and the work continues to this day. It is thought that this was the burial ground for the dead from a vast area. The formation of the tombs differs; this probably corresponds to the economic means of the person buried, however, most are ornately decorated and contain vases, ceramic utensils, and jewelry. These finds are preserved in the National Etruscan Museum of Tarquinia. The most important tombs have been sealed and can no longer be visited. The tombs of the Lionesses of Polyphemus, the Bear, the Augurs, the Bulls, and the Leopards were richly decorated with wall paintings and are now protected against further deterioration.

Some tombs are faithfully reconstructed at Etruscopolis, a large underground cave of tufa rock at the gates of the city. It is the work of Omero Bordo, an artist who likely is more knowledgeable about Etruscan art than many other more qualified art critics. He comes by his knowledge in an interesting way. In order to survive during the difficult postwar years, Bordo became a "tombarolo," or a grave robber. He dug through the earth to the chambers below and stole statues and vases that had been made thousands of years before; he then sold these to collectors. Inside the tombs he learned to recognize the characteristics of Etruscan art. He studied their ceramic-making and painting techniques; after all, he was, and still is, a great artist. He tried to replicate the bronzes and ceramics. Some of his work is so authentic looking that it is now exhibited in museums and private collections in Italy and abroad. He became known as the "king of pottery," and his fame was recognized by kings, such as Gustav of Sweden, who invited him to court despite his shady background.

Eventually, Bordo's past caught up to him, and he was imprisoned for several years. His present activity, a legal one, is the result of those past experiences. He is a consultant to the office of fine arts and history for Rome and Lazio; he is considered *the* expert on Etruscan art. His tombs at Etruscopolis have been carefully painted and are filled with high-quality replicas of utensils and jewelry. In addition, he is the director of the School of Artistic Ceramics of the city of Tarquinia, where he has a studio and sells his work; his ceramics come with a declaration of authenticity signed by the "Last Etruscan."

Omero Bordo's workshop is in the center of the old city in Tarquinia. "Signed" copies of Etruscan ceramics and bronzes can be purchased there. Also in Tarquinia, Todi makes sculptures in tufa rock. The goldsmith Rosito at Fiuggi produces handmade jewelry and precious objects. In Rome the Bottega Mortet specializes in engraving.

Working with gold, in two distinctly different forms and markets, has been an important activity in Lazio for many centuries. In the capital, there was a preference for classical production, influenced by the church and the noble families. Today this has given rise to the jewelry that sparkles in the windows of Via Condotti and Via Veneto. But in the countryside, there was always a need to display one's wealth, and showy jewelry was popular: great pendants, coral necklaces, solid gold chains, rings studded with large precious stones. The latter work has almost completely disappeared, but it has been replaced with very inventive objects inspired by Etruscan and Roman jewelry, particularly in the Castelli Romani, the Frosinone Valley, and at Circeo and Tarquinia.

facing page
The Winged Horses, symbol of Tarquinia, in the National Museum in Palazzo Vitelleschi.

below
A potter working the wheel.

CASTELLI

EARTHENWARE MASTERPIECES

THE LINE BETWEEN CRAFTSMANSHIP AND ART IS SOMETIMES FINE, and the ceramics of Castelli are an example of this. Ceramics have been made for centuries in this village in the province of Teramo. The museum is housed in the former Santa Maria degli Angeli Convent and displays plates and large vases that hold their own with the sculptures and paintings. Ceramics made in Castelli during the sixteenth century—the most florid period—are also preserved in the Museo del Palazzo Venezia in Rome, at the Victoria and Albert Museum in London, and in hundreds of private collections.

Although Castelli is in a mountainous area, at the foot of Mount Camicia and with the Gran Sasso range in the distance, Castelli is relatively low-lying, in a landscape of green hills scored by ravines of gray clay. These ravines attracted the attention of a community of Benedictine monks from San Vincenzo al Volturno, and in around AD 1000, they founded the imposing monastery San Salvatore, which is nearby. The monks began making terracotta and ceramic objects, and taught the technique to the farmers in the area. At the end of the fifteenth century, a special kind of ceramic making started. The technique was known as "*engobed* and scratched"—a mixture of diluted white clay and water was applied as a coating to the pottery, which was then colored and scratched. Majolica was then added to the kinds of objects produced. This satisfied a wealthier, more demanding clientele. They appreciated the refined quality obtained by the application of a decorated glaze with motifs inspired by the popular Umbrian ceramics. In the sixteenth century, the artisans of Castelli acquired even more sophisticated techniques, creating a style of their own that did not reflect the decorative influences of Umbrian ceramics. It became very popular among Europeans. Castelli's greatest period of ceramic craftsmanship was from the end of the fifteenth to the end of the eighteenth century. Thanks to the workshops of masters such as Grua, Fuina, Gentili, and Ceppelletti, who made exceptionally beautiful plates and pitchers, this work found a place among the most important ceramics on the international scene. Today's ceramics tend to be more traditional, decorated with the classic Renaissance colors

Lace-making with bobbins at Pescocostanzo.

facing page
Detail of hand-painted ceramic ware typical of Castelli.

Lace-making is another important craft in the region. Scanno and Pescocostanzo are the major producers of lace there. In the eighteenth century, nuns from Cluny taught the local women a special technique, similar to that used in Bruges in Belgium; the technique is still used today. The design is made with bobbins and a "tombolo," or stuffed pillow, onto which the stretched thread from the spindle is pinned. The "tombolo aquilano" method is particularly appreciated because the work is continuous and made in such a way that the background and the decoration blend into each other seamlessly. Both the technical precision of the product and the elegance of the traditional decorations are admired. They are a reminder of the stylistic method of the Gothic floral of Abruzzo that can also be seen at the entrances to the churches.

of blue, yellow, and ochre. But modern creations signed by famous artists are also made. This level of craftsmanship spread from Castelli to other areas in the region, including Ortona, Palena, Fara Filiorum Petri, and Raiano, where it is still possible to visit workshops.

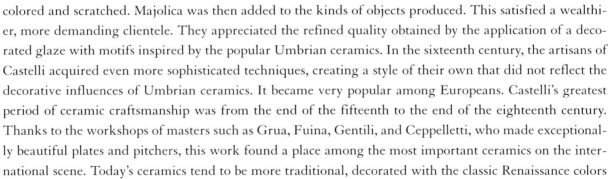

Each summer Castelli hosts an exhibition and market of local crafts. The ceramic work of Vera Tobia uses traditional colors and designs. The Simonetti factory is large, whereas that of Melchiorre is very small. Located in the ancient Franciscan Santa Maria Convent, a few steps from the Institute of Ceramic Art, a museum of ceramics features exhibits on the development of this art form over the centuries. On the nearby hill, in San Donato Church, there is a beautiful example of a coffered ceiling in ceramic tiles.

L'AQUILA

THE SHEEPHERDING INDUSTRY

FRENCHMAN PIERRE LAVEDAN IS THE AUTHOR OF A MAJOR WORK about urban development in the Middle Ages. He believes that the foundation of L'Aquila was one of the most important events in Europe. The city did not form by chance and did not grow slowly like other places. It grew as a result of a kind of "industrial" development. The basin in which it was built had already been inhabited in the Roman era—not because it was a crossroads for commercial traffic or for pilgrims but because the region possessed what one could call the first economic-industrial structure in history. This structure focused on sheepherding. Sheep farming requires a large investment of capital and coordination of many different specialized activities; it is not a subsistence activity. In L'Aquila, the sheep tracks made by the flocks between lowland and mountain pastures were about 330 feet wide and stretched from the slopes of the Gran Sasso mountain range as far as the Puglia region, where the "Dogana per la mena delle pecore" (customs house for the management of the sheep), was located. As they were moved, thousands of sheep needed to be protected against raids; pastures needed to be available along the way; and fenced areas were necessary so that the animals could be counted for tax reasons. Peltuinum, Altilia, and other towns were built for this purpose. Sheep migrations enabled the animals to graze throughout the year. In Roman times it was an industry in which even the emperors took part. After the fall of the Empire, raids were common and the farming towns were abandoned. A punishment of death meted out for stealing sheep did not stop the problem; neither did the intervention of saints, as was written in the *Dialogues* of Gregory I the Great. It was the Normans who reinstated the migrations, clear-cutting the lush forests of Puglia and thus providing a large area for grazing. Halfway through the twelfth century, ninety-nine entrepreneurs formed an association and decided to build the city of L'Aquila to manage the reborn "industry." This led to another interesting development. Shepherds spent long hours watching the flocks and solitary evenings around the fire; as a way to occupy their time, they began to carve objects from wood. They made objects that could be used in their daily lives, such as sticks, water bottles, stools, collars for the animals, ladles, and bowls, and they decorated them with geometric designs, religious symbols, or flowers and garlands. Eventually, these objects were being created on a higher artistic level. This was encouraged by schools for etching, where beautiful utensils, bas-relief and statues for churches and convents, as well as objects for everyday use—lovely works of art—were created.

One of the two main roads in Atilia, the Roman city that was an important junction for the herding of flocks from summer to winter pastures.

Wool weaving and tanning were two activities also connected with farming. They were entrusted to the patient hands of experts rather than to machines. At first, textiles were functional, needed for protection from inclement and cold weather; plainer textiles then gave way to those embellished with country scenes or religious icons. Woven materials as well as wall hangings and tapestries can be found in Teramo, L'Aquila, Pretoro, Guardiagrele, and Castel di Sangro. Leather is worked between Teramo and L'Aquila. High-quality saddles, saddle packs, reins, hats, and bags are made, as well as other items. At one time these objects were used by shepherds; today they are made for enthusiasts of horsebackriding and trekking with horses, which is a popular activity in the region.

During the first week in August, a regional crafts exhibition takes place in L'Aquila. The monthly "Mercatino" of Abruzzo is held in Chieti, Lanciano, Ortona, and Pescara. Lace is made in Scanno and Pescocostanzo, where one can buy items or commission one's own designs. The best wood engravers are in Pretoro, Popolu, Pescocostanzo, Ovindoli, and Loreto Aprutino. Kitchen furniture is made in Arischia.

facing page
Excellent quality leather results in the production of saddles of every kind.

SULMONA

TOO GOOD TO EAT

SUGARED ALMONDS ARE A CROSS BETWEEN A CULINARY AND DECORATIVE ART. They have been made in Sulmona since the fifteenth century, when the Santa Chiara Monastery started creating them. But this is not the reason there is a ship in the museum of the Columbus Foundation in New York entirely made of a mosaic of sugared almonds. This remarkable sculpture was made in Sulmona by a confectioner named D'Alessandro to celebrate the five-hundredth anniversary of Columbus's voyage to America; it is only one of the many examples of the skill of Sulmona confectioners. The creativity and imagination shown in their work is incomparable. D'Alessandro specialized in *panelle*-making. Panelle are panels made of sugared almonds that look like they are woven into a mosaic. He was commissioned to decorate the table at the summit meeting of the G7 in Naples. He also created the full-size figure of a baseball player to honor Joe DiMaggio when he visited Italy.

The Confetti Pelino-Sulmona was founded in 1783 and is among the oldest companies specializing in the art of making Sulmona sugared almonds. One part of the factory is a museum, presenting the history of this tradition. Old machinery is displayed in a room that has been reconstructed as an eighteenth-century workshop. Antique tools and other items are displayed along with old photographs and certificates attesting to the quality of the company's products. It is well worth a visit to the museum to learn about the origin of these famous sweets and their history in Sulmona.

Making these sweet treats started when the town was a flourishing commercial center. Venetian merchants came to exchange goods brought from the East for those made in Conca Peligna; one of the items they brought was sweet sugarcane syrup. This syrup led to the creation of the almonds. At the end of the fifteenth century, a Sulmona confectioner discovered by chance that when the sugarcane syrup was warmed it turned into a white paste that became hard and crystallized. He tried to cover almonds, hazelnuts, and citrus peel with it. Because they keep well, sugared almonds have become a symbol of celebrations and are given at special occasions. Different colors have different meanings: pink and blue almonds are for births and christenings; white ones are for weddings; green ones are for engagements; gold and silver ones are for wedding anniversaries; and red ones commemorate scholastic achievements. There are still five factories in Sulmona that make sugared almonds entirely with sugar syrup—no starch or flour added. The almonds, or hazelnuts or pistachios, are covered with this sugar and sometimes even filled with liqueurs or chocolate. They are sold loose, in gift boxes, or incorporated into colorful compositions that become decorative objects in and of themselves.

Fifty-four different kinds of sugared almonds can be purchased at the Pelino company. Besides D'Alessandro, artistic decorations in sugared almonds and some very original gift boxes can be found at the Fabbrica Confetti Panfilo Rapone. Wrought ironwork is available in Guardiagrele at Domenico di Sciascio. The works of the artisans of the Maiella are on display at a fair in August. Another fair featuring copper and wrought iron objects is held at Tossicia at the end of July.

Sugared almonds aren't the only things Sulmona is known for. Copper objects are made here as well. This activity originated in the gypsy communities that once populated the Adriatic Coast; they were very skilled at this work. The craft still thrives in the region and Alfadena, in the province of L'Aquila, and Ortona and Vasto, in the province of Chieti. The highest-quality wrought ironwork can be found in Pescocostanzo, Chiarino, and Guardiagrele. The many little workshops and stores of these old villages make large pots and frying pans in copper, molds for cakes, and other useful kitchen items and decorative objects. They also produce wrought-iron andirons, vases, and light fixtures for indoor and outdoor use.

AGNONE
BELLS RINGING

PIETRABBONDANTE COUNTY, OF WHICH AGNONE WAS PART, is now just a village in the valley of the Verrino River, but, judging by the archaeological excavations in the area, it must have been important in the past. The foundation of an Ionic temple, which was destroyed by Hannibal in 217 BC, has been discovered there. A fascinating ancient Italian theater has also been unearthed. The concave auditorium and the ruins of the stage are all that is left of this theater, which could hold twenty-five hundred spectators in stone-carved seats.

Metalworking has been an activity in this region for more than two thousand years, as evidenced by the third century BC *Tabula Anglonensis*, preserved in London's British Museum. Although the oldest bell, signed by Nicodemo Marinelli, is dated 1339, we know that the Marinelli foundry, with a specialty in sacred bronze objects, has been in operation in Agnone for one thousand years. It is the oldest foundry in the world, where bells are molded as they were centuries ago, following a strict, ancient process. In 1924 Pope Pius XI gave permission for them to bear the title Pontificia.

Bells were probably invented by the Chinese around 1000 BC, and are cited in the Bible and by Greek and Latin authors, but it was in Christianity that they assumed an important liturgical function. The technique of molding was systematized midway through the sixteenth century in *De Tintinnabulis*, the "bible" of the art of bell-ringing. It was written in Latin by Girolamo Maggi and was then translated into every European language. It takes three months to make a bell. A core of bricks is covered with well-shaped clay, which produces the internal profile. A temporary bell in wax, with all the necessary inscriptions and artistic decorations, is built over this. It is then covered with layers of fine clay until the required thickness is obtained (this is called the mantle). This mold is heated to melt the wax, leaving negative impressions of the decorations inside the mantle. It is then placed in a hole in the ground (called the casting ditch) near the furnaces and the bronze is poured into the space between the core and the mantle. This is the most intense moment in the foundry, when even small imperfections become evident. While the workmen near the furnace guide the pouring toward the mouth of the mold using long iron poles, they break the silence by invoking the Madonna, the holy symbol of birth, with the repeated intonation of Santa Maria. The model is allowed to cool; the bell is taken from the casting ditch, freed from the core and the mantle, and cleaned and chased before the iron clapper is applied; musical testing takes place at this time.

The theater in the Santuario Italico at Pietrabbondante.

facing page
Testing the sound of the bells at the Marinelli bronze foundry.

Small souvenir bells can be purchased at the Marinelli Museum shop. There is another interesting bell museum in Montegalda, in the Vicentino area. La Ramera in Agnone works with various metals. Isernia is the capital of the province and is famous for lace, which can be purchased at Castiello or at Sassi Buccigrossi.

The Marinelli Museum is worth a visit. It is attached to the foundry and dedicated to Pope John Paul II, who honored it with a visit. Bells from the year AD 1000 to the present day are displayed, as are copies of famous bells, such as the bell used to celebrate the centennial of the unification of Italy; the bell used during the perestroika, the meeting between Pope John Paul II and Mikhail Gorbachev; celebrations of Christopher Columbus; and the peace bell that was donated by John Paul II to the United Nations on the organization's fiftieth anniversary. This bell was cast with shell casings collected by Albanian children after the war, and it was placed in the main square of Tirana. At the end of a visit to the museum, there is a demonstration ringing of the bells cast in this foundry, with a small improvised "hammer" concert near the exit; the sound produced is extraordinary.

SCAPOLI

SOUNDS OF THE PIPE

SCAPOLI IS A SMALL VILLAGE WITH ABOUT ONE THOUSAND INHABITANTS. It is located at the foot of the Mainarde mountain range, in the heart of the Molise. Its name is derived from the Latin *scapula*. Today it is one of the few places where bagpipes are made using traditional methods and natural materials. Here the talk of the town is not about football or politics but about bagpipes and reed flutes. Locals do not take sides for or against genetically modified crops in their fields, but they do on the use of plastic to make reed pipes.

The bagpipe is an ancient wind instrument. Julius Caesar used bagpipes to frighten the horses of the Britons; bagpipes were then brought to Scotland. The shepherds who went to the manger in Bethlehem played this reeded flute. It is an instrument common to many European countries, with variations in shape and name: it is a *piva* in northern Italy, a *surdulina* among the Albanians of Calabria and Sicily, a *lunedda* in Sardinia, a pipe in Scotland and Ireland, and a *gaita* in Spain, Portugal, and Turkey. The type of flute primarily made in the workshops of Fonte Costanza in Scapoli has four wooden reeds, which are made from olive wood, cherry, ebony, or mountain ash. Two reeds, called *ritta* and *manca* (right and left), are conical and of different lengths. They have double metal tongues that

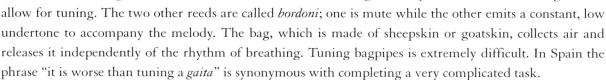

allow for tuning. The two other reeds are called *bordoni*; one is mute while the other emits a constant, low undertone to accompany the melody. The bag, which is made of sheepskin or goatskin, collects air and releases it independently of the rhythm of breathing. Tuning bagpipes is extremely difficult. In Spain the phrase "it is worse than tuning a *gaita*" is synonymous with completing a very complicated task.

According to legend, the pipers of the Molise were nomads. They wore dark felt hats or pointed hats and shoes held in place with crossed bands, like those worn by bandits. They were like "merchants of pastoral music," who traveled throughout Europe and even as far as Russia. It is said that they wandered on foot from city to city during the winter months. But the reality is that they were migrant workers who hoped to earn a little money in the towns they passed through. They would play their bagpipes at local fairs and during the *novene*, the cycle of nine days of prayer that precedes the Christmas holidays. Scapoli has a permanent exhibition of bagpipes and reed flutes. There is a national museum of bagpipes, and there is a cultural association that publishes an international periodical (*Utriculus*) dedicated to ethnic music and the bagpipe-related instruments of the world.

The traditional bagpipes of Scapoli.

Frosolone is a farming village in the mountains of the Matese. Blade-making here dates back to ancient times when the natural caves above the village were used as forges. They are called *fulsulae*, from fulgent or radiant. The blacksmiths of the village made swords and sabers for the Lombards, who had conquered areas this far south. Today, the little workshops and factories of the town specialize in making knives, daggers, scalpels, and scissors. There is a museum of cutting instruments; it displays the most representative locally made tools, as well as those from other parts of Italy and around the world. In August, there is a national exhibition of scissors and knives; there is also an event called the Feast of Forging.

Scapoli is the site of the International Bagpipe Festival, as well as a fair and market that takes place on the last Sunday in July. Arte e Tradizione in Scapoli's historic district sells bagpipes. Handmade knives can be purchased at Rocco Petrunti in Frosolone, and scissors are sold at Artigianato Forbici. Nicola Francescone is one of the few craftsmen in the world who creates perforated and decorated steel blades; these are rare pieces and have been given as gifts to many American politicians. His work can be found in Campobasso.

facing page
Aerial view of the ancient hamlet of Scapoli, nestled deep in the unspoiled countryside.

The Elephant Rock on the island of Pantelleria.

SOUTHERN *Italy* AND THE ISLANDS

AMALFI
HANDMADE PAPER

THE AMALFI COAST ON THE TYRRHENIAN SEA IS A STRETCH OF ROCKY coastline of incomparable natural beauty. Abundant, lush gardens in the beautiful villages here have very thin soil; according to legend the soil was brought by ship from the banks of the Nile. Amalfi became a rich and powerful town in the eleventh century and was one of the four maritime republics. The town's maritime codes and laws are described in the *Tabula amalphitana* preserved in the civic museum. The people established solid commercial bases in Tripoli and at Constantinople; they founded the Order of St. John (the origins of the Knights of Malta) in Jerusalem.

The invention of the compass, in 1302, was attributed to Flavio Gioia, or Flavio of Amalfi; this instrument led to great strides in navigation and exploration. In the thirteenth century, as a result of contact with the Arab world and the resulting dissemination of knowledge, Amalfi began to produce paper in the Valle dei Mulini (Valley of the Windmills). Some date the start of papermaking in the area to 1231. Amalfi continued to produce handmade paper and to export it in large quantities until the eighteenth century, when larger manufacturers elsewhere began to dominate the market. Twenty-six paper mills remained active there until 1954, when a flood destroyed almost everything.

Amalfi papermaking occurs in a few phases. Cloth is shredded, collected in stone vats, and mixed until it becomes gluelike. The resulting goo is placed in wooden vats where it adheres to a mold; from there it is transferred to woolen felts, where a stock of alternating felt-paper sheets is obtained. It is then pressed to squeeze out excess water. The sheets of paper are removed one at a time from the felt, left to dry in the open air, ironed, and packed. Watermarks are a characteristic element of Amalfi paper. The watermarks are different for each producer—a signature of the paper mill; they make it possible to trace the history of each mill. The oldest example of an Amalfi watermark dates back to 1376; this watermark is still used. A letter or symbol is made out of very thin metal wire that is placed in the center of a paste mold.

Today only about ten paper mills exist in the Valley of the Windmills. Two of the mills still make paper of the same refined quality that was produced centuries ago, with the same silky texture and distinctive watermarks that have made Amalfi paper famous for centuries.

A view of the Amalfi Coast from the hotel San Pietro in Positano.

facing page
Handmade paper from the Amatruda factory.

There is an interesting museum of handmade paper in Amalfi. The manufacturer Amatruda produces handcrafted paper. Nearby, at Castel San Giorgio, some craftspeople reproduce artistic photographic prints on sheets of Amalfi paper that have been emulsified by hand. Woven-straw items can be found in the markets during the summer months.

Weavers living in the inland farming area in Montoro and Summonte in Campania, work with straw, raffia, and reeds. The objects made—baskets for bread and fruit, jewel boxes, fans, and hats—also are found in tourist areas such as Ischia. Many craftspeople in Irpinia continue to weave. They are independent from the market, because their work is solely made for folklore fairs and religious purposes; for example, a straw obelisk twenty-five feet tall is supported by the Statue of the Madonna of the Misericordia at Fontanarossa. "The lily" is built for the feast of San Rocco at Filumeri. It is about fifty feet tall and made of a series of braided stalks of wheat supported by a wooden frame. At Mirabello Eclano, an obelisk made with threads of woven straw is eighty-two feet tall and weighs twenty tons; it supports the Statue of the Madonna Addolorata.

CAPODIMONTE

THE FINEST PORCELAIN

LIFE-SIZE BOUQUETS OF FLOWERS THAT LOOK SO REAL one thinks they should smell fragrant, groups of miniature statuary where even the expression of the eyes contributes to the character of the figures, work of such fine detail one fears they will break into pieces just by looking at them: this captures the exquisite work of the porcelains of Capodimonte, a place that specializes in one of the highest forms of ceramic art in the world.

A shop in Vietri sells local ceramics.

facing page
A bouquet of flowers, typical of the rare and refined porcelain of Capodimonte.

Bourbon king Charles III opened a prestigious ceramics factory in 1739 when he married Maria Amalia of Saxony, niece of the founder of the Meissen porcelain factory. His goal was to decorate his palace in Naples with objects more beautiful than those of the courts in Paris and Vienna, and more beautiful than those produced by the Vezzi factory in Venice and the Rossetti in Turin. Clay was brought in from Calabria. It was very fine and kaolin-free (clay with kaolin is hard to work with if fine details are desired). The resulting white porcelain was translucent with a compact, reflecting glaze and velvetlike colors. The king ordered a blue lily, a symbol of purity, to be made. Twenty years later, when he ascended the throne of Spain and moved to Madrid, the factory was abandoned.

Activity at the factory resumed about a decade later when the Real Fabbrica Ferdinandea (Royal Factory of Ferdinand) was established in Naples; it stopped producing goods for the court in 1805. However, Capodimonte's famed porcelains had become famous beyond the borders of the kingdom, and individual craftspeople set up workshops to supply the European market. In 1738 Charles III built the grand building that is home to the National Museum of Capodimonte. Its purpose was to house the collection of art that he had inherited from his mother, Elisabetta Farnese. In 1758 the paintings were placed in the twelve rooms on the *piano nobile* (second floor); his successor, Ferdinand IV, added other works of art from the Farnese Palace in Rome and art from the Neapolitan school. (Parts of the building were looted by Napoleon's troops.) Later, Gioacchino Murat set up the Galleria Napolitana with works that were acquired when the monasteries were suppressed. Today, researchers and collectors from around the world go to see the collections of porcelain and majolica in the museum. Tableware and ornamental objects from the royal palaces of Naples are on display, in addition to eighteenth- and nineteenth-century porcelains of biscuit of Sèvres, Vienna, Meissen, and Capodimonte, and majolicas from the Real Fabbrica di Napoli (Royal Factory of Naples). The rococo sitting room, with three thousand pieces of porcelain, is a masterpiece. Charles of Bourbon requested it as a gift for his wife, and it was destined for the royal palace at Portici.

Ceramics are sold at Antica Manifattura Capodimonte. San Giorgio a Cremano specializes in characteristic Capodimonte figures made by Alfonso Esposito. Figures can also be found at Ponti Rossi, Arzano, Calvizzano, Casalnuovo, Casoria, and Naples. Glazed tiles and other ceramics are produced at Cava de' Tirreni, Nocera, and Salerno. Eighteenth-century styles and decorations can be found in San Lorenzello and Cerreto Sannita in the province of Benevento. The National Museum and the collection at Villa Floridiana are not to be missed.

Vietri a Mare is at the southern end of the Amalfi Coast, near Salerno. It is the major area for traditional ceramic production in the province of Campania. Shops abound and some factories sell their products on site. The Ceramics Museum of Vietri is housed in some of the rooms of Villa Guariglia at Raito, a little village that overlooks Vietri. It has a wide range of representative objects, as well as an exhibition of the work of world-renowned ceramicist Guido Gambone. Also displayed are older works, particularly objects created in the 1920s and 1930s. This was known as the "German period" because it was influenced by the style of Max Melamerson, a particularly enterprising artist who made Vietri a center for ceramicists from Northern Europe.

CASERTA

SILKS FOR THE PALACE

FERDINAND IV OF BOURBON WAS AN AMBITIOUS AND ENLIGHTENED KING, and wanted his palace in Caserta to be so imposing and sumptuous that it would eclipse Versailles. He also wanted it to be a safe place for the government of Naples. The inauguration of the great palace and immense garden necessitated the production of exquisite objects that further ensured the prestige of the Bourbons: ceramics from Capodimonte, semi-precious stones from San Carlo alle Mortelle, weapons from Torre Annunziata. In 1789, before people understood that the preservation of nature and industrial-scale production were mutually exclusive activities, the king built the Royal Colony of San Leucio, in the valley of the Civicorno; it was in the middle of the royal park. This was a center for textile production with strict regulations on civic life—libertarian in today's style—and efficiently organized. Philosopher Benedetto Croce regarded the Bourbon project as "madness," a "royal toy" to pass the time between one hunt and another. But it was a courageous experiment that made the village prosperous and still bears fruit.

The little village of Torre and the Belvedere rise on the mountain of San Leucio, from which the colony took its name. It was the home of the dukes of Acquaviva and was purchased in 1759 to ensure the flow of water to the palace gardens. King Ferdinand then rebuilt the Belvedere and transformed the main salon into a parish church. He brought in silkworms, installed a silk mill in the courtyard, built a cowshed for the manufacture of silk (making use of the Caroline aqueduct built by the architect Vanvitelli), and created a system to sell the silk items produced. The over two hundred inhabitants of the village lived in the San Ferdinando and San Carlo areas. All of the houses were identical and were lined up along the main road. A progressive statute was passed. It decreed obligatory education, earnings based on merit, and the foundation of a charity for the old and the infirm, among other things. The intention was for the colony to become a "city of silk," supplying the palace with damasks and brocades; it was to be called Ferdinandopolis. The project was never completed, but San Leucio prospered anyway. More "factories" were added; forward-looking rules and regulations governed them. Modern machinery was also introduced. Among these machines: perforated cardboard invented at the beginning of the 1800s by Frenchman Joseph Maria Jacquard; it was used to produce tapestries for the king. The velvets and brocades that hung in the palace were renowned throughout the European courts. An extraordinary collection is on display in eleven rooms of the Appartamento Vecchio, or Old Apartment.

The Fountain of Ceres in the park of the Palace of Caserta. The Great Waterfall is in the background.

facing page
Brocade linings from the San Leucio silk works.

The historic Antico Opificio Serico De Negri (silk factory) stands in Piazza della Seta in San Leucio. Textiles and other objects such as cushions, tablecloths, clothes, and dolls are sold in the I Sorrisi shop. The Il Telaio dei Sogni di Sant'Agnelli factory produces decorated tapestries, carpets, and cushions. Nearby, Nola specializes in papier-mâché objects, such as picture frames, jewel boxes, masks, and Nativity scenes. Sant'Anastasia makes barrels and other wooden objects, as well as copper bowls.

Caserta Palace, built by Luigi Vanvitelli and his son, Carlo, is one of the largest and most sumptuous residences in Italy. It was built between 1754 and 1774, using the labor of slaves and convicts; it cost six million ducats. The palace covers approximately 485,000 square feet. Contained on its five floors are twelve hundred rooms overflowing with stucco, marble, statues, and paintings; thirty-three staircases in addition to a central stairway; a court theater; and a chapel. There is an extraordinary view from the atrium looking out into the garden. The garden was requested by Marie Caroline of Hapsburg and designed in the style of those of the European courts, with approximately two miles of basins and groups of statues, including the fountain of Diana and Actaeon, and a waterfall that is almost 262 feet tall and is fed by water from the Caroline aqueduct twenty-five miles away.

NAPLES

ARTS AND CRAFTS

THE HISTORIC CENTER OF NAPLES HAS BEEN DECLARED A WORLD HERITAGE site by UNESCO, but this is not the reason the city is unique. Nor is it because of Piedigrotta and Posillipo (which means "the place to forget all pain"); nor San Gennaro, whom the Catholic church has removed from the calendar of saints but who continues to perform miracles despite this banishment. It is the natives of Naples, and their adaptability and versatility, that make the city unique. The people from the Bassi (lower quarter) and from Via Spaccanapoli are able to do any kind of work and to invent a "trade" for themselves, even when there is no work—and in Naples there is often no work. People in Naples understand the "art of making the best of things." Until recently, "painter of fish eyes" was listed as a job: this person was employed to freshen up the eyes of fish that had not been sold at market the day before. In the streets of Naples there is a *fanfellicaro*, a man who sells slices of apple, as well as a shoe shop that caters to "the most difficult feet" and sells unpaired shoes. The *maruzzaro* sells tasty snails; the *galantaro* sells trinkets; and the *assistito* offers dreams and lottery numbers. But Naples also has "real" trades and forms of craftsmanship. One of these is the making of Nativity figurines. These are produced by artisans in Via San Gregorio Armeno, in the center of the old city, who are part of a consortium that protects their work. It is thought that this type of work originated, at least officially, in 1478. This is documented in a notarized contract belonging to the Duke of Calabria, who commissioned sculptors Giovanni and Pietro Alemanno to make forty-one large painted and gilded wooden figures to be placed in the Nativity scene in the private chapel of the Church of San Giovanni at Carbonara. Since then a series of commissions were given to the best artists of the period to beautify public churches and private chapels. Sculpting techniques have evolved over the centuries. From monolithic wooden sculptures came models in wood with moveable arms and legs; then came figures made out of wire frames and dressed in cloth costumes. Wire frames enabled craftspeople to make figures in all kinds of poses. Aristocratic patrons were intent on amazing their guests, and incredibly realistic Christmas decorations were designed for them. The Neapolitan Nativity scene took root and became famous the world over. The figures were about sixteen inches tall, made partly in modeled and fired clay, painted with bright colors, and mounted on wire frames and dressed in silk clothes and gold embroidery. Along with these "noble" figures, representations of everyday people were added and inserted into scenes of taverns, craftsmen's workshops, or the market square.

The elegant Piazza del Plebiscito at night; the neoclassical church of San Francesco di Paolo is in the background.

facing page
The Galleria Umberto I, built at the end of the nineteenth century.

Mariano Rubinacci's London House in Via Filangeri was opened by his father; today, the company has shops in Milan, Rome, and London. Custom-made contemporary suits can be finished in a few weeks; they cost a few thousand dollars. Vintage styles of the thirties, forties, or fifties—clothes that dressed Tyrone Power and Cary Grant—can also be made, if preferred; these cost a bit more. Another tailor, Ciro Paone, has been using fabrics from London or Biella for fifty years. He produces custom clothes in his factory at Arzano, near Naples. Measurements for jackets and pants (and also shirts, ties, and shoes) are taken in Kiton shops around the world—from New York to Osaka and Shanghai; the 330 tailors in the company make them.

Fratelli Sinno, in the heart of the old city, sells Nativity and other figures; these can also be purchased at Ulderico Pinfildi and Il Mondo della Ceramica. A yearly exhibition in December features the art of the Nativity scene. Beautiful Nativity scenes are displayed in the churches of Gesù Vecchio, Santa Maria, and San Nicola. The Nativity scene exhibited at the Royal Palace has 210 figures, and one of the most spectacular is at the San Martino Museum. There are many precious-metal workshops in the Borgo degli Orefici (ignore the signs outside their shops that declare We Buy Gold rather than We Sell Gold).

above, left
Nativity scenes, shepherds, and other objects for sale in via San Gregorio Armeno.

above, right
The Scarabattola, in via Tribunali, is a workshop that hand produces Nativity figurines and Pulcinella or Punch puppets.

right
A stall in via San Gregorio Armeno, the street that is home to the Nativity craftsmen.

facing page
The stall of a greengrocer.

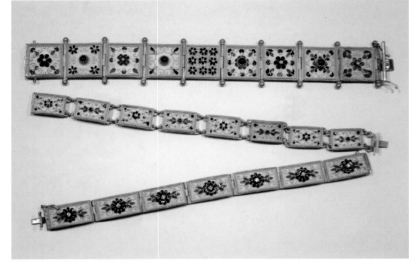

Carved coral, cameos on shells, and gold-leaf decorations with semiprecious stones, are some of the lovely jewelry pieces made in Naples.

facing page
Open-air show of antiques from a shop in via Tribunali.

Borgo Orefici lies behind the port, between Corso Umberto and Via Marina. In the thirteenth century there was a group of Neapolitan goldsmiths' workshops here, and when they were officially recognized by Joan I of Anjou they founded their first guild. The artists learned their technique from the French goldsmiths who worked for the court and the aristocracy, and accented their designs with their own Neapolitan imagination and creativity. Today a consortium of roughly one hundred craftsmen guarantees quality and authenticity. Antique jewelry from Pompeii as well as modern pieces are on display in the many shop windows.

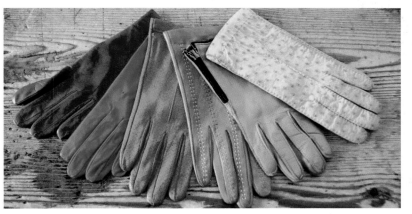

facing page
Via Chiaia, Naples' Rodeo Drive.

above, left
Exclusive Marinella ties owe their uniqueness to the fine fabrics used to make them for more than ninety years.

above, right
The Marinella shop. Natural skin and dyed handmade gloves from "Omega Produzione Guanti" in via Stella.

Handmade leather gloves are one of the traditional and world-famous crafts still maintained in Naples. Begun in the eighteenth century, leather glove-making reached its pinacle in the nineteenth century when Naples was the Bourbon capital of the Kingdom of the Two Sicilies. Prime-quality untreated leather is still used today. Before they reach the window of a shop, a pair of gloves is worked on by fifteen different skilled artisans in twenty-five separate operatons. The only way to check that a pair of gloves has indeed been handmade is to examine the stitching inside and out. The skin must be slightly elastic widthwise, but never in length. To keep the hands warm, a wool or cashmere or silk lining should be inserted after the glove has been made so that the fingers are fully insulated.

SOLOFRA

THE SMOOTHEST LEATHER

REMAINS OF PREHISTORIC SETTLEMENTS—ANCIENT ITALIAN TOMBS dating to the fifth century BC, Roman aqueducts and *villae rusticate* (farms), and remnants from the Lombards—were scattered among the small villages in the Picentini Mountains. Unfortunately, an earthquake devastated the Irpinia region in 1980.

In Solofra, the most important area in the upper valley of the Irno River, restoration has been undertaken on the palazzos that were built by the Tricarico families in the thirteenth century, the Filangeri in the fourteenth century, and the Orsini in the sixteenth century. These prosperous noble families prompted the rise of goldsmithing and silversmithing, painting workshops, and stonecutting in Solofra. The name of the village derives from the Oscan word *solofri*, meaning wholesome; ironically, since the eleventh century the economic engine of the village has been the production of leather, which creates pollution. The connection of the village with leather craftsmanship was the result of local resources: there was easy access to plants such as chestnut, hazelnut, and Turkey oak that contain the tannin necessary to cure skins; the rocks were used to produce lime; and water was plentiful.

Leather work from the craftsmen of Solofra, among the greatest stylists since the eleventh century.

facing page
The ruins of Pompeii in the shadow of Vesuvius.

Tanneries were built along the river banks; and animal skins to be washed, skinned, and stripped were immersed in brick vats filled with water and lime. They then passed through a series of barrels containing more potent tannin solutions. The length of time needed to tan skins depended on how the leather was to be used; for example, to make soles for shoes, the skins were kept in the basins and pressed with stones for as long as two years. They were then beaten to make them even harder. The finishing, dyeing, and drying of the skins on frames happened in workshops. Skins were stretched and nailed to the frames to fix their shape, and then softened with a greasy substance. At the beginning of the sixteenth century, there were dozens of *apotheche de consaria* that supplied gilded skins to Amalfi to promote commerce. They also sent cured skins to Salerno; these were used to make rigging, paper (the specialty of Solofra), and clothing. Skins became important in Naples for the manufacture of shoes. The tanning tradition was passed down within families and has been perfected over the centuries—and still is today. Solofra continues to be one of the most important leatherworking regions in Italy, at a comparable level with Arzignano in the Veneto area and Santa Croce in Tuscany. There are hundreds of companies in Solofra that tan and cure skins from South Africa, Latin America, the Middle East, and New Zealand; they re-export the finished products all over the world. Solofra specializes in tanning sheepskin and goatskins and in working the "flower," the softest part of the skins.

Among the many tanneries in Solofra that produce and sell leather clothing are Confezioni Anna, New Age Leather, Pelle d'Oro, and Euro Moda. The tanneries of Gaeta Nicola and di Maio provide leather for clothing. In and around Vesuvius, many craftspeople make decorative objects from volcanic slate, including Ranieri in Naples and Clipeus Art in San Giorgio a Cremano.

Using volcanic slate is widespread in villages around Vesuvius. In the past, its hardness and its resistance to wear made it ideal for paving roads and building oil presses and mills, as well as for entryways and other architectural details. In fact, volcanic slate can be seen in the houses of Pompeii. In the eighteenth century slate was widely used for the entrances to the great palazzos, the stairways and colonnades of villas, and the statues in the gardens at Portici, Torre del Greco, San Giorgio a Cremano, and Herculaneum. Today the volcanic slate from Vesuvius is still used for road paving and for architectural ornaments such as columns and doors, but it is primarily used to make fountains, park benches, tables, decorative items, and even jewelry.

SORRENTO
THE NOBLE ART OF MARQUETRY

MARQUETRY IS A CRAFT IN WHICH SMALL CUT AND SHAPED PIECES OF WOOD are embedded in a wooden base (a table, a decorative object, or a hanging panel) to create elaborate geometric patterns or pictorial representations. At one time, pieces of natural wood, such as dark walnut, pale ash, or reddish cherry, were used to create the various shades of the pattern, and sometimes gold leaf and precious stones were added.

The golden harbor of Marina Piccola.

facing page
The fine inlay work on the Pyramid Box by Alessandro Fiorentino.

Today, dyed pieces of veneer, not wood, are used.

Raphael and Michelangelo were masters of the art of inlay, and until the eighteenth century the courts of Europe vied with one another for the works of the most famous artists. But the "noble art of inlay" as it was called, began to lose favor. The only school of marquetry that still exists in Italy was, and still is, in Sorrento, where it is believed this craft tradition started around the fifth century AD. The monks of the Sant'Agrippino Monastery used the wood of lemon, orange, and walnut trees to decorate furniture and to make hanging panels. The technique spread outside the monastery. It was embellished and perfected until it became known as the "inlay of Sorrento" which, in the nineteenth century, reached its most refined level; work reproduced Neapolitan costumes or the frescoes that were unearthed during the excavation of Pompeii.

The Amalfi Coast was a favorite place for intellectual elites and thanks to them the fame of the local marquetry artists spread throughout Europe; their skill was officially recognized when Francis I of Bourbon commissioned them to restore the furniture in the Royal Palace. Today, most of Sorrento's marquetry is produced by about one hundred companies with seven hundred employees. The results are excellent but certainly not comparable to the seventeenth-century inlay on display in the sacristy of the Certosa of San Martino in Naples, now a national museum. But there are workshops today where masters of the art create beautiful pieces.

In the 1990s, a marquetry museum and workshop opened; displayed is a collection of nineteenth-century inlay collected by Alessandro Fiorentino, the owner of a company that promotes a cultural and commercial appreciation of wood marquetry. The museum presents the history of marquetry, and the workshop produces decorative objects and offers classes where students can learn traditional marquetry techniques.

The origin of the name Sorrento (Surrentum) is connected to mermaids or sirens, whose bewitching song enchanted sailors and caused their ships to run aground on the rocks. This ancient connection makes Sorrento the object of thousands of romantic songs, the most famous of which is *Turna a Surriento*, immortalized by the great Enrico Caruso. The rooms at the Grand Hotel Excelsior, where Caruso stayed in 1921, have been preserved as they were at that time, with the piano and the score of the song and photographs of the artist hanging on the walls. One can sleep in these rooms, but it is not easy: each year at a fundraising auction for the Metropolitan Opera in New York, wealthy Americans vie for a stay in this suite.

Carlo de Nicola, Giuseppe Esposito, and Francesco Maione are marquetry masters in Sorrento. Rolo, in the province of Reggio Emilia, is also an important center of production; it has a museum of marquetry as well. Good-quality keepsakes of all kinds can be found around Sorrento: tapestries are produced at Sant'Agnello, and handmade beeswax candles of every size and type are available. Objects made from woven straw and raffia, as well as ceramics and embroidered cloth, are produced on the islands of Capri, Ischia, and Procida.

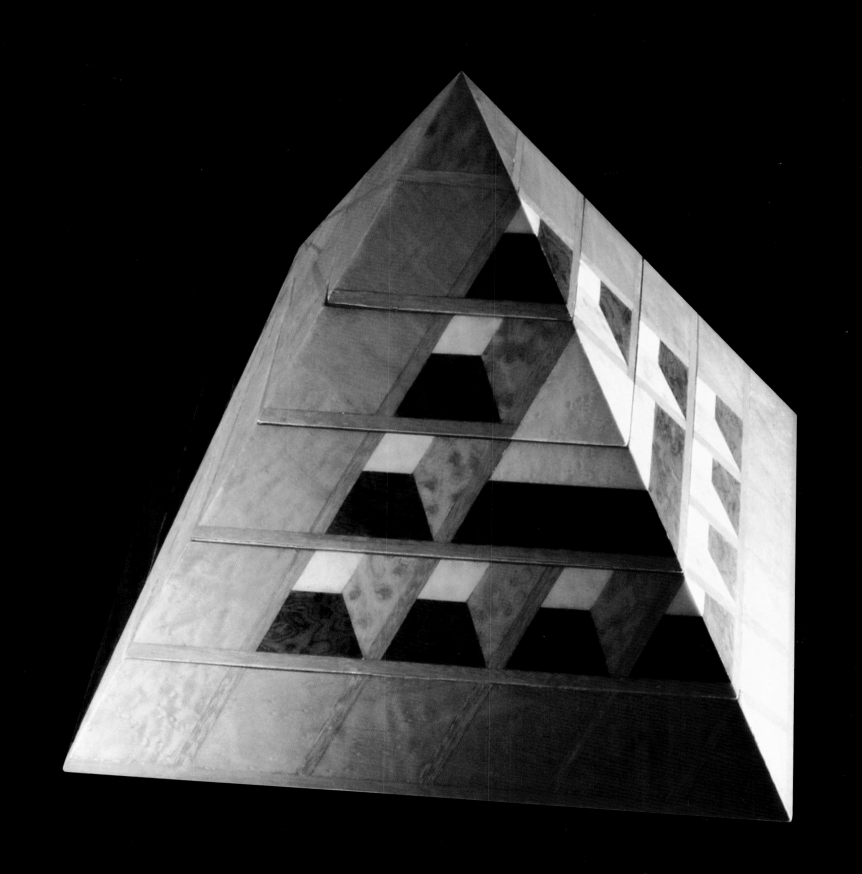

TORRE DEL GRECO RED GOLD

CORAL IS INTRIGUING, SENSUAL, AND MYSTICAL; IN AND AROUND NAPLES, it is an amulet worn to bring good fortune. In Christian theology it is associated with the figure of Christ and often the Christ child appears in the arms of the Madonna wearing a coral necklace. In mythology, after Perseus decapitated the Gorgon, he went to the sea to wash off the blood; the drops that fell into the water turned into stone trees.

It is said that this "red gold," staunches hemorrhaging and cures madness, impotence, and leprosy. Coral debris is still sent to India where it used to make aphrodisiacs, and Australian scientists are experimenting with chemical substances extracted from coral in the hope of finding a cure for cancer and AIDS. Its structure made it mysterious and magical. It looks like a small tree and therefore was thought to be a marine vegetable; it becomes hard and can be worked like a stone—alchemists thought it was a mineral. But coral is a coelenterate, like a jellyfish and sea anemone. In 1723 a doctor from Marseilles, Jean André Peyssonel, settled the plant/animal debate.

Coral belongs to the group of the anthozoans (from the Greek *antos zeton*, animal in the shape of a flower) and is subdivided into two groups based on the number of polyps it has: the octocorals (eight polyps) of the Mediterranean and the seas around Japan (these are used to make jewelry); and the esacorals (six polyps) that form the coral barrier reefs of the Pacific and are too fragile to be worked. Instead, esacorals were used to make decorative objects (collecting this coral has been banned for many years). Collection of red coral *(corallium rubrum)* is still legal, although it is strictly controlled. In Roman times this economic resource was fished along the Neapolitan coast; it was made into cameos or pendants for necklaces and bracelets. There were the *tondi*, which looked like pearls, the two-inch-long *frange* or fringes, the shorter *corti*, and the *botticelle*, which were cylindrical.

In the eighteenth century Torre del Greco, a village overlooking the Bay of Naples, was the main supply center for this precious material, but it was only at the beginning of the next century that the first laboratory opened. Thanks to Cardinal Paolo Bartolomeo Martiri, who had obtained an exclusive license from the Bourbon government, cameos were made here by master engravers. Martiri also founded a school to teach coral craftsmanship; this ensured distinctive, high-quality products. Working with coral continues to flourish; cameos are made with coral from Asia but also with mother-of-pearl, malachite, and tortoise shell.

The House of Neptune and Amphitrite at Herculaneum. The splendid mosaics in the Nympheum have been exquisitely preserved.

The Oromare Consortium (Oromare means "gold of the sea") represents 150 companies located between Torre del Greco and Naples; one of these is Petrosino. Basilio Liverino is a museum that contains one of the best personal collections in the world; it runs the School for Craftsmen in Torre del Greco. Giovanni Ascione's workshop is the oldest cameo-making business. Mondial Coral makes particularly beautiful jewelry, combining coral with gold and diamonds. There are coral museums in Torre del Greco, Naples, and Ravello.

Between Pompeii and the Lattari Mountains (Gragnano, Casola di Napoli, and Santa Maria La Carità) there are many family businesses that produce souvenirs and objects such as sandals and hats, but the main product is bathing suits. The large-scale manufacture of bathing suits began in the 1970s thanks to the proximity of popular beaches on the peninsula of Sorrento and the Amalfi Coast. Today there are five to six thousand people employed in this business and they make about five million suits per year, some of which are supplied to the big distributors and exported all over Europe. Gragnano bathing suits are particularly stylish.

facing page
Elegant cameos and refined coral jewelry from the clever hands of the craftsmen of Torre del Greco.

GROTTAGLIE
DECORATIVE TERRACOTTA

RED CLAY CAVES ARE SCATTERED THROUGHOUT THE PUGLIA REGION, which is why making terracotta objects has flourished there. Many companies manufacture roofing tiles and perforated bricks; tiles for flooring; and objects for everyday use such as plates, bowls, jugs, and the large water pitchers, called *quartare*, that can hold about twenty-six gallons of liquid and today are used as garden decorations. Making elegant ceramics—plates, household utensils, and other objects—also is a tradition. In Capurso and Ostune, whistles are made in the shapes of priests, members of the military, and little dogs; these are then decorated in bright colors. In Surano there is a doll- and oil-lamp-making tradition; in Galatina, trumpets and bells; in Gravina di Puglia and at Monte Sant'Angelo, figurines for Nativity scenes. Ceramic flower baskets are also made; the work is reminiscent of the porcelains of Capodimonte, and it is inspired by the Greeks and imitates those found at Siponto. The ceramic objects are glazed in vibrant greens or in white, similar to the ceramics of Faenza. It is the decoration, and above all the coloring, that differentiates one workshop from another. Indeed, if one craftsperson stops working, his methods for making a particular color disappear with him. In Grottaglie, the most important area of production, terracotta ceramics have been produced for centuries. Historians believe the refugees of Rudiae—the flourishing center of Puglia's Messapian people, which was destroyed by the Vandals—excelled at terracotta craftsmanship.

Terracotta objects—dishes, water jugs, and containers for oil—have been made in Grottaglie since ancient times. In order to improve their technique, the local craftspeople went to the school in Taranto, one of the most famous of Magna Grecia, and these styles are still being made today. Dozens of artisan workshops can be found beside the Palazzo Vescovile (the bishop's palace). Their caves are carved out of the tufa rock and called *camenn'ri* (from chimney stacks), where muted interior colors contrast with the display of vibrantly colored objects in the courtyards or on the streets. Master ceramicists pass down the craft to their sons. Their secret baking techniques are particularly important, as they give objects durability over time.

The ceramic work at Grottaglia is almost always of a rustic nature, refined by blue or yellow lines and with the typical blue cockerel with red crest. There are also more refined examples, with highly decorated baroque shapes—a reminder of the time when these products were destined for the homes of local aristocrats. Whistles featuring caricatures of famous people, including politicians and celebrities, are also abundant.

The Ceramics Museum is housed in the Castello Episcopio.

facing page
Vincenzo del Monaco's ceramic statuettes are beautiful and provocative.

The majolica museum at the State Institute of Art at Grottaglie offers a complete history of this Puglian craft tradition. Visitors learn about the different types of majolica objects and the artistic evolution of local ceramic products; understanding the work increases appreciation of it. It is a destination not only for tourists but students and researchers. One of the first exhibits features a collection of local ceramics (bowls and platters for daily use, devotional objects, bricks). A second exhibit focuses on the work of master artisans. Another exhibit displays student work, particularly objects that have been entered in international competitions.

A ceramics exhibition takes place at the Castello Episcopio in August. The largest factory in the town, which is a warren of caves connected by stone staircases, is that of Nicola Fasano. Ceramic workshops can be found throughout Puglia. The Del Monaco workshop is carved out of the tufa rock and dates back to 1416. Orazio Patronelli was the first workshop to use a computerized oven. Giuseppe di Fazio specializes in large handmade plates. The ceramics of Anna Trani and Giuseppe Fazio are beautiful, and are in the tradition of "Puparieddu," a ceramics craftsman.

LECCE

PAPIER-MÂCHÉ STATUES

MAKING PAPIER-MÂCHÉ STATUES FOR RELIGIOUS CELEBRATIONS has been a custom in Lecce for hundreds of years; the tradition was imported from Spain, but only here has this papier-mâché work developed into an art form. Today, the most spectacular constructions are made for outdoor festivals, including the floats for the carnival in Putignano, in the province of Bari, or for the holy day of the Madonna della Bruna in Matera.

Lecce is a very Church-oriented city; traditions related to the Church, such as making papier-mâché statues, began in the second half of the sixteenth century. After the Council of Trent, the Counter-Reformation recalled the faithful to the Catholic church. New churches were built in the city, chapels were built on farms and in country residences, and many saints were canonized, making it necessary to create statues before which people could kneel to pray. The Church wanted this to be done as quickly as possible in order to consolidate its hierarchy and counteract Lutheran Protestantism. But apart from the fact that marble was unaffordable to the people in this area, it also took a long time to sculpt. Moreover, the supply of local tufa rock was barely sufficient for the construction of buildings and façades. So the local artists and craftspeople used a different material, filling the churches with papier-mâché statues; an inexpensive material was elevated to a level worthy of representing holy figures. Statues of the Madonna and the saints, sometimes as tall as sixteen feet, were made with remarkable attention to detail. The statues also incorporated the exuberant floral decorations of baroque Lecce.

The best papier-mâché sculptures in Lecce were made in the nineteenth century, and the techniques used then are still in use today. Wastepaper was moistened to soften it. It was then treated with disinfectants and worm repellents, put in the sun to dry, and then cooked in water mixed with cellulose, starch, chalk, and resin. The result was a paste that was either shaped by hand or put in terracotta molds. Finished sculptures were treated with sealing wax to make them more waterproof and then decorated by hand; painted decorations were combined with the application of decals and gold inlay. The art of papier-mâché flourished over the centuries, because it was necessary to maintain and restore existing statues. In Lecce there are many artisan workshops that make religious figures, shepherds for Nativity scenes, or favorite traditional characters. There is also a school to teach young people the art form.

facing page
A papier-mâché Nativity scene with hand-painted figurines.

below
Detail of a facade of a Baroque palazzo in Lecce. The pink stone of Lecce is soft and easy to work.

Lecce stone is soft, easy to work, and slightly pink, which gives it a warm quality. It is the ideal stone for the graceful baroque style—exuberant but not overwhelming—that is characteristic of the churches and palazzos of a city. All over the city are decorations and statues that look like they are carved out of wax. The stone of the Murge is most common. It was used for the construction of the trulli typical of the landscape of the countryside around Bari. These constructions have an unusual history. In the sixteenth century the Count of Conversano, lord of the lands, wanted to develop his fiefdom without having to pay the king of Naples taxes on the construction of new houses. He therefore decreed that the people should build their houses in dry stone, so that they could be dismantled and rebuilt quickly in case tax inspectors came. It was only in 1797, when the people were freed from the yoke of the counts, that the "casa dell'amore" (house of love) was built at Alberobello, the first to be made of ashlar bound with lime and mortar.

Small papier-mâché objects can be found in many shops in the city. Beautifully worked statues of all sizes can be purchased at the Galleria Giuseppe de Tommasi or at the Arte della Cartapesta. Eugenio Galli and Artefare make objects out of papier-mâché and stone. Lecce stone is sculpted by Arredi d'Arte in Pietra.

MATERA
NATIVITY SCENES

THE MOST POPULAR SOUVENIR SOLD IN MATERA IS THE TERRACOTTA WHISTLE, called a *cuccu*, in the shape of a cock. It is a very simple musical instrument that makes a low sound and is customarily used during the Madonna di Pacciano Feast on the first Sunday in May. It is actually a ritual object of pre-Christian origin that symbolizes virility and is given as a declaration of love to a single woman who is not yet betrothed.

The cuccu comes in many sizes—sometimes very large. The cock has a showy red cockscomb that is sometimes accompanied by horns; the elongated tail is the mouthpiece of the whistle. After it is fired, the whistle is painted white with whitewash or tempera, and then decorated with colored stripes that must never cross each other; this wards off the evil eye. Whistles are also made in other shapes, and in other towns in southern Italy—it is a centuries-old tradition. In the Middle Ages, for example, whistles were used to caricature public personalities, politicians, and the aristocracy. They were given to children as toys. Nowadays they mostly caricature celebrities.

Papier-mâché is another Materan craft that is related to a popular local tradition. Artisans build huge floats for the Madonna della Bruna Feast on July 2. The setting is spectacular. Old and New Testament scenes are depicted with life-size statues transported on brightly painted floats; these accompany the statue of the Madonna and Child seated on a throne on the largest and most beautiful float. The artwork is fairly crude because the statues last only one day; they appear in the procession around the duomo and at the end of the celebration they are dismantled and torn into pieces that are taken home by the faithful or sold the next day in the market as souvenirs.

The same craftspeople make lovely Nativity scenes out of papier-mâché. These are in the form of small dioramas, usually forty by twenty inches but also much smaller, so they can be displayed on a table; they include the main features and figures: the hut with Mary, Joseph, Baby Jesus, the ass, the ox, the Three Kings, the shepherds, and so on. These Nativity scenes are less exuberant than the Neapolitan ones, and the papier-mâché used here is painted when it is cold; it is not fired, as it is in Lecce. The craftspeople who make the papier-mâché also create finely wrought decorations that are finished and painted.

The white, colored or natural *cuccù*, (whistles) from the Geppetto shop are made in the shape of a young hen.

The "city of stones" has been declared a World Heritage site by UNESCO; it is the most complete and representative example of a cave-dweller settlement in the Mediterranean. It is built on an intricate series of passages, stairways, and caves dug out of the tufa rock and includes houses with arches and balconies, vegetable gardens, stables, and barns. Facing the city, beyond the Gravina di Matera, is a naturally formed rocky plateau of cliffs and deep ravines. It almost looks deserted but it is witness to human life that dates to the Paleolithic era, as can be seen from the ruins in the Bat's Grotto. The area is now an archaeological park and contains some interesting churches built into the rocks by Greco-Byzantine monks during the eighth through thirteenth centuries. Many are completely underground; some are lavishly decorated with frescoes.

Papier-mâché whistles can be found at Michele Pantasuglia. Various ceramic and papier-mâché objects are available at Nicola Festa or at Pietro Gurrado. Matera's archaeological museum is dedicated to Domenico Ridola, a local doctor and archaeologist who discovered prehistoric objects, including sarcophagi, vessels decorated with figures, statues, weapons, necklaces, and coins.

facing page
The churches of the Madonna dell'Idris and of San Giovanni Caveoso at the top of the *sassi* of Matera.

SAN PAOLO
ALBANESE

NATURE AND INDUSTRY

THE SCENTED BROOM (*SPARTIUM JUNCEUM L.*) IS AN ELEGANT SHRUB that grows wild on the arid lands of Mediterranean countries. Since ancient times, it has been used for many purposes: the long fibers of the plant's stalks were made into matting and ropes, bags and saddle packs, and fabrics for clothing; the flowers were used to make scented essences, hair dyes, and diuretic brews.

Natural fibers are used to weave baskets of all shapes and sizes.

facing page
The National Park of Pollino with the mountains on the Piana di Sibari.

Today it is used to make other products, including cellulose pulp. And research that is partly funded by the European Union is revealing the unique qualities of the fiber obtained from the strong, flexible green stalks (*vermene*). Although experts believe broom will be seen on the catwalks at fashion shows, its most promising use seems to be in the automobile industry. In fact, some major companies such as Fiat, Mercedes, and BMW, have already replaced non-recyclable fiberglass, used to make car-body parts, with a plastic-broom fiber material. Moreover, vermene is almost completely non-flammable, and if a car should catch fire it does not emit toxic gases.

But in Southern Italy, there are people who are still attached to the old uses of broom. The *arbëreschë* communities scattered across part of Monte Pollino are home to Albanian exiles who arrived five centuries ago, driven out by the armies of Mehmed II. These ethnic minorities are integrated into the socioeconomic fabric of the region, but they have kept their customs, traditions, language, and culture. San Costantino Albanese and San Paolo Albanese can be found in the Sarmento Valley, on the Lucania side of Monte Pollino. They face each other on the banks of the river, twin "islands" that strenuously protect their identity. In these two villages one hears a dialect that is not spoken anywhere else in the neighboring villages. Women wear costumes embroidered with gold and silver thread. The main church is decorated with Byzantine icons and the Greek Orthodox rite is celebrated. Broom grows abundantly on the dry land around San Paolo Albanese. Every family harvests it at the end of the summer and after the flowering season. It is transformed into fabric for sacks and rucksacks that are used by farmers and shepherds. The community still gathers around the fires to boil and strip the stalks—con-

Broom items include saddlebags for donkeys, and sieves and combs to dry pasta and figs. Stone, wood, wicker, or reed objects are made by the craftspeople of the Albanian communities. They also make bagpipes and dolls wearing traditional costumes. Weavers work in the home with ancient tools; they primarily make carpets and traditional costumes. Avigliano is the place to make any purchases.

Although traditional fabrics and woven materials are found throughout Lucania, their use has not spread beyond the region; they are made for personal use and are not sold. The village of Pignola—in the mountains of the Materano—is an exception; Giovanni Murat built large factories for textile-making here. The people produced a lovely cloth, called *filandina*, in many different shades; but today this fabric is no longer made here. The artisans of Avigliano in the Potenza area still make knotted carpets. In Trecchina, craftspeople weave with reeds, cane, and willow. This village is also noted for the manufacture of tin objects, particularly toys.

tinuing an ancient custom that was almost completely forgotten—to meet and talk, and to sing traditional songs. Today use of these fibers and the resulting crafts are becoming increasingly popular as the market grows; this type of artisan activity attracts tourists as well.

COSENZA

CENTER OF CRAFTSMANSHIP

IN CONTRAST TO OTHER CITIES IN SOUTHERN ITALY, COSENZA gained importance even though it was far from the sea and any commercial routes. Although tucked away in impassable mountains, it became the economic and cultural capital of Calabria. The city was built on the slopes of the Sila Plateau. Its forests of tall straight trees provided good material for building ships and churches. It was far from the Ionian Sea, which was sandy and malaria-ridden, and where pirates frequently invaded. Although it was difficult to find safe harbor on the Tyrrhenian Coast, ships did pass and ideas were disseminated from Naples and Rome. Many colonialists came to the city, but this process was slower than in other places. As a result of the relative calm, there was no need to wall the city; surrounding areas were not walled either but connected by winding roads that had first been walked by the ancient Romans, whose planning skills were unparalleled. In 1452, historian Leandro Alberti described Cosenza as *continovata città,* or a city in which cultural activities were concentrated around the castle on Pancrazio Hill. The people built sumptuous palaces and residences outside the town—they did not want to attract envy and resentment—while the artisans and merchants were scattered throughout the area. But

An antique carpet-making frame.

facing page
The flourishing art of embroidery is evident in these delicate designs.

within the city there were strong factions of noble families with special privileges: the "sartori" owned a palazzo where their children were educated, and the tanners taught their working techniques as far away as the court of Maximillian of Austria. Textile production was particularly important. Longobuco, for example, produced fine silks that were sold in the best markets in Europe. Every step of the silk-production process happened there, beginning with the cultivation of the silkworm. Today this charming village is still an important textile center. The silks have unique designs, such as the "king's head," a green vase on a gold-yellow background; the colorful "judge's point," two birds balanced on a pair of scales; "the vineyard," bunches of grapes and vine leaves in dark green and lilac; and "the procession," a man and a woman in traditional dress. In Amantea, embroidery is equally important. San Giovanni in Fiore is known for fine textile craftsmanship—especially its production of knotted carpets in the style of the Caucasus. This has almost

San Giovanni in Fiore is associated with the Gioacchino abbot who lived in the twelfth century and whom Dante described in the *Divine Comedy* as "the gifted prophetic spirit." The village developed around the saint's monastery, with modest stone houses inhabited by shepherds and woodcutters who could tolerate the terrible winters and the strict rules imposed by the monks. In fact, women to this day wear the traditional costume with a white linen head cover. The abbey had a tumultuous history—the site of raids and fires, demolitions and renovations—that culminated with the monks being driven out by Napoleonic laws. The entire complex was looted at that time. The remains are particularly interesting: the imposing walls and the façade of the church, which contains a monumental thirteenth-century portal.

completely replaced the art of goldsmithing and silversmithing that was once the principal activity of the town; today these objects are made mostly to decorate traditional clothes. Master goldsmiths still work in the city, and their filigree is particularly beautiful. However, Crotone's filigree work is the most renowned in the region.

In San Giovanni in Fiore, gold jewelry can be purchased at Giovanni Battista Spadafora or at the Pertichini jewelers; carpets are sold at the Carpet School—Suola Tappeti Domenico Caruso—or at the Tiano crafts center. For embroidery, go to Amantea at the Piccolo Mondo Antico and at Mario Celestino in Longobuco. Good-quality briar pipes are made in Mandatoriccio.

CALTAGIRONE

A TALE OF CLAY AND COLOR

There are about a hundred places in Italy that are famous for their ceramics, twenty- eight of them belonging to the Italian Association of Cities of Ceramics, with its rules and regulations and famous logo that guarantees the production of "Traditional Artistic Ceramics." Caltagirone falls into this group, but very few of the other members have lived with ceramics for so many thousands of years. In the twelfth century the city was subdivided into areas that were inhabited by various ethnic groups each corresponding to a different kind of ceramics production: To the north, along the walls, the Muslim *cannatari* produced glazed earthenware pots; tile and brick-makers were located in the south, outside the medieval walls between the Porta del Vento (Gateway of the Wind) and the place where the church of San Giovanni once stood; bowls and other vessels were produced around the church of San Giuliano; isolated by an edict of 1312, the Jewish community stood outside the Norman walls, but they were reunited with the other districts because of ceramic production. Ancient documents testify to meaningful steps taken in history: privileges conceded by King Alfonso in 1432 allowed the sale of Calatese ceramics all over the island, tax free; in 1518 the viceroy forbade the mining of clay near the city walls because they were in danger once again of collapsing. Two hundred years earlier a landslide had buried all the ceramic-makers workshops in the San Giovanni district. In 1528, when the craftsmen's guilds were more powerful than ever and the *cannatari* had their own chapel in the Chiesa Madre and a privileged position at court, Charles V called the city "magnificent." At that time, colored glazes decorated the palazzos of the powerful, public and private monuments, fountains, wayside shrines, and crossroads all over Sicily. Before this, however, Caltagirone had a long story to tell. In 827 the city was conquered by the Arabs who were already masters of highly refined ceramic-making methods, such as glazing, a technique which was in use in Syria and Persia where for centuries the people had taken advantage of the region's high-quality clay. Honey was widely available in the area and artisans immediately set about making great jars for storing it. The origins of ceramic-making date back even further. During the early years of the twentieth century, a beautiful bowl or crater was discovered at San Luigi. The black and red figures represent a ceramist forming a vase on a wheel turned by an assistant. During excavations at the San Gregorio monastery some decades later, the remains of a kiln and broken pieces of vases were found bearing the same decorative style. Both of these date back to the fifth century BC.

facing page
Characteristic colored ceramics from the Ceramiche dell'Aquila company.

below
The stairway of Santa Maria del Monte. Each riser is decorated with ceramics tiles.

The 142 steps of the stairway that connects the municipal building to Santa Maria del Monte can be seen from Piano di San Giuliano in the center of Caltagirone. The risers are covered with beautiful majolica tiles that seem to form a multicolored wall. It is a striking image and full of meaning; a monument to the ceramic art of Caltagirone that begins in the ancient workshops clustered around the Palazzo dell'Aquila and stretches down to via Roma, to the State Institute of Art, founded by Don Luigi Sturzo in 1918, where the modern ceramics craftsmen receive their training. The cooperative of the majolica craftsmen of Caltagirone is housed in a building in the little square of San Giorgio. There is also a museum that exhibits rare ceramic pieces and the best work of the students. A rich collection of Caltagirone majolica and a complete review of Sicilian ceramics (about 2,500 pieces) is housed in the Regional Ceramics Museum in the public gardens. Unfortunately, the greater part of the collection was destroyed during an earthquake in 1693.

Various Caltagirone ceramics, bearing Renaissance motifs in particular, are on sale at the Bottega del Decoro di Sammartino e Delfino. Traditional and modern pieces are available at the Ceramiche Artistiche Romano, and hand-decorated blocks at Ceramiche Artistiche Silva. Ceramiche d'Arte Alessi offers innovative colors, while Ceramiche d'Arte Patri specializes in terracotta figures and reproductions of antique ceramic pieces. Copies of the pieces in the Ceramics Museum can be bought at Varsallona Ceramiche Artistiche. Donnarte is a cooperative of women who produce traditional textiles and brocades with embroidery in gold and silver. The long stairway of Santa Maria del Monte is decorated with thousands of flowers in May, and in July, for the feast of San Giacomo 4000, "coppi" or colored cardboard cylinders, lit from inside with little oil lamps, form a carpet of colored lights.

CATANIA

HEROIC PUPPETS

THE FAMOUS SICILIAN *PUPI*, A KIND OF PUPPET, IS OF ANCIENT ORIGIN. In fact, these puppets existed in the fourth century BC in the Symposium by Xenophon, as referred to by the Greek term *neurospata*. They reappeared in southern Italy (in Rome and Naples) in the first half of the nineteenth century, when poems of chivalry were rediscovered; these poems had themes that were worthy of the most modern soap operas: great loves, affairs, duels, and bewitchment. Neapolitan puppeteers brought them to Catania, in Sicily, between 1850 and 1860. The *History of the Paladins of France* became the canvas on which the *cuntisti* narrators orally described the deeds of Orlando. Public performances were improvised and enriched with local news; performances were geared to adults not children.

Pupi are constructed by different craftspeople, requiring a close collaboration: the carpenter builds the structure; the blacksmith and the tinsmith make the armor; the tailor cuts and sews the satin and velvet clothes. The engraver, who makes the wooden heads, has to be particularly clever as he must accentuate the characteristics of the players: Charlemagne has an austere face framed with white hair and a white beard; Orlando has a squint; Rinaldo is mocking; Gano di Magonza is grim and scarred.

Every *pupo* is different and every city uses its own technique to make them: the pupi of Catania are five feet tall and weigh about seventy-five pounds; they are simpler than those of Palermo or Messina, which are about three feet tall but have particularly elaborate armor, helmets with mobile visors, and banners that flutter. They are all dressed in the war costumes of the sixteenth century. The characters representing the Turks have no armor; they are dressed in uniforms that are less showy and they carry a round shield (never the triangular shield typical of the Crusaders). The female figures are always in sweet and dignified poses. The important detail that distinguishes pupi from other marionettes is that the paladins, called *pupi armati* (armed pupi), have the right sword arm guided by a rigid metal rod rather than a string. This enables the arm to be quickly drawn from the scabbard, enabling the simulated duels and fights to be particularly furious and vigorous. Traditional pupi are produced today by only a few puppeteers who still perform in theaters or for collectors. The Teatro di Santa Rosalia in Palermo is the most interesting and accomplished, and the company takes its show on tour throughout the world. Smaller, more simply finished pupi are made as souvenirs and can be found in cities and tourist meccas.

The feast of Sant'Agata in Catania is a combination of cult, devotion, folklore, and tradition.

The elephant fountain is the focal point of the central square of Catania's duomo. The *liotru*, the elephant, is the symbol of the city; the elephant can be found exuberantly decorated, sculpted in lava from Etna and probably dating to the Roman era. In Catania, working in lava stone is an ancient tradition and still flourishes throughout Etna; this is particularly true in Giarre and in Bronte, where the black stone's brilliant sheen has always been admired. There is also deep respect for the stone, because it comes from Etna; the volcano dominates the landscape and life of the region. In addition to its use as a building material—for balustrades, columns, and fountains—many craftspeople in the Etna area produce artistic objects and souvenirs.

There is a theater-museum of Sicilian pupi in Caltagirone and a museum of marionettes in Palermo. Tables and decorative objects made from lava stone can be purchased at the Efesto di Biancavilla workshop and at Merlo in Santo Stefano di Camastra. In the style of the pupi, hand-decorated, non-moveable military figures (*carabinieri*) can be found with their mustaches and plumed headgear. Some of them are six feet tall. Also available are Greek-inspired theatrical masks carved in wood.

facing page
The technique of engineering the puppets has been passed down through generations. Sicilian puppets, or *pupi*, have been added to the World Heritage list, acknowledging their value as a form of traditional and popular culture.

THE ISLANDS OF SICILY

SACRED BLACK STONE

SEVERAL ARCHIPELAGOS SURROUND SICILY: THE EOLIAN IN THE NORTH, the Egadi to the west, and the Pelagie, in the Sicilian channel, to the south. The villages on these islands are heavily touristed—and geared to tourism—but many ancient crafts are still preserved. These crafts originally were produced as objects for everyday use, because the isolation of the islands did not permit them to be purchased elsewhere. Now locals have been given a new incentive—to produce souvenirs for the tourists. Although isolated, it did not prevent the development of very ancient and flourishing civilizations, as can be seen from the history of Mozia, a Carthaginian colony, or Lipari, the largest and most populous of the Eolian islands. These are the "seven sisters" that were formed from volcanic eruptions under the sea. In the seventeenth-century fortress on Lipari, there is an important museum that houses ceramics painted in three colors dating from the fourth century BC. Sarcophagi, masks from the Greek tragedies, and vases painted with mythological and godlike figures are also housed here. The various strata of the excavations on the island have enabled scientists and historians to unearth and substantiate six thousand years of history, from colonization by the Greeks, the Romans, the Spanish, and the Normans. Lipari owes its good fortune to obsidian, a volcanic rock that is either a shiny black or dull green. It looks more like glass than stone, and was mined here and formed into cutting tools that were exported throughout the Mediterranean. Ancient people called it *liparia*, and believed it to be more precious than gold; they thought the god Vulcan himself had made it. It was considered sacred, with magical powers, because of its presumed origin and its rarity; this is mentioned in many texts of the ancient Greeks. Obsidian was highly prized all over the world. It is the "sacred stone" of Mecca, and the Native Americans of the Mississippi Valley walked for days to reach Yellowstone to get the smallest pieces of it for use in their sacred rituals. A Native American fable tells the story of a princess who received a shard of the stone as a gift. She announced that she would give her hand only to the man who could climb the "glass mountain" from which the shard came. The myth still resonates: According to New Agers, obsidian has the power to staunch hemorrhages, eliminate mental and spiritual blocks, cure intestinal cramps, and more. It is worth having a piece solely for its beauty. Lipari and Pantelleria are among the few places where it can be found, since they are islands that were created from volcanic eruptions and where nature has much more to offer: landscapes of lava stone, which is used to make millstones, sculpture, and decorative objects; and the sea bed, where fishermen dive for branches of coral that is sold unpolished.

A view of Lipari

facing page
Jewelry will be made from this piece of uncut obsidian.

Obsidian can be found on Lipari at L'Ossidiana or among the souvenirs of Grazia Famularo. Pau, in Sardinia (Oristano), is also known for its obsidian, and there is a museum of "the black gold of prehistory." Bartolo Lauria and Stefano Panza produce distinctive ceramics on Lipari. On Ustica, brightly colored bags are sold at I Colori del Mare. Decorative ceramics can be found at Ceramica Insana at Santo Stefano di Camastra.

All of the little harbor villages of the islands have shops where locally made crafts—from woven cloth to printed fabrics and ceramics—are sold. Most of the ceramic sold on the islands, however, comes from Santo Stefano di Camastra, in the province of Messina, which is the main area for Sicilian production. Tufa stone objects can be found in Favignana. Pantelleria sells bags and straw baskets, lobster cages, and *lamparas*, large lights mounted on fishing boats used to attract calamari at night. Sponges are sold in many shops on Lampedusa. They are soft and long lasting and are among the most valuable in the world. There was a time when the boats stayed out to sea for months, fishing with nets set as deep as 100 to 130 feet; today, fishing is strictly regulated.

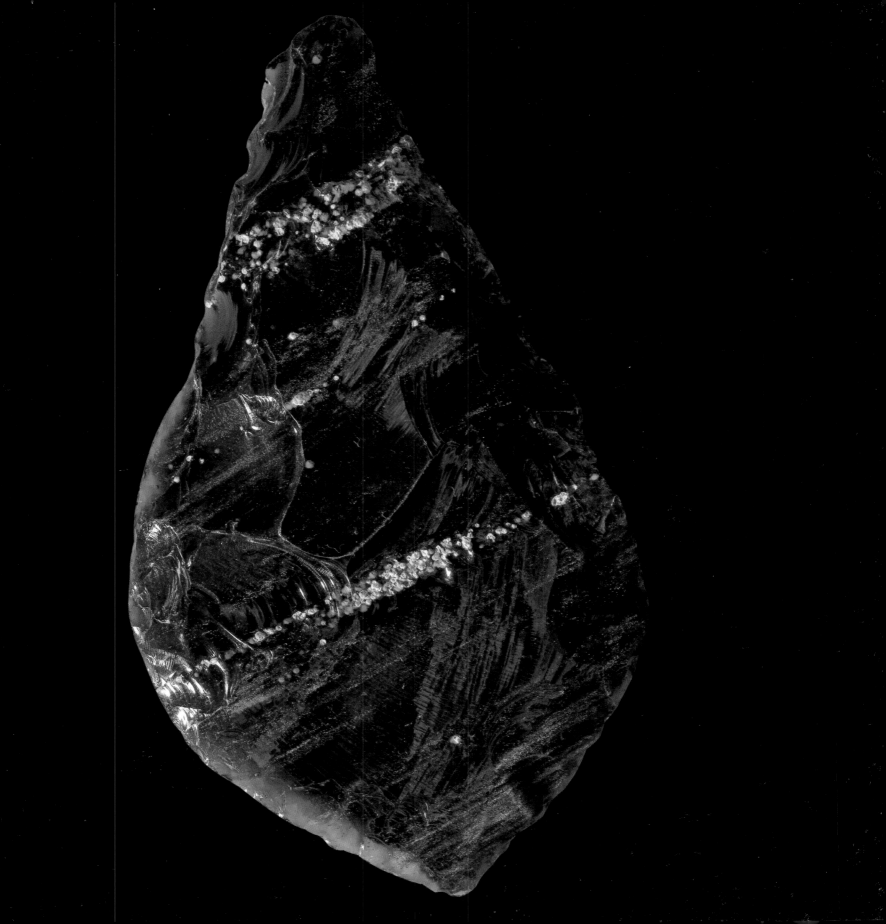

PALERMO

ROMANTIC CARRIAGES

THE MOST ORIGINAL CREATION OF SICILIAN CRAFTSMANSHIP IS THE PAINTED CART. These carts were once seen everywhere on the island, but they are now relegated to museums or great houses, displayed under the front porches. Some beautiful examples are exhibited at the Terrasini Museum. About five thousand were used in Palermo in the 1930s. Twenty years later they could be seen only on the farms in the interior. In the city, badly adapted side sections of the carts are fixed to modern three-wheeled delivery vans; people's pride in the old carts prompts them to continue to use them, even though their inconvenience is widely recognized. The rest of the cart panels end up on the stalls of secondhand furniture dealers; it is still possible to find them here. Or they can be seen in the best antique dealers' shops.

The decorated cart appeared in Sicily in the nineteenth century. Until the seventeenth century only the richly decorated carriages of wealthy landowners were used in the cities; the farmers who worked in their service could only afford basic wooden carts, which they used to transport goods. A century later, however, roads were improved and even the farmers began to use their carts to take their families to Mass on Sundays, cleaning them up so as not to dirty their best Sunday clothes. In the mid-nineteenth century some farmers began to decorate their carts. First came painted representations of saints; then, with the renewed interest in chivalric poetry, came scenes of epic and romantic episodes from the cycle of Orland and his paladins.

Making painted carts became a popular, specialized, and complex craft, involving the work of more than one artisan; workshops were almost always concentrated in certain areas of the city: in Palermo, workshops along the Corso dei Mille in the Zisa area, and the workshops of Bagheria, were famous for their decorations. First the *carradore* chose the wood and built the several parts, assembled with a belt of wrought iron. The blacksmith also made the box decorated with arabesques and the other metal parts. In turn, the engraver sculpted in bas-relief the heads of knights and ladies in the corners, on the connection between the two shafts, and on the borders. The surface of the lateral sides, both front and back, were then painted. The workshop assistants first painted two or three coats of a base color, and then sketched out a line decoration in geometric patterns or rosettes. The master then proceeded with the real painting, executed in a crude style in which all the characters were placed in the foreground or with a barely suggested perspective, without shadows or shades of color. This technique made the paintings unique.

The lovely cloister of Monreale, with its central Arabic-style fountain.

facing page
Detail of the side of a colorful Sicilian cart with bas reliefs of the knights of Charlemagne.

Typical area crafts can be found in Aris, and pieces for Nativity scenes at Sicily Folk. In Cefalù, cart souvenirs are sold at Chez Nino and pupi in wood and embossed copper are sold at the Piccolo Mondo Antico. Typical Sicilian cloth caps, as well as more contemporary hat styles by designers such as Missoni and Gianfranco Ferré, are sold in Palermo at Coppola Storta.

Palermo is known for its Vucciria. It is held every day between Piazza Caracciolo and Piazza San Domenico. Vucciria is not only a market but a vital part of the city's life, displaying a wealth of vibrant colors and energy that reflects the diversity of its residents. There are women with Greek features or women wearing necklaces and rings that look like they are on loan from an Asian palace; small-boned, aesthetic-looking men like the prophets of the Sinai, or imposing men with blond hair and blue eyes—descendents of the northern Normans. All together they constitute a raucous crowd. The word *vucciria* means noisy—an uproar or a tumult of life—and inspired a famous painting by Renato Guttuso. It is here, rather than in the *salotto rosso* or the Via Ruggero Settimo, that we discover the real Palermo.

SYRACUSE

PAPYRUS: A MEANS OF COMMUNICATION

ACCORDING TO THE ROMAN ORATOR CICERO, SYRACUSE was the "most beautiful of the Greek cities." A few miles from here is a little river of mythological origin. It was created by the love of the nymph Ciane, who was transformed by the god Pluto into a spring of clear water for the river god Anapo. The place is enchanting and has seduced many Roman, Arab, English, and Italian poets. It is here that the largest number of papyrus plants in Europe can be found; they were probably brought by the Arabs. The *Cyperus papyrus Linneo* plant is very elegant and is not to be confused with the *Cyperus alternifolius*, which is a house plant. Papyrus grew spontaneously in the shallow waters of the Nile and Niger rivers, and in Egypt, where the name means "that which belongs to the king." It was cut into strips and used to make mats, vats, boats, sails, sandals, paper, hats, boxes, and ropes. The roots were dried and used as fuel. The juice was imbibed; the ashes were considered therapeutic. If writing delineates the passage of human society from prehistory to history, the invention of writing paper made from papyrus facilitated communication among peoples. Before this time, humans wrote on columns of stone, bronze or wood tablets, or strips of leather. Papyrus was easy to use and revolutionized writing. For more than two thousand years it was the material of choice for recording information and for communicating across the globe.

Grotesque masks, monsters, and other strange faces support the balcony of the Baroque palazzo of Ludica, near Syracuse.

Latin historian Pliny the Elder (who lived during the first century AD) describes the processing of a sheet of papyrus: "the stem was cut lengthwise into thin strips placed one beside the other on a board until it formed the size of the sheet required. Other strips were placed at right angles across the lower layer. It was then bathed in the muddy waters of the Nile, beaten with a mallet and pressed, laid out to dry, and then evened out with a smooth stone." The stems were processed at once, near where they were harvested, so that the lymph within them glued the fibers together. This was the basic preparation technique. Sheets of papyrus have been made this way since 1781. At that time, the Institute of Papyrus was founded; it supported the cultivation and transformation of the precious plant into a variety of products. Exhibitions and seminars are also organized to showcase this extraordinary plant and its uses. The soft, natural-colored sheets make high-quality writing paper; this paper is being used to reproduce the illuminated codices and Egyptian paintings that are preserved in museums in Cairo and Turin. Parchment is also used for diplomas, certificates, cards, and wedding invitations.

The Papyrus Museum in Syracuse opened in 1989 with works from a private collection; in recent years the museum's holdings have grown and today it offers a complete record of the history of papyrus and its uses. The museum's primary activity is the recovery, conservation, and publication of historical documents written on papyrus. It also conducts scientific research into the plant and the manufacture of parchment, as well as the problems of conservation and restoration of ancient documents. Documents from the fifteenth century BC to the eighth century AD are preserved in the museum. There are samples of the parchment made in Syracuse, a document on herbs, and various objects made from papyrus, such as sandals, vessels, matting, and boats from the Tana and Chad lakes. Also on display are writing instruments and historical documents on the origins of papyrus and its evolution in Egypt and Syracuse.

facing page
From the Papyrus Institute, an elegant writing set of pen, inkpot, and sheets of papyrus.

Writing paper made from papyrus—both plain and decorated with prints or hand-painted—can be purchased at the Institute of Papyrus, at Papyrus, and at Carolina de Santis. The Izzo brothers' company, Oro Design, creates copies of baroque and ancient Greek jewelry. The Aretusa and Gorgone collections make gold reproductions of the antique coins of Syracuse and the masks of the Greek theater.

ALGHERO

GOLD AND SILVER COSTUMES

IN SARDINIA, GOLD AND SILVER WERE USED FOR A VERY SPECIFIC PURPOSE: they were the final touch on ceremonial costumes; gold was for the women and silver was for the men. Embroidery, brooches, chains, and buttons were often filigreed and enriched with precious stones, adding luxuriousness to the clothes. Many objects were mounted in gold, from crosses and rosaries to pendants and amulets that were made from materials such as precious stones but also pieces of glass. The *lasu*, of Spanish origin, is a pendant in the shape of a butterfly; it is made of laminated, perforated, and decorated gold and is tied around the neck with a velvet ribbon. The granulated-filigree wedding ring is also a common style, and has become a classic souvenir. Goldsmiths abound in Alghero. They are dedicated mostly to working with precious coral and make objects of rare beauty. Traces of the Sumerians, Assyrians, Phoenicians, Romans, and Celts can be seen in coral work. In the East it was considered one of the most precious objects for exchange, far more valuable than gold coins. The King of Benin still wears a ceremonial costume woven with corals that weighs about one hundred pounds.

Alghero is a fascinating city, probably the most noble in Sardinia, and owes much of its history to the Catalans. Its name, from *Alguer*, or a place full of algae, is not very evocative. But it owes its traditions and architecture and even its language to Catalonia. The streets are called *carrer*, the ramparts *murralla*.

Neptune's Grotto can be found at Capo Caccia, near Alghero. It is the most beautiful in Sardinia, with its fantastic shapes and clear blue waters.

The surrounding sea is still rich with precious *corallium rubrum*, which is used to make jewelry. This coral is a red or pink marine animal (coelenterate) that looks like a little tree and forms colonies that look like a miniature forest. It takes years for a colony to form and for this reason fishing coral is regulated and is carried out by divers who descend up to 328 feet into the sea to find it. At one time people from the region of Campania came to collect it, taking it back to Torre del Greco and Torre Annunziata, where master craftspeople worked with it. (Coral grew on their coasts as well, but that of Alghero was more precious because it was larger and was not worn down by the volcanic ash of Vesuvius.) Today coral is worked in the most elegant shops in Alghero's city center, around the medieval Plaia Civica and the Santa Maria Church. Companies offer underwater trips to see the coral in its natural state. It can even be found at a depth of thirty-three to fifty feet.

From the city walls of Alghero, Capo Caccia can be seen on the other side of the gulf. It is one of the most beautiful places in Sardinia—a rocky promontory overlooking the sea and pounded by blue-violet waves. This was the habitat of monk seals, although these animals have not been seen for many years. It is the only place in Italy where the Griffon vulture, a predatory bird with a wingspan of ten feet, nests. The white rock, covered with Mediterranean brush and dwarf palms, is a perfect place for these birds. The view is spectacular from the road leading to the lighthouse. At water level are the Neptune Grottoes, described by the Duke of Buckingham as "a prodigy of the gods." In order to visit the Scala del Cabrio caves, visitors must descend 656 steps; boats from Alghero also bring visitors to the entrance.

Gold and coral jewelry is sold at the Casa del Corallo, at the Marogna brothers' studio, at Franco Marras, at Ferraro Gioielli, or at Leo Carmela. These stores are all in the center of the old city. Splendid examples of goldwork of past centuries can be found in the collections of museums in Calgari, Sassari, and Nuoro. Other important makers of coral jewelry are housed in Sicily, in Trapani, and in Campania, at Torre del Greco.

facing page
Coral is often used for elegant necklaces.

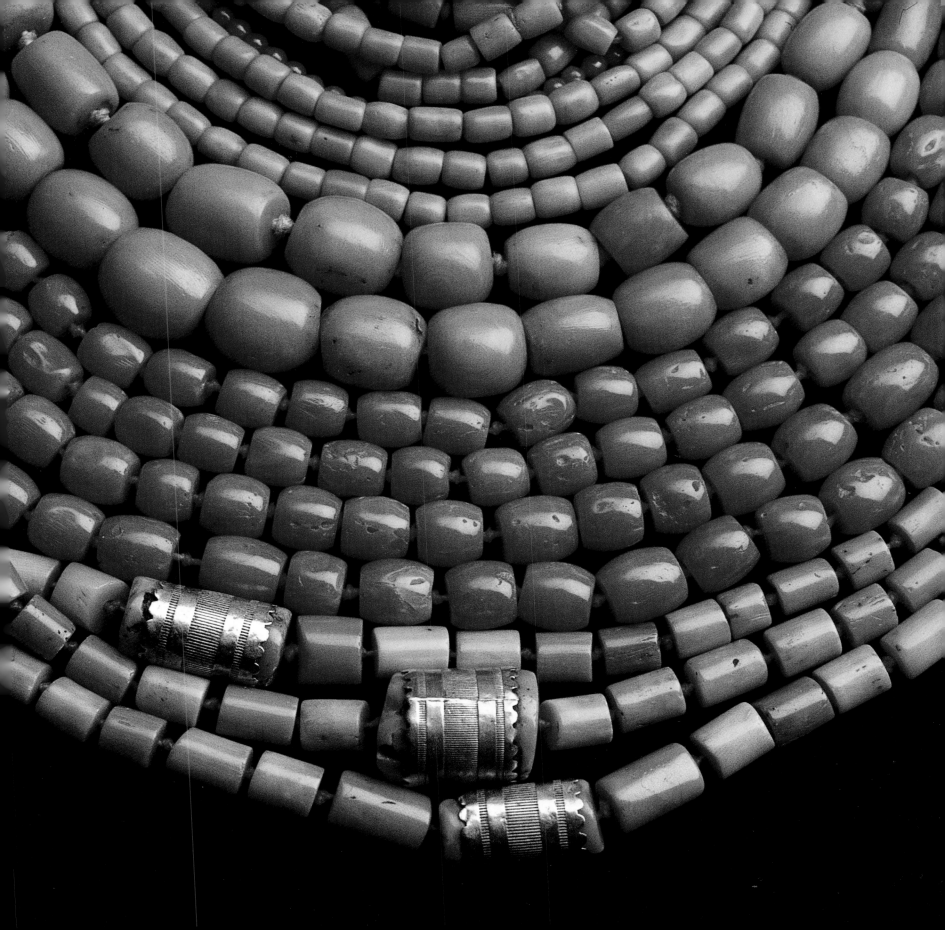

GALLURA

WHERE CORK COMES FROM

THE LANDSCAPE OF THE PLATEAU OF THE GALLURA IN NORTHERN SARDINIA is dominated by cork oak trees. This evergreen has adapted to arid soil and is resistant to fires. The trunk is twisted and the branches contorted. It can reach a height of sixty-five feet and the trunk can be as wide as sixteen to nineteen feet; it is a majestic tree. The cork oak (*quercus suber*) has a rust-red color on its smooth trunk. This type of oak, which grows in temperate climates and on rocky, dry soil, is the only tree from which cork is produced. Cork is a product exclusively made in the Mediterranean. Gallura's cork industry makes Italy the fourth most important producer, after Portugal, Spain, and North Africa. There are hundreds of activities connected with cork. This is where the Experimental Station for Cork has been established; it studies the problems of this wood, as well as its possible uses.

Beautiful hand-painted ceramic tiles from Cerasarda.

facing page
Cork-oak trees.

Cork is obtained in the following way: The first stripping takes place on trees that are at least twenty-five to thirty years old; the cork (called "male" and "virgin") is gray and of poor quality. The next extraction is from female trees only and takes place after another ten to twelve years. This is called "softwood," or "reproductive" wood, and is a higher quality product. Stripping is done by hand because no machinery equals the skill of Gallura's *su ogadori*. With their hatchets they carve the bark of the trunk just below the first bifurcation of the branches. They do not touch the "second skin" of the tree, which is less than one-quarter-inch thick; if it is cut, the tree dies.

Cork is a natural product with exceptional properties. It is light, insulating, biodegradable, recyclable, non-toxic, and immune from infestations of fungi and bacteria; it also repels insects and rats, and it does not melt when it is burned. It does not drip or emit toxic gases. One of the unique characteristics of cork is that when it is put under pressure it contracts and can be lengthened without modifying its width. As soon as the pressure is released, any deformaties disappear. Although it is a material of infinite possible uses (no other artificial material has equal properties), 80 percent of cork is used in the wine industry for the manufacture of bottle corks. What remains is used to make shoe soles, insulation for buildings and for the automobile industry, flooring tiles, decorative panels, and wall coverings (the surface does not need to be covered); very thin sheets are used for clothing. Craftspeople use cork to make jewelry boxes, picture frames, and decorative containers.

The traditional knife used to strip cork trees, made in Guspini, is called *sa guspinesa*. It is characterized by a very thin blade, a blunt point, and a wood or horn handle with an engraved double ring. The typical Pattada knife (*sa pattadesa*) is, by far, the most beautiful knife made in Italy. The blade is leaf shaped for stripping; the handle is made from the horn of sheep. There is no spring. It is sometimes decorated with engraved studs. There is a museum of the Sardinian knife in Arbus. The *s'arburesa* knife is made there. This knife has a bulbous blade and is used for stripping and branding. The *s'aresoja* or *resolsa*, the most typical of the Sardinian knives, is a switchblade with a steel blade and ram-horn handle.

Every two years in
September the
National Fair of Cork
is held at
Calangianus. In
Pattada, knives are
sold at the shop of
the Fogarizzu
brothers or at
Raimondo Sistigu;
they also can be
purchased at Paolo
Pusceddu in Arbus.
Roberto Monni
produces knives in
Sinnai as does the
Coltelleria
Artigianale
Guspinese in
Guspini in the
Cagliari area. A
crafts market is held
in Guspini during
the second half of
July. The
market/exhibition of
Sardinian knives is
held from July to
August every other
year.

ORISTANO

CANE AND MARSH REEDS

THE MISTRAL BLOWS IN FROM THE SEA AND PUSHES BACK THE TIRSO RIVER, and this gives Oristano its wealth. Just as the Nile did in ancient Egypt, the river floods the plain depositing precious silt that fertilizes the soil and fills the depressions in the land; fish-filled lagoons form. It was this phenomenon that led humans to settle in the area more than eight thousand years ago, the evidence of which includes the burial sites at Cùccuru Is Arrius, the *domus janus* of the Neolithic age, the megalithic dolmen, the nuraghi, and the remains of the great city of Tharros, which was inhabited by the Phoenicians, the Carthaginians, and the Romans. The tip of the promontory of the Sinis Peninsula parts the wind, making it an ideal harbor. In the second half of AD 1000, in order to avoid the continuing incursions of the Saracens, the inhabitants of Tharros built a new city in between the lagoons, where there was a small settlement of fishermen; Aristanis, "among the pools"—Oristano's Byzantine name—was built. It developed into the capital of the Giudicato of Arborea, the most highly developed of all the medieval European courts. The *Carta de logu*, a legal codex issued by Eleonora, wife of the ruling judge/governor, took effect all over Sardinia. The rights of women and the less fortunate were emphasized; for example, it regulated communal property in marriage and recognized the legal rights of servants.

Today, Oristano is a town full of monuments among which the most important is the Gothic Santa Maria Assunta Cathedral, founded in the thirteenth century but rebuilt in the eighteenth century. The octagonal bell tower is from the fifteenth century. The town's economy is based primarily on agriculture and fish breeding. There is also a one-thousand-year-old craft tradition that takes advantage of the abundant natural resources of the area. Clay from the lagoons is fired in wood-burning ovens and beautiful terracotta objects are made for home use. Wicker baskets, hampers, and mats are made from marsh canes. Women sit at their front doors by the side of the village's roads, weaving the carefully chosen and prepared reeds and long stalks of grain with great dexterity; they make storage baskets for bread, fruit, and other foods. These objects are made with such delicacy that they look like jewel boxes. Sometimes they are decorated; other times the focus is on the natural material and the weave. Canes were once tied tightly in bunches to make *frassonis*, the boats used by the fishermen of the lagoons at Cabras and Santa Giusta. Today these boats are used only during the regattas that take place in the lagoon at Santa Giusta.

The passion for horses and their tackle is long-standing in Oristano. The *Sa Sartiglia* takes place in the city on the last Sunday of Carnival. It is a joust in which masked horsemen must pierce a star-shaped ring with their lances. The *Sartigliedda* happens on the following day. During this event, which also takes place in August, young riders mount the horses of the Giara di Gesturi. Also during Carnival the *Sa carella 'e nanti* takes place at Santulussurgiu; the Feast of the Horse is in June. Similar competitions are held at San Vero Milis, at Paulilatino, Bonacardo, Sanugheo, Busachi, and Abbasanta. In July the Ardia is held at Sedilo. It is a spectacular race in honor of San Constantino, who actually was not a saint but an emperor (there is a sanctuary dedicated to him).

facing page
Traditional Sardinian carpets and tapestries are hand woven on ancient frames at the Su Trobasciu cooperative in Mogoro, near Oristano.

below
Canes surrounding the Santa Giusta pool with the village in the background.

An important wickerwork fair is held in Sinnai during the first two weeks of August. Textiles made on traditional horizontal looms can be found in the area: look for carpets in Samugheo and tapestries in Mogoro. The large village of Mogoro also produces wood and ceramic crafts, and it hosts an annual fair. The carpets and tapestries are made by a cooperative of women. There is an interesting museum of Mediterranean weaving in Castelsardo.

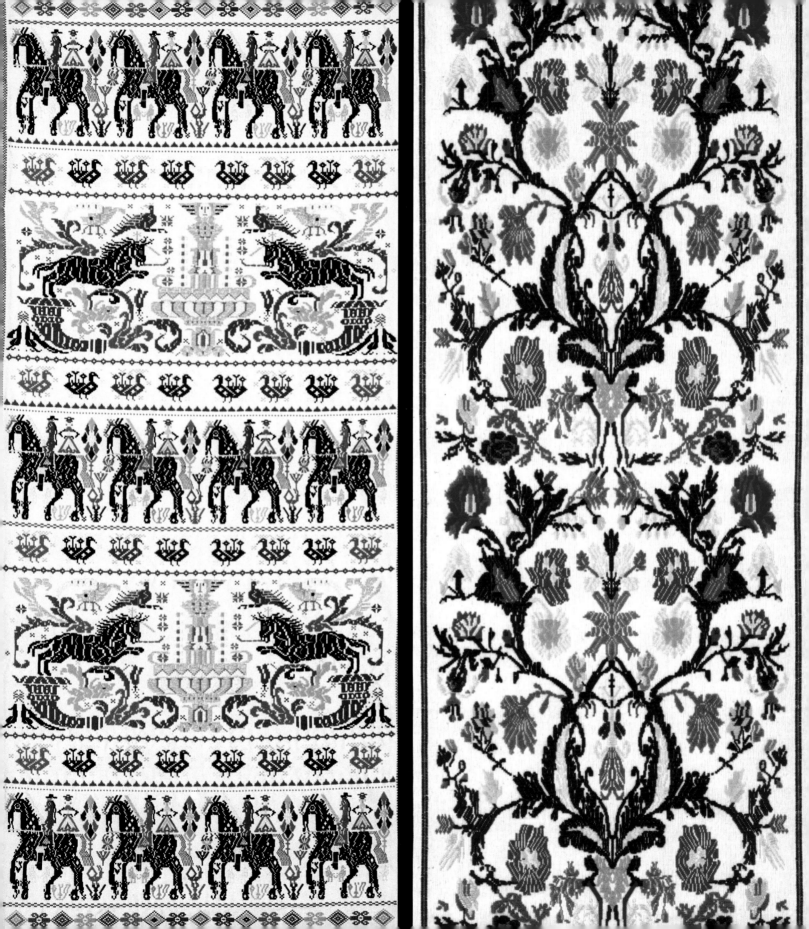

ADDRESSES

abbadia lariana (lombardy)

Museo Setificio Monti
via Nazionale 113
23821 Abbadia Lariana (LC)
phone +39 0341.731241
www.museoabbadia.it

agnone (molise)

Tourist Information
via Farinacci 9
86170 Isernia
phone +39 0865.3992
www.regionemolise.it

Hotel Sammartino
largo P. Micca 44
86061 Agnone (IS)
phone +39 0865.77577

Fonderia Marinelli - Museo storico della campana
via F. d'Onofrio 14
86081 Agnone (IS)
phone +39 0865.78235
info@campanemarinelli.com
www.campanemarinelli.com

La Ramera
via Marconi 1
86081 Agnone (IS)
phone +39 0865.779086

agordo (veneto)

Tourist Information
via 27 Aprile 5A
32021 Agordo (BL)
phone +39 0437.62105
agordo@infodolomiti.it

Hotel Villa Imperina
via Pragrande 5
32021 Agordo (BL)
phone +39 0437.62046
imperina@imperina.it
www.villaimperina.it

Luxottica
località Valcozzena
32021 Agordo (BL)
phone +39 0437.6441
www.luxottica.it

Dieffe Occhiali
via Faion 11
32021 Agordo (BL)
phone +39 0437.63340

Dieffe Unisex
via XXVII Aprile 10
32021 Agordo (BL)
phone +39 0437.641332

La Muda
località La Muda 10
32030 La Valle Agordina (BL)
phone +39 0437.640450
lamuda@libero.it

ala di trento (trentino–alto adige)

Tourist Information
corso Rosmini 6
38068 Rovereto (TN)
phone +39 0464.430363
rovereto@apt.rovereto.tn.it
www.apt.rovereto.tn.it

Hotel Leon d'oro
via Tacchi 2
38068 Rovereto (TN)
phone +39 0464.437333
info@hotelleondoro.it

Ristorante San Colombano
via Vicenza 30 (SS 46)
38068 Rovereto (TN)
phone +39 0464.436006
sancolombano@tin.it

Museo del pianoforte antico
via S. Caterina 1
38061 Ala (TN)
phone +39 0464.670636
www.museodelpianoforteantico.it

albisola (liguria)

Tourist Information
Passeggiata E. Montale 21
17012 Albissola Marina (SV)
phone +39 019.4002008
albisola@inforiviera.it

Hotel Garden
viale Faraggiana 6
17012 Albissola Marina (SV)
phone +39 019.485253
garden@savonaonline.it

Ristorante Al Cambusiere
via Repetto 86
17012 Albissola Marina (SV)
phone +39 019.481663
info@cambusiere.it

Ristorante Au Fundegu
via Spotorno 87
17013 Albisola Superiore (SV)
phone +39 0184.80341

Giuseppe Mazzotti 1903
viale Matteotti 29
17012 Albissola Marina (SV)
phone +39 0194.89872

Casa dell'arte
via Colombo 91
17013 Albisola Superiore (SV)

Studio Erman Design
corso Mazzini 77
17013 Albisola Superiore (SV)
phone +39 0194.80000

Casa museo Jorn
via d'Annunzio 6
17012 Albissola Marina (SV)
phone +39 019.40029281

Museo della ceramica Manlio Trucco
corso Ferrari 191
17012 Albisola Capo (SV)
phone +39 19.482741

Ceramiche IMA
via alla Contrada 3
17013 Albisola Superiore (SV)
phone +39 0194.81657

Maria Gaggero
via Spotorno 9
17013 Albisola Superiore (SV)
phone +39 0194.91626

Ceramiche San Giorgio
via Matteotti 5
17012 Albissola Marina (SV)
phone +39 0194.82747

alessandria (piedmont)

Tourist Information
via Cagliaudo 2
15100 Alessandria
phone +39 0131.234794
info@comune.alessandria.it

Hotel Europa
via Palestro 1
15100 Alessandria
phone +39 0131.236226
info@hoteleuropaal.com

Ristorante La Fermata
via Vocchieri 120
15100 Alessandria
phone +39 0131.251350
lafermata@aliceposta

Fondazione Borsalino
via G. Savonarola 71
15100 Alessandria
phone +39 0131.234122
www.borsalino2000.it

Space Cannon Vh
strada per Felizzano 14
15043 Fubine (AL)
phone +39 0131.772288
info@spacecannonvh.com
www.spacecannon.it

Officina delle memorie
(first Sunday of the Month)
Centro Storico
15100 Alessandria
phone +39 0131.40035

alghero (sardinia)

Tourist Information
piazza Porta Terra
07041 Alghero (SS)
phone +39 079.979054
infotourism@infoalghero.it

Hotel Villa Las Tronas
Lungomare Valencia 1
07041 Alghero (SS)
phone +39 079.981818
info@hvlt.com

Ristorante Il Pavone
piazza Sulis 3
07041 Alghero (SS)
phone +39 079.979584

Atelier Orafo Fratelli Marogna
piazza Civica 34
07041 Alghero (SS)
phone +39 0799.84814

Franco Marras
via Carlo Alberto 67
07041 Alghero (SS)
phone +39 0799.80093

Ferraro Gioielli
via C. Alberto 49
07041 Alghero (SS)
phone +39 0799.979268

Leo Carmela
piazza Civica 18
07041 Alghero (SS)
phone +39 0799.980893

Casa del Corallo
piazza Porta Terra 2
07041 Alghero (SS)
phone +39 0799.975392

almè (lombardy)

Trussardi Factory Outlet
via Milano 40
24011 Almè (BG)
phone +39 035.634146
marco.maggi@trsevolution.bg.it
www.trussardi.it

almenno san bartolomeo (lombardy)

Antica Osteria Giubì
via Cascinetto 2
24030 Almenno S. Bartolomeo (BG)
phone +39 035.540130

Museo del falegname Tino Sana
via Papa Giovanni XXIII 59
24030 Almenno San Bartolomeo (BG)
phone +39 035.554411
www.tinosana.com

alpette (piedmont)

Tourist Information
corso Vercelli 1
10015 Ivrea (TO)
phone +39 0125.618131
info@canavese-vallilanzo.it
www.canavese-vallilanzo.it

Hotel Sirio
via Lago Sirio 85
10015 Ivrea (TO)
phone +39 0125.424247
info@hotelsirio.it

Ecomuseo del rame
via Sereine
10080 Alpette (TO)
phone +39 0124.809122
www.comunealpette.it

altare (liguria)

Ristorante Quintilio
via Gramsci 23

17041 Altare (SV)
phone +39 019.58000
quintilio@libero.it

Museo del vetro e dell'arte vetraria
piazza S. Sebastiano 1
17041 Altare (SV)
phone +39 0195.84734
www.isvav.it

amalfi (campania)

Tourist Information
corso Roma 19
84011 Amalfi (SA)
phone +39 089.871107
www.aziendaturismoamalfi.com

Hotel Santa Caterina
via Nazionale 9
84011 Amalfi (SA)
phone +39 089.871012
info@hotelsantacaterina.it

Ristorante Marina Grande
viale delle Regioni 4
84011 Amalfi (SA)
phone +39 089.871129
marina-grande@tiscali.it

Cartiera Amatruda
via delle Cartiere 100
84011 Amalfi (SA)
phone +39 0898.71315
www.amatruda.it

Museo della carta
via delle Cartiere 23
84011 Amalfi (SA)
phone +39 0898.304561
www.museodellacarta.it

amantea (calabria)

Tourist Information
via V. Emanuele 11
87032 Amantea (CS)
phone +39 0982.41785

Hotel La Tonnara
via Tonnara 13
87032 Amantea (CS)
phone +39 0982.424272

Piccolo Mondo Antico
corso V. Emanuele 87
87032 Amantea (CS)
phone +39 0982.425356
www.mondoantico.net

andreis (friuli–venezia giulia)

Museo d'arte e civiltà contadina
piazza Centrale
33080 Andreis (PN)
phone +39 042.776007

angera (piedmont)

Hotel dei Tigli
via Paletta 20
21021 Angera (VA)

phone +39 0331.930836
www.hoteldeitigli.com

Museo della bambola e della moda infantile
Rocca Borromeo
21021 Angera (VA)
phone +39 0331.931300
www.borromeoturismo.it

aosta (valle d'aosta)

Tourist Information
piazza Chanoux 45
11100 Aosta
phone +39 0165.235343
piazza Arco d'Augusto
11100 Aosta
phone +39 0165.33352
aptaosta@aostashop.com
www.aostashop.com/apt.htm

Hotel Europe
piazza Narbonne 8
11100 Aosta
phone +39 0165.236363
hoteleurope@ethotels.com
www.ethotels.com/hoteleurope.html

Hotel Holiday Inn Aosta
corso Battaglione Aosta 30
11100 Aosta
phone +39 0165.236356
hotelholidayinn@ethotels.com
www.ethotels.com

Hotel Villa Novecento
viale Monte Bianco 64
11013 Courmayeur (AO)
phone +39 0165.843000
villa-novecento@romantikhotels.com
www.romantikhotels.com/courmayeur

Ristorante Le Foyer
corso Ivrea 146
11100 Aosta
phone +39 0165.32136
fax +39 0165.239474

Ristorante Vecchio Ristoro
Via Tourneuve 4
11100 Aosta
phone +39 0165.33238

Angolo creativo
via Gramsci 22
11100 Aosta

Dorino Ouvrier
frazione Epinel 64
11012 Cogne (AO)

Napapijri Geographic
località Amerique
11020 Quart (AO)
phone +39 0165.773576
www.napapijri.com

Ceramica Marina Torchio
Regione Chabloz 20
11100 Aosta
phone +39 0165.552559

K100
via de Tillier 21
11100 Aosta
phone +39 0165.31884

Jaccod
via Monte Solarolo 5
11100 Aosta
phone +39 0165.44585

arbus (sardinia)

Museo del coltello sardo
via Roma 15
09031 Arbus (CA)
phone +39 070.9759220
www.museodelcoltello.it

Pusceddu
via Roma 15
09031 Arbus (CA)
www.coltellosardo.com

arezzo (tuscany)

Tourist Information
piazza Risorgimento 116
52100 Arezzo
phone +39 0575.23952
piazza della Repubblica 28
phone +39 0575.377678
info@arezzo.turismo.toscana.it
www.turismo.toscana.it

Ristorante Il Falconiere
località San Martino 370
52044 Cortona (AR)
phone +39 0575.612679
info@ilfalconiere.com

Hotel Cavaliere Palace
via Madonna del Prato 83
52100 Arezzo
phone +39 0575.26836
info@cavalierehotels.com

Hotel Val di Colle
località Bagnoro
phone +39 0575.365167
52100 Arezzo
valdicolle@tin.it

Ristorante Buca di San Francesco
via San Francesco 1
52100 Arezzo
phone +39 0575.23271

Agriturismo Fattoria Montelucci
località Montelucci 8
52020 Pergine Valdarno (AR)
phone +39 0575.896525
info.montelucci@.it
www.montelucci.it

Trattoria La Capannaccia
località Campriano 51c
52100 Arezzo
phone +39 0575.361759

Trattoria Il Saraceno
via Mazzini 6a
52100 Arezzo
phone +39 0575.27644
info@ilsaraceno.com

Unoaerre
via Fiorentina 550
52100 Arezzo
phone +39 0575.925862
www.unoaerre.com

Carniani
via del Gavardello 62
52100 Arezzo
phone +39 0575.381847

Fiera Antiquaria
(every first sunday of the month)
piazza Grande
52100 Arezzo
phone +39 0575.21869

argenta (emilia–romagna)

Grazia del Pozzo
via Garibaldi 12
44011 Argenta (FE)
phone +39 0532.804919

arluno (lombardy)

Griffe Diffusion
via Guido Rossa 1
20010 Arluno (MI)
phone +39 02.90119004
www.griffesdiffusion.it

ascoli piceno (marche)

Tourist Information
via Thaon de Revel 4
60100 Ancona
phone +39 071.3589902
aptr@regione.marche.it
www.le-marche.com/italia/marche
Palazzo dei Capitani, piazza del Popolo
63100 Ascoli Piceno
phone +39 0736.253045
iat.ascolipiceno@regione.marche.it

Hotel Villa Seghetti Panichi
via San Pancrazio 1
63031 Castel di Lama (AP)
phone +39 0736.812552
info@seghettipanichi.it
www.seghettipanichi.it

Hotel Pennile
via G. Spalvieri
63100 Ascoli Piceno
phone +39 0736.41645
hotelpennile@tin.it

Ristorante Castel di Luco
località Castel di Luco
63040 Acquasanta Terme (AP)
phone +39 0736.802319
luco@abitarelastoria.it

Ristorante Gallo d'Oro
corso Vittorio Emanuele 13
63100 Ascoli Piceno
phone +39 0736.253520

Mercatino dell'Antiquariato e Collezionismo
(every third weekend of the month)
Chiostro Maggiore
63100 Ascoli Piceno

asolo (veneto)

Hotel Villa Cipriani
via Canova 298
31011 Asolo (TV)
phone +39 0423.523411
villacipriani@sheraton.com

Ristorante ai Due Archi
via Roma 55
31011 Asolo (TV)
phone +39 0423.952201

Scarpa
via Fermi 4
31010 Asolo (TV)
phone +39 04235284
www.scarpa.net

Scuola asolana di antico ricamo
via Canova 331
31010 Asolo (TV)
phone +39 0423.952906

Mercatino dell'Antiquariato
(every second saturday and sunday of the month)
Centro Storico
31010 Asolo (TV)
phone +39 0423.55967

Tessoria Asolana
via Canova 317
31010 Asolo (TV)
phone +39 0423.952062

assisi (umbria)

Tourist Information
piazza del Comune 12
06081 Assisi (PG)
phone +39 075.812534
info@iat.assisi.pg.it

Hotel Subasio
via Frate Elia 2
06082 Assisi (PG)
phone +39 075.812206
info@hotelsubasio.com

Ristorante Buca di S. Francesco
via Brizi 1
06081 Assisi (PG)
phone +39 075.812329

Angelucci Ornella
via S. Francesco 28a
06081 Assisi (PG)
phone +39 075.816146

Bolletta Danilo
Piaggia S. Pietro 9
06081 Assisi (PG)
phone +39 075.812528

asti (piedmont)

Tourist Information
via Grandi 5
14100 Asti
phone +39 0141.353034
piazza Alfieri 29
14100 Asti
phone +39 0141.530357

Hotel Reale
piazza Alfieri 6
14100 Asti
phone +39 0141.530240
www.hotel-reale.com

Hotel Salera
via Monsignor Marello 19
14100 Asti
phone +39 0141.410169
salera@tin.it

Ristorante Gener Neuv
lungo Tanaro dei Pescatori 4
14100 Asti
phone +39 0141.557270
www.generneuv.it

Ristorante La Grotta
corso Torino 366
14100 Asti
phone+39 0141.214168

Arazzeria Scassa
via dell'Arazzeria 60
14100 Asti
phone +39 0141.271352
ugscassa@tin.it
www.arazzeriascassa.com

Vittoria Montalbano
corso Matteotti 28
14100 Asti
phone +39 0141.592182

Antiquario di Asti
piazza S. Secondo
14100 Asti
phone +39 0141.399461

auronzo di cadore (veneto)

Tourist Information
via Roma 10
32041 Auronzo di Cadore (BL)
phone +39 0435.400198
auronzo@infodolomiti.it

Ristorante Cacciatori
via Ligonto 26
32041 Auronzo di Cadore (BL)
phone +39 0435.97017

G5 di Lozza G&C
via Stadio 4
32041 Auronzo di Cadore (BL)
phone +39 0435.400370

Centro ottico fratelli G. Lozza
via Ospitale 3
32041 Auronzo di Cadore (BL)
phone +39 0435.99418

avenza (tuscany)

Hotel Carrara
via Petacchi 21
54031 Avenza (MS)
phone +39 0585. 857616

Dino Felici
via Aurelia 1
54031 Avenza (MS)
phone +39 0585.858310

avigliano (basilicata)

Aviliart
corso Gianturco 105
85021 Avigliano (PZ)
phone +39 0971.81168

Eden Art
via Don Minzoni
85021 Avigliano (PZ)
phone +39 0971.57904

Il Filo di Arianna
via S. Maria del Carmine 18
85021 Avigliano (PZ)
phone +39 0971.700375

Lovallo Tommaso
contrada Vallebona
85021 Avigliano (PZ)
phone +39 0971.82170

bassano del grappa (veneto)

Tourist Information
largo Corona d'Italia 35
36061 Bassano del Grappa (VI)
phone +39 0424.524351

Bonotto Hotel Belvedere
piazzale G. Giardino 14
36061 Bassano del Grappa (VI)
phone +39 0424.529845
belvederehotel@bonotto.it

Hotel Ristorante Villa Ca' Sette
via Cunizza da Romano 4
36061 Bassano del Grappa (VI)
phone +39 0424.383350
info@ca-sette.it
www.ca-sete.it

Ristorante Hotel Al Camin
via Valsugana 64
phone +39 0424.566134
36022 Cassola (VI)
info@hotelalcamin.com

Ristorante Al Ponte
via Volpato 60
36061 Bassano del Grappa (VI)
phone +39 0424.219274
info@alpontedibassano.com

Ristorante Da Bauto
via Trozzetti 27
36061 Bassano del Grappa (VI)
phone +39 0424.34696

Ristorante Al Castello Superiore
via Cansignorio della Scala 4
36063 Marostica (VI)
phone +39 0424.73315

ABC Ceramiche
vicolo Ca' Erizzo 15
36061 Bassano del Grappa (VI)
phone +39 0424.524364
ceramicheabc@libero.it

Perdomello
viale Vicenza 93C
36061 Bassano del Grappa (VI)
phone +39 0424.502118

Museo della ceramica-Palazzo Sturm
via Schiavonetti
36061 Bassano del Grappa (VI)
phone +39 0424.524933
www.museobassano.it

bellagio (lombardy)

Tourist Information
piazza Mazzini
22021 Bellagio (CO)
phone +39 031.950204
prombell@tin.it

Grand Hotel Villa Serbelloni
via Roma 1
22021 Bellagio (CO)
phone +39 031.950216
inforequest@villaserbelloni.it

Ristorante Barchetta
Salita Mella 13
22021 Bellagio (CO)
phone +39 031.951389

Mortelmans
via degli Artigiani 16
22021 Bellagio (CO)
phone +39 031.951115
www.mortelmans.it

Pierangelo Masciadri
Salita Mella 19 - Salita Plinio 6
22021 Bellagio (CO)
phone +39-031-950067
fax +39-031-682965
www.masciadri.tv
pmasciadri@tiscalinet.it

belluno (veneto)

Mercatino Cose di Vecchie Case
(every forth sunday of summer)
Centro Storico
23100 Belluno
phone +39 0437.913509

bergamo (lombardy)

Tourist Information
viale Vittorio Emanuele II 20
phone +39 035.210204
24121 Bergamo
aptbg@apt.bergamo.it
www.apt.bergamo.it

Hotel Excelsior San Marco
piazza della Repubblica 6
24122 Bergamo
phone +39 035.366111/366159
info@hotelsanmarco.com

Starhotel Cristallo Palace
via B. Ambiveri 35
24100 Bergamo
phone +39 035.311211
reservations@starhotels.it

Ristorante Da Vittorio
viale Papa Giovanni XXIII 21
24121 Bergamo
phone +39 035.213266
info@davittorio.com

Ristorante Lio Pellegrini
via San Tomaso 47
241210 Bergamo
phone +39 035.247813
info@liopellegrini.it
www.liopellegrini.it

Taverna Colleoni e Dell'Angelo
località Città Alta
piazza Vecchia 7
24129 Bergamo
phone +39 035.232596
colleonidellangelo@uninetcom.it
www.colleonidellangelo.com

bertiolo (friuli–venezia giulia)

Alverio Savoia
via Udine 24
località Pozzecco
33032 Bertiolo (UD)
phone +39 0432.917426

biancavilla (sicily)

Efesto, la Fucina degli Dei
via Scirfi 24
95033 Biancavilla (CT)
phone/fax +39 095.981226
www.efestosnc.it
(show room: Sant'Alessio Siculo,
via Nazionale 212)

biella (piedmont)

Tourist Information
piazza V. Veneto 3
13900 Biella
phone +39 015.351128
info@atl.biella.it

Hotel Agorà Palace
via Lamarmora 13A
13900 Biella
phone +39 015.8407324
info@agorapalace.it

Ristorante Zenzero
via Belletti Bona 17
13900 Biella
phone +39 015.2524549
info@zenzero-restaurant.com

Lanificio F.lli Cerruti
via Cernaia 40
13900 Biella
phone +39 015.351144
Lfcoutlet@lancerr.com
www.lanificiocerruti.com

Fratelli Graziano
via Martiri Libertà 84
13888 Mongrando (BI)
phone +39 0156.66122
postmaster@graziano.it
www.graziano.it

Liabel
via Padre Greggio 8
13900 Biella
phone +39 015.8487426
www.liabel.it

Mercato di antiquariato e brocante
Zona Riva
13900 Biella
phone +39 015.351128

bienno (lombardy)

Museo del ferro
via Artigiani 13
25040 Bienno (BS)
phone +39 0364.300307
www.comune.bienno.bs.it

bologna (emilia–romagna)

Tourist Information
piazza Maggiore 1
40121 Bologna
phone +39 051.246541
touristoffice@comune.bologna.it

Grand Hotel Baglioni
via dell'Indipendenza 8
phone +39 051.225445
40121 Bologna
ghb.bologna@baglionihotels.com
baglioni.hotel-bologna.net/it/

Hotel Internazionale
via dell'Indipendenza 60
phone +39 051.245544
40121 Bologna
internazionale.res@monrifhotels.it

Hotel Dei Commercianti
via de' Pignattari 11
40124 Bologna
phone +39 051.7457511
commercianti@inbo.it
www.bolognarhotels.it

Trattoria Battibecco
via Battibecco 4
40123 Bologna
phone +39 051.223298

Ristorante Diana
via dell'Indipendenza 24
40121 Bologna
phone +39 051.231302
diana@softer.it

Ristorante Biagi
via Della Grada 6
40122 Bologna
phone +39 051.553025
ristorantebiagi@hotmail.com

Ducati Motor Holding
via Cavalieri Ducati Antonio 74
40132 Bologna
phone +39 051.401646
www.ducati.com

Museo nazionale del soldatino Mario Massacesi
Villa Aldovrandi Mazzacorati
via Toscana 19
40141 Bologna
phone +39 051.6234703
www.museodelsoldatino.cbj.net

Mercato dell'Antiquariato
(every second weekend of the month)
piazza S. Stefano
40132 Bologna
phone +39 051.246541

Mercato della montagnola
(friday and sunday)
piazza 8 Agosto - via Irnerio
40100 Bologna
phone +39 051.246541

bolzano (trentino–alto adige)

Tourist Information
piazza Walther 8
39100 Bolzano
phone +39 0471.307000
info@bolzano-bozen.it

Hotel Greif
piazza Walther
39100 Bolzano
phone +39 0471.311000
info@laurin.it

Ristorante Kaiserkron
piazza della Mostra 1
39100 Bolzano
phone +39 0471.970770
kaiserkron@dnet.it

Thun Store
via Galvani 29
39100 Bolzano
phone +39 0471.245111
infothuniversum@thun.it
www.thuniversum.com

Oberrauch-Zitt
via Portici 67
39100 Bolzano
phone +39 0471.972121

Mercato del Sabato
piazza Centrale
39100 Bolzano

borgomanero (piedmont)

Hotel Ramoverde
via Matteotti 1
28021 Borgomanero (NO)
phone +39 0322.81479
hotelramoverde@tiscalinet.it
www.hotelramoverde.it

Ristorante Pinocchio
via Matteotti 147
28021 Borgomanero (NO)
phone +39 0322.82273
bertinotti@ristorantepinocchio.it

Maglificio di Borgomanero
via Curti 7
28021 Borgomanero (NO)
phone +39 0322.81612

Tessuti Chic
via Matteotti 104
28021 Borgomanero (NO)
phone +39 0322.835446

bracciano (lazio)

Mercato di Antiquariato e Artigianato
(every second sunday of the month)
Centro Storico
00062 Bracciano (RM)
phone +39 06.9043374

breganze (veneto)

Liuteria Centro Musica
via Castelletto 25
36042 Breganze (VI)
phone +39 0445.300672

brendola (veneto)

Marzotto Factory Store
via Einaudi 5
36040 Brendola (VI)
phone +39 0444.492422
www.marzotto.it

brescia (lombardy)

Tourist Information
piazza della Loggia 6
25121 Brescia
phone +39 030.2400357
turismo@comune.brescia.it
www.comune.brescia.it

Hotel Vittoria
via delle 10 Giornate 20
25121 Brescia
phone +39 030.280061
info@hotelvittoria.com

Ristorante Castello Malvezzi
via Colle S. Giuseppe 1
25133 Brescia
phone +39 030.2004224
info@castellomalvezzi.it

Ristorante La Sosta
via S. Martino della Battaglia 20
25121 Brescia
phone +39 030.295603
lasosta@tin.it

Museo delle armi L. Marzoli
via del Castello 9
25121 Brescia
phone +39 030.293292
www.comune.brescia.it/musei

bressanone (trentino–alto adige)

Tourist Information
viale Stazione 9
39042 Bressanone (BZ)
phone +39 0472.836401
info@brixen.org

Hotel Elefante
via Rio Bianco 4
39042 Bressanone (BZ)
phone +39 0472.832750
info@hotelelephant.com
www.hotelelephant.com

Ristorante Oste Scuro-Finsterwirt
vicolo del Duomo 3
39042 Bressanone (BZ)
phone +39 0472.835343
info@finsterwirt.com

Boutique Peter Öhler
via Portici Minori 8a
39042 Bressanone (BZ)
phone +39 0472.201180

brianza (lombardy)

Hotel de la Ville
viale Regina Margherita 15
20052 Monza (MI)
phone +39 039.382581
info@hoteldelaville.com

Ristorante Derby Grill
viale Regina Margherita 15
20052 Monza (MI)
phone +39 039.382581

Arflex International
Via Don Rinaldo Beretta 12
20034 Giussano (MI)
phone +39.0362.853.043
fax +39.0362.853.080
www.arflex.com
info@arflex.it

Molteni & C
Via Rossini 50
20034 Giussano (MI)
phone +39 0362 359.1
Fax +39 0362 354448
customer.service@molteni.it
www.molteni.it

Area International
via Nuova Valassina 20
20058 Carate Brianza (MI)
phone +39 0362.903861
www.areainternational.it

Minotti
via Indipendenza 152
20036 Meda (MI)
phone +39 0362.343488
www.minotti.com

Tisettanta
via Furlanelli 96
20034 Giussano (MI)
phone +39 0362.319330
fax +39 0362.319300
www.tisettanta.com

Busnelli
via Kennedy 34
20020 Misinto (MI)
phone +39 02.96320221
www.busnelli.it

Fontana Arte
Alzaia Trieste 49
20094 Corsico (MI)
phone +39 02.45121
www.fontanaarte.it
info@fontanaarte.it

brunico (trentino–alto adige)

Tourist Information
via Europa 26
39031 Brunico (BZ)
phone +39 0474.555722
info@bruneck.com
www.brunico.it

Hotel Rosa d'oro-Goldene Rose
via Bastioni 36b
39031 Brunico (BZ)
phone +39 0474.413000
info@hotelgoldenerose.com

Kunter Ceramica
via Bruder Willram 31
39031 Brunico (BZ)
phone +39 0474.411164

Lanificio Mössmer
via W. Von der Vogelweide 6
39031 Brunico (BZ)
phone +39 0474.411267
info@moessmer.it
www.moessmer.it

Franz Tessitura Artistica
via M. Pacher 9
39031 Brunico (BZ)
phone +39 0474.555385
info@tessiturafranz.it
www.tessiturafranz.it

budrio (emilia–romagna)

Sport Hotel
via Massarenti 10
40054 Budrio (BO)
phone +39 051.803515
htlsport@tin.it

Fabio Menaglio
via Zenzalino Sud 6
40054 Budrio (BO)
phone +39 051.800958

Museo dell'ocarina e degli strumenti musicali in terracotta
via Garibaldi 35
40054 Budrio (BO)
phone +39 051.6928281
www.comune.budrio.bo.it

Museo dei burattini
via Mentana 19
40054 Budrio (BO)
phone +39 051.6928281
www.comune.budrio.bo.it

bulgarogrosso (lombardy)

B&B Cravatte
via Montale 1
Zona Industriale
22070 Bulgarogrosso (CO)
phone +39 031.934228

burano (veneto)

Ristorante da Romano
via Galuppi 221
isola di Burano

30012 Venezia
phone +39 0541.730030

Casa del Merletto
via S. Martino Sinistro 462
isola di Burano
30012 Venezia
phone +39 041.730801

Dalla Lidia Merletti
via S. Martino Destro 215
isola di Burano
30012 Venezia
phone +39 041.730073

Museo del Merletto
piazza Galuppi 187
isola di Burano
30012 Venezia
phone +39 0541.730034
www.comune.venezia.it/museicivici

caltagirone (sicily)

Tourist Information
via Volta Libertini di S. Marco
95041 Caltagirone (CT)
phone +39 0933.53809
www.comune.caltagirone.ct.it

Grand Hotel Villa San Mauro
via Portosalvo 14
95041 Caltagirone (CT)
phone +39 0933.26500
reservation.vsm@framon-hotels.it

Il Casale delle rose
contrada S. Stefano
95041 Caltagirone (CT)
phone +39 0933.25064

Museo regionale della ceramica
via Roma
95041 Caltagirone (CT)
phone +39 0933.52783

Istituto statale d'arte per la ceramica Luigi Sturzo
via Madonna della Via 5
95041 Caltagirone (CT)
phone +39 0933.21094

Ceramiche Dell'Aquila
Via Reburdone 7
95041 Caltagirone (CT)
phone +39 093334076 - 093350022
Fax +39 093340507
ceramiche@dellaquila.ct.it
www.dellaquila.ct.it

La Scala
scala Santa Maria del Monte 8
95041 Caltagirone (CT)
phone +39 0933.57781

Bottega del Decoro
via Roma 32
95041 Caltagirone (CT)

Romano
via Principe Amedeo 16
95041 Caltagirone (CT)

Silva
piazza Umberto I 19
95041 Caltagirone (CT)

Alessi
via Principe Amedeo 9
95041 Caltagirone (CT)

Patrì
via Roma 17
95041 Caltagirone (CT)

Varsallona
via Discesa Collegio 1
95041 Caltagirone (CT)

Donnarte
via Collegiata 7
95041 Caltagirone (CT)

camerano (marche)

Raccolta di fisarmoniche d'epoca
Palazzo Comunale
via San Francesco 24
60021 Camerano (AN)
phone +39 071.730301

camisano vicentino (veneto)

GT Erre
via degli Alpini 5
36043 Camisano Vicentino (VI)
phone +39 0444.611224

campo ligure (liguria)

Effe Erre
via Valle Calda 7
16013 Campo Ligure (GE)
phone +39 010.921381

Pisano F&C
via Saracca 72
16013 Campo Ligure (GE)
phone +39 010.920427

Rizzo
via Saracco 23
16013 Campo Ligure (GE)
phone +39 010.921172

Giuseppe Oliveri
via M. oliveri 17
16013 Campo Ligure (GE)
phone +39 010.921080

Museo della filigrana
via della Giustizia 5
16013 Campo Ligure (GE)
phone +39 010.920891
www.museofiligrana.org

Eredi Bongera
via Saracco 1
16013 Campo Ligure (GE)
phone +39 010.920570

F.P. Filigrana
via Don Minzoni 47
16013 Campo Ligure (GE)
phone +39 010.920570

canneto sull'oglio (lombardy)

Hotel Margot
via Tazzoli
46013 Canneto s/O (MN)
phone +39 0376.709011

Ristorante Dal Pescatore
località Runate
46013 Canneto s/O (MN)
phone +39 0376.723001
santini@dalpescatore.com

Trattoria del Cacciatore
piazza Gramsci 12
46013 Canneto s/O (MN)
phone +39 0376.723500

Museo del giocattolo G. Superti Furga
Centro Sociale
piazza Gramsci
46013 Canneto s/O (MN)
phone +39 0376.70175
cannetocultura@libero.it
www.mantova.org/comunecanneto

Fairplast
via Roma 34
46013 Canneto s/O (MN)
phone +39 0376.723223

cantù (lombardy)

Hotel Canturio
via Vergani 28
22063 Cantù (CO)
phone +39 081.716035
info@hotelcanturio.it

Ristorante Al Ponte
via Vergani 25
22063 Cantù (CO)
phone +39 081.712561

Pipe Castello
via Fossano 44
22063 Cantù (CO)
phone +39 031.714176

Cooperativa produzione merletti
corso Unità d'Italia 6
22063 Cantù (CO)
phone +39 031712265

capodimonte (campania)

Tourist Information
Stazione Centrale
80142 Naples
phone +39 081.268779
ept@netgroup.it
Stazione Mergellina
80142 Naples
phone +39 081.268779
piazza dei Martiri 58
80131 Capodimonte (NA)
phone +39 081.405311

Hotel Villa Capodimonte
via Moiariello 66
80131 Capodimonte (NA)
phone +39 081.459000
www.villacapodimonte.it

Ristorante Ciro
via S. Brigida 71
80131 Capodimonte (NA)
phone +39 081.5524072

Antica manifattura Capodimonte
via De Feo 2
80022 Arzano (NA)
phone +39 081.7318341
info@ceramicheamc.com
www.ceramicheamc.com

Museo e gallerie nazionali di Capodimonte
via Miano 1
80131 Capodimonte (NA)
phone +39 081.7499111 - +39 848.800525
capodimonte.spmn.remuna.org

Museo Duca di Martina
Villa Floridiana
80131 Capodimonte (NA)
phone +39 081.5788418

L'Airone
contrada Squillace 26
80022 Arzano (NA)
phone +39 0817.310719

NRS Capodimonte
via R. de Feo 4
80022 Arzano (NA)
phone +39 0817. 34422

CDC
via G. Amato 10
80026 Casoria (NA)
phone +39 0817.575577

La Capodimonte Artistica
via V. Emanuele 50
80026 Casoria (NA)
phone +39. 0817.576336

La Nuova Orchidea
via V. Emanuele 12
80026 Casoria (NA)
phone +39 0817.587584

carpi (emilia-romagna)

Hotel Touring
viale Dallai 1
41012 Carpi (MO)
phone +39 059.653701
info@hoteltouringcarpi.it

Ristorante L'Incontro
via per Correggio 43
41012 Carpi (MO)
phone +39 059.664581
ristorantelincontro@libero.it

Frarica-Dino Erre
via Anna Frank 6
41012 Carpi (MO)
phone +39 59.687056
dinoerre@dinoerre.com
www.frarica.it

Italo Confezioni
via Ama di Quartirolo 48b
41012 Carpi (MO)
phone +39 059.643191
info@italoconfezioni.191.it
www.italoconfezioni.com

Lepel
via Nuova Ponente 25b
41012 Carpi (MO)
phone +39 059.635140
www.lepel.it

Migor Camicerie
via C. Colombo 5
41012 Carpi (MO)
phone +39 059.694222
info@migor.it
www.migor.it

Museo di xilografia
Piazza Martiri 68
41012 Carpi (MO)
phone +39 059.649955
www.carpidiem.it

carrara (toscana)

Ristorante Ninan
via L. Bartolini 3
54033 Carrara (MS)
phone +39 0585.74741
ninan@tiscalinet.it

Museo civico del marmo
via XX Settembre
località Stadio
54033 Carrara (MS)
phone/fax +39 0585.8457460
giove.snuce.cnr.it/museo.html

casalgrasso (piedmont)

Centro Liquidazione Mobili
via Saluzzo 41
12030 Casalgrasso (CN)
phone +39 011.975175

casalmaggiore (lombardy)

Museo del bijou
via Porzio 9
26041 Casalmaggiore (CR)
phone +39 0375.43682
www.museodelbijou.it

casalmoro (lombardy)

Calze Filodoro Outlet
via Brescia 6
46040 Casalmoro (MN)
phone +39 0376.728290
www.filodoro.it

caserta (campania)

Tourist Information
corso Trieste 39
phone +39 0823.321137
81100 Caserta
enturismo.caserta@virgilio.it

Hotel Amadeus
via Verdi 72
phone +39 0823.352663
81100 Caserta
hotelamadeus@libero.it

Hotel Belvedere
Località Vaccheria/S. Leucio
via Nazionale Sannitica 87 (km 31)
81100 Caserta
phone +39 0823.304925

Ristorante Le Colonne
via Nazionale Appia 7/13
81100 Caserta
phone +39 0823.467494
info@lecolonnemarziale.it
www.lecolonnemarziale.it

Ristorante La Cucinotta
via Pollio 14
81100 Caserta
phone +39 0823.442807
www.lacucinotta.com

casette d'ete (marche)

Della Valle-Tod's
corso Garibaldi 134
63019 Casette d'Ete (AP)
phone +39 0734.871671
www.tods.com
info@tods.it

Ikam Italia
via Nenni 72
63011 Casette d'Ete
phone +39 0734.871313

Amaranti
via Nenni 105 A
63011 Casette d'Ete
phone +39 0734.861008

Kid's Heaven
via L. da Vinci 10
Zona Industriale Brancadoro
63011 Casette d'Este (AP)
phone +39 0734.871030

Zintala
contrada Mostrapiedi
63011 Casette d'Ete (AP)
phone +39 0734.810213

Pelletteria Torresi
via Parri 143
63011 Casette d'Ete
phone +39 0734.871244
www.torresi.com

casirate d'adda (lombardy)

Antichità Pirovano
via Dante 41
24040 Casirate d'Adda (BG)
phone +39 0363.87179

casnate con bernate (lombardy)

Emporio Pinto
via Roma 9
22070 Casnate con Bernate (CO)
phone +39 031.398624
www.achillepinto.com

castagnole monferrato (piedmont)

Peschera
via V. Emanuele II 5
14030 Castagnole Monferrato (AT)
phone +39 0141.292133

castelfidardo (marche)

Tourist Information
via Thaon de Revel 4
60100 Ancona
phone +39 071.3589902
aptrr@regione.marche.it
servizio.turismo@regione.marche.it
www.le-marche.com/italia/marche
Stazione Marittima
60100 Ancona
phone +39 071.201183
iat.ancona@regione.marche.it

Hotel Ristorante Il Fortino Napoleonico
località Portonovo
via Poggio 166
60100 Ancona
phone +39 071.801450
fortino@fastnet.it

Ristorante Al Rosso Agontano
via Marconi 3
60100 Ancona
phone +39 071.2075279

Ristorante Boccon Divino
via Matteotti 13
60100 Ancona
phone +39 071.57269

Megascini Nello
via Adriatica 41
60022 Castelfidardo (AN)
phone +39 0717.820247

D&D Fantini
via IV Novembre 61
60022 Castelfidardo (AN)
phone +39 071.7822787

Museo internazionale della fisarmonica
via Mordini 1
60022 Castelfidardo (AN)
phone +39 0717.808288
www.accordions.com

Mercatino Castellano
(every friday on July and August)
60022 Castelfidardo (AN)
phone +39 0717.80071

Victoria Accordions Company
Via IV Novembre 57/A
60022 Castelfidardo (AN)
phone +39 071.780004
fax +39 071.7822593
victoria@accordions.it
www.accordions.it

castellamonte (piedmont)

Castellamonte Crea
via Nigra 28
10081 Castellamonte (TO)
phone +39 0124.515160

Ceramiche Cielle
via Educ 4
10081 Castellamonte (TO)
phone +39 0124.582642

Maria Teresa Rosa
via G. Romana 38
10081 Castellamonte (TO)
phone +39 0124.582583

castelli (abruzzo)

Tourist Information
Comune di Castelli
piazza Roma 11
64041 Castelli (TE)
phone +39 0861.979142

Hotel Paradiso
località S. Gabriele dell'Addolorata
64045 Isola del Gran Sasso (TE)
phone +39 0861.975864

Ristorante La Volta Antica
via Barnabei
64041 Castelli (TE)
phone +39 0861.970708

Museo delle ceramiche
via Convento
64041 Castelli (TE)
phone +39 0861.979398

Ceramica Vera Tobia
via Antoniano 1
64041 Castelli (TE)
phone +39 0861.970655

Melchiorre
bivio Villa Rossi
64041 Castelli (TE)
phone +39 0861.974957

Simonetti
Villaggio Artigiano
64041 Castelli (TE)
phone +39 0861.979493
www.ceramichesimonetti.it

Centro Ceramico Castellano
località Villaggio Artigiano
64041 Castelli (TE)
phone +39 0861.979121
www.castelliceramica.com

Deros'arte
località Casette Faiano
64041 Castelli (TE)
phone +39 3333070241

Di Silvestre ceramiche
Villaggio Artigiano
64041 Castelli (TE)
phone +39 0861.979494

Graziana Pistocchi
bivio Villa Rossi
64041 Castelli (TE)
phone +39 0861.974947

castelli calepio (lombardy)

Mariano Carrara
24060 Castelli Calepio (BG).
phone +39 035.4425415
info@marianocarrara.it

castelsardo (sardinia)

Museo dell'intreccio mediterraneo
via Marconi
07031 Castelsardo (SS)
phone +39 0794.71380

castenaso (emilia—romagna)

Ferrareccia del Ferro Battuto
via Nasica 118
40055 Castenaso (BO)
phone +39 051.6052238

catania (sicily)

Tourist Information
via Cimarosa 10
95124 Catania
phone +39 095.7306233
apt@apt.catania.it
www.apt.catania.it

Excelsior Grand Hotel
piazza Verga 39
95129 Catania
phone +39 095.7476111
excelsior-catania@thi.it

Hotel Villa del Bosco
via del Bosco 62
95125 Catania
phone +39 095.7335100
info@hotelvilladelbosco.it

Osteria Antica Marina
via Pardo 29
95100 Catania
phone +39 95.348197

Ristorante Il Carato
via V. Emanuele II 81
95131 Catania
phone +39 095.7159247
info@ilcarato.it
www.ilcarato.it

Osteria i Tre Bicchieri
via San Giuseppe al Duomo 31
95124 Catania
phone +39 095.7153540
info@osteriaitrebicchieri.it
www.osteriaitrebicchieri.it

Ristorante La Siciliana
viale Marco Polo 52/a
95126 Catania
phone +39 095.376400
lasiciliana@tiscalinet.it

cavalese (trentino—alto adige)

Artigianato Fiemmese
località Masi, via Chiesa 40
38033 Cavalese (TN)
phone +39 0462.231353

cefalù (sicily)

Tourist Information
corso Ruggero 77
90015 Cefalù (PA)
phone +39 0921.421050
info@cefalu-tour.pa.it

Hotel Riva del Sole
Lungomare Colombo 25
90015 Cefalù (PA)
phone +39 0921.421230
lidia@rivadelsole.com

Ostaria del Duomo
via Seminario 5
90015 Cefalù (PA)
phone +39 0921.421838

Chez Nino
corso Ruggero 145
90015 Cefalù (PA)

Piccolo mondo antico
via V. Emanuele 91
90015 Cefalù (PA)

cembra (trentino—alto adige)

Artigianato artistico
viale 4 Novembre 22
38034 Cembra (TN)
phone +39 0461.683283

cenaia (tuscany)

Punto Vetro
via V. Veneto 3
56040 Cenaia (PI)
+39 050.644070
puntovetro@katamail.com
www.puntovetro.it

centallo (piedmont)

Vegezzi-Bossi
via Marconi 48
12044 Centallo (CN)
phone +39 0171.214176

champorcher (valle d'aosta)

Cooperativa Lou Dzeut
località Chardoney
11020 Champorcher (AO)
phone +39 0125.37327

chiavari (liguria)

Tourist Information
corso Assarotti 1
16043 Chiavari (GE)
phone +39 0185.325198

Hotel Monte Rosa
via Monsignor Marinetti 6
16043 Chiavari (GE)
phone +39 0185.314853
info@hotelmonterosa.it

Ristorante Lord Nelson
corso Valparaiso 27
16043 Chiavari (GE)
phone 0185.302595

Adriano Podestà
via Gastaldi 17
16043 Chiavari (GE)
phone +39 0185.308208

F.lli Levaggi
Via Parma 469
16043 Chiavari (GE)
phone/fax +39 0185.383092
info@levaggisedie.it
www.levaggisedie.it

Mostra Mercato dell'Antiquariato
(every second week end of the month)
via Martiri della Liberazione
16043 Chiavari (GE)
phone +39 0185.3095588

chiesa valmalenco (lombardy)

Fratelli Gaggi
via Roma 2
23023 Chiesa di Valmalenco (SO)
phone +39 0342.451283

chieti (abruzzo)

Mercantico d'Abruzzo
(every fourth sunday of the month)
corso Marrucino
66100 Chieti
phone +39 085.7672513

cicagna (liguria)

Consorzio Artigiano Ardesia Fontanabuona
via Alberogrosso 10
16044 Cicagna (GE)
phone +39 018.592394

Cuneo & C.
via Molinazzo 21
16044 Cicagna (GE)
phone +39 018.5929983

Ecomuseo dell'ardesia.
La via della pietra nera
viale Italia 25
località Chiapparino
16044 Cicagna (GE)
phone +39 0185.971091
www.galfontanabuona.it

città della pieve (umbria)

Antiqcarta
(every second week-end of the month)
06062 Città della Pieve (PG)
phone +39 075.8409366

città di castello (umbria)

Tourist Information
piazza Matteotti-Logge Bufalini
06012 Città di Castello (PG)
phone +39 075.8554922
info@iat.citta-di-castello.pg.it

Hotel Tiferno
piazza Raffaello Sanzio 13
06012 Città di Castello (PG)
phone +39 075.8550331

Ristorante Il Bersaglio
viale Orlando 14
06012 Città di Castello (PG)
phone +39 075.8555534

Tela Umbra
via S. Antonio 3
06012 Città di Castello (PG)
phone +39 075.85543.37

Arte Ferro
via Argenti
località Cerbara
06012 Città di Castello (PG)
phone +39 0758.510877

Emanuele Emiliani
via Mattei 24
06012 Città di Castello (PG)
phone +39 0758.5558477

Camiceria Etrusca
viale Romagna 73
06012 Città di Castello (PG)
phone +39 0758.8518087
negozio@camiceriaetrusca.com
www.camiceriaetrusca.com

Raccolta del laboratorio di tela umbra
via S. Antonio 3
06012 Città di Castello (PG)
phone +39 0758.554337

cividale (friuli–venezia giulia)

Tourist Information
corso Paolino d'Aquileia 10
33043 Cividale (UD)
phone +39 0432.731461
arpt-cividale@regione.fvg.it

Hotel Roma
piazza Picco 17
33043 Cividale (UD)
phone +39 0432.731871

Locanda Al Castello
via del Castello 12
33043 Cividale (UD)
phone +39 0432.733242

Julia Marmi
viale Gemona 230
33043 Cividale (UD)
phone +39 0432.733280

cogliate (lombardy)

Giochi Preziosi
via delle Primule 5
20020 Cogliate (MI)

phone +39 02.964751
www.giochipreziosi.it

cogne (valle d'aosta)

Atelier d'Art et Metiers
via Grappein 100
11012 Cogne (AO)
phone +39 0165.74296

colle val d'elsa (tuscany)

Tourist Information
via Campana 43
53034 Colle Val d'Elsa (SI)
phone +39 0577.922791
pro.loco@comune.collevaldelsa.it
www.comune.colle-val-d-elsa.si.it

Relais della Rovere
via Piemonte 10
53034 Colle Val d'Elsa (SI)
phone +39 0577.924696
dellarovere@chiantiturismo.it

Hotel Villa Belvedere
località Belvedere
53034 Colle Val d'Elsa (SI)
phone +39 0577.920596
email@villabelvedere.com
www.villabelvedere.com

Ristorante Arnolfo
via XX settembre 50
53034 Colle Val d'Elsa (SI)
phone +39 0577.920549
arnolfo@arnolfo.com

Colle Cristallo
località S. Marziale
53034 Colle Val d'Elsa (SI)
phone +39 0577.909711
info@collecristallo.com

Vilca
località S. Marziale
53034 Colle Val d'Elsa (SI)
phone +39 0577.929188
vilca@vilca.it, www.vilca.it

Compagnia del Cristallo
località Pian dell'Olmino
53034 Colle Val d'Elsa (SI)
phone +39 0577.928279

Cristallerie Mezzetti
via Oberdan 13
53034 Colle Val d'Elsa (SI)
phone +39 0577.920395
e-mailcristalleriemezzetti@email.it

Mario Belli
via Diaz 10/14
53034 Colle val d'Elsa (SI)
phone +39 0577.920784

Boreno Cigni
Vicolo delle Fontanelle 8
53034 Colle Val d'Els
phone +39 0577.920326

como (lombardy)

Tourist Information
piazza Cavour 17
22100 Como
phone +39 031.3300111
lakecomo@tin.it

Grand'Hotel di Como
via per Cernobbio
22100 Como
phone +39 031.5161
info@grandhoteldicomo.com

Hotel Villa Fiori
via per Cernobbio 12
22100 Como
phone +39 031.33820
info@hotelvillafiori.it

Ristorante Navedano
via Pannilano
località Camnago Volta
22100 Como
phone +39 031.308080

Ristorante Terrazzo Perlasca
piazza de Gasperi 8
22100 Como
phone +39 031.303936
terrazzoperlasca@virgilio.it

Diffusione Seta Outlet
via Paoli 3
22100 Como
phone +39 031.523800
www.incomo.com

Emporio della seta Frey
viale Risorgimento 49
22073 Fino Mornasco (CO)
Phone +39 031.927538
www.frey.it

Guarisco Store
statale dei Giovi 66
22070 Grandate (CO)
phone +39 031.399111
guarisco@guarisco.it
www.guarisco.it

Museo tessile Ratti
Lungolario Trento 9
22100 Como
phone +39 031.2332224

Ratti
Via Madonna, 30
22070 Guanzate (CO)
phone +39 031 35351
Fax: +39 031 3535316
fashion@ratti.it
www.ratti.it

Museo didattico della seta
via Valleggio 3
22100 Como
phone/fax +39 031.303180
www.museosetacomo.com

Museo dei treni in miniatura
via Pio XI 157
22100 Como
phone +39 031.541541

Mercato di antiquariato e brocante
(every first saturday of the month)
piazza S. Fedele
22100 Como
phone +39 031.3300111

coreglia antelminelli (tuscany)

Museo della figurina di gesso
via del Mangano 17
55025 Coreglia Antelminelli (LU)
phone +39 0583.78082

cornuda (veneto)

Calzaturificio Flavis
via del Commercio 6
31041 Cornuda (TV)
phone +39 0423.639401

La Reginetta
via del Commercio 9
31041 Cornuda (TV)
phone +39 0423.639521

Lotto Factory Outlet
via Padova 23
31041 Cornuda (TV)
phone +39 0423.821400
lss.cornuda@tin.it

The North Face Outlet
via Padova 21
31041 Cornuda (TV)
phone +39 0423.839133
outlet.it@thenorthface.com

Tipoteca italiana
via Canapificio 3
31041 Cornuda (TV)
phone +39 0423.86338
info@tipoteca.it
www.tipoteca.it

cosenza (calabria)

Tourist Information
corso Mazzini 92
87100 Cosenza
tel +39 0984.27485
aptcosenza@virgilio.it

Holiday Inn Cosenza
via Panebianco
87100 Cosenza
phone +39 0984.31109
holidayinn.cs@virgilio.it

Hotel Centrale
via del Tigrai 3
87100 Cosenza
phone +39 0984.75750
hotelcentrale@tin.it

Ristorante L'Arco Vecchio
piazza Archi di Ciaccio 21
87100 Cosenza
phone +39 0984.72564

Ristorante L'Antica Osteria dell'Arenella
piazza Arenella 9
87100 Cosenza
phone +39 0984.76573

Bottega sartoriale Valentini
Contrada Pantoni
87100 Cosenza
phone +39 0984.939804
info@valentini-bs.it
www.valentini-bs.it

cossato (piedmont)

Bottega Artigiana
via Ranzoni 10
13014 Cossato (BI)
phone +39 0159.25622

creazzo (veneto)

Carion Vetrate Artistiche
via Cima 12, 23
36051 Creazzo (VI)
phone +39 0444.520657
piero.modole@tin.it

cremona (lombardy)

Tourist Information
piazza del Comune 5
26100 Cremona
phone +39 0372.23233
info@aptcremona.it
www.cremonaturismo.com

Delle Arti Design Hotel
via Bonomelli 8
26100 Cremona
phone +39 0372.23131
info@dellearti.com
www.dellearti.com

Hotel Impero
piazza della Pace, 21
26100 Cremona
phone +39 0372.413013

Agriturismo Lo Stagno
via Cascina Gerre del Pesce
26049 Stagno Lombardo (CR)
phone +39 0372.57055 - 2495603
info@lostagno.it
www.lostagno.it

Ristorante Al Caminetto
via Umberto I, 26
26047 Scandolara Ripa d'Oglio (CR)
phone +39 0372.89589
www.ristorantealcaminetto.com

Ristorante Il Violino
via Sicardo 3
26100 Cremona
phone +39 0372.461010
www.ilviolino.it

Museo Stradivariano
via Ugolani Dati 4
26100 Cremona
phone +39 0372.407269

Museo del violino
via Palestro 17
26100 Cremona
phone +39 0372.2461886

Collezione violini di Palazzo Comunale
piazza del Comune 8
26100 Cremona
phone +39 037.222138

Consorzio Liutai A. Stradivari
piazza Stradivari 5
26100 Cremona
phone +39 0372.464490

Brugnini & Beck
via Bissolati 48
26100 Cremona
phone +39 0372.463048
www.cremonaliuteria.it

crocetta del montello (veneto)

Camiceria Arcadia
via Canapificio 12
Crocetta del Montello (TV)
phone +39 0423.665002
www.arcadiashirt.com

cunardo (lombardy)

Manifattura ceramiche
località Camartino
21035 Cunardo (VA)
phone +39 0332.716018

cureggio (piedmont)

Granital
via Novara 24
28060 Cureggio (NO)
phone +39 0322.839376

delta del po (emilia–romagna)

Tourist Information
Castello Estense
44100 Ferrara
phone +39 0532.209370
infotour@provincia.fe.it
www.comune.fe.it
Piazza Folegatti, 28
44022 Comacchio (FE)
phone +39 0533.310161
iat@comune.comacchio.fe.it

Hotel Duchessa Isabella
via Palestro 70
44100 Ferrara
phone +39 0532.202121
info@duchessaisabella.it
www.duchessaisabella.it

Hotel Annunziata
piazza Repubblica 5
44100 Ferrara
phone +39 0532.201111
info@annunziata.it
www.annunziata.it

Ristorante Quel Fantastico Giovedì
via Castelnuovo 9
44100 Ferrara
phone +39 0532.760570

Ristorante Antica Trattoria Volano
viale Volano 20

44100 Ferrara
phone +39 0532.761421
anticatrattoriavolano@interfree.it

Hotel Logonovo
viale delle Querce 109
44024 Lido degli Estensi (FE)
phone +39 0533.327520
logonovo@libero.it

Hotel Caravel
località Lido di Spina
viale Leonardo 56
44024 Lido degli Estensi (FE)
phone +39 0533.330106
hotelcaravel@tin.it

Ristorante Aroldo
località Lido di Spina
viale delle Acacie 26
44024 Lido degli Estensi (FE)
phone +39 0533.330948
belsandro@libero.it

Ristorante La Barcaccia
piazza XX Settembre 41
44022 Comacchio (FE)
phone +39 0533.314080
trattoriabarcaccia@libero.it

deruta (umbria)

Tourist Information
Pro Deruta
piazza dei Consoli 4
06053 Deruta (PG)
phone +39 0759.711559
www.proderuta.it

Hotel Asso di Coppe
SS E45
06053 Deruta (PG)
phone +39 0759.710205

Ristorante La Fontanina
piazza dei Consoli
06053 Deruta (PG)
phone +39 0759.724112

Germano Bettini
via Tiberina Sud 320
06053 Deruta (PG)
phone +39 075.9710550
www.terrecottederuta.com

La Bottega del Vasaio
via Tiberina 119
06053 Deruta (PG)
phone +39 075.9711284

Ubaldo Grazia Maioliche
via Tiberina 181
06053 Deruta (PG)
phone +39 075.9710201

Maioliche Marina Montanari
piazza dei Consoli 16
06053 Deruta (PG)
phone +39 075.972315

Museo regionale della ceramica
largo S. Francesco
06053 Deruta (PG)
phone +39 0759.711000
www.sistemamuseo.it

dolomiti bellunesi (veneto)

Tourist Information
piazza Duomo 2
32100 Belluno
phone +39 0437.940083
belluno@infodolomiti.it

Hotel Villa Carpenada
via Mier 158
32100 Belluno
phone +39 0437.948343
fax +39 0437.948345

Hotel Valgranda
via Pecol 11
32010 Zoldo Alto (BL)
phone +39 0437.789151
valgranda@dolomiti.it
www.dolomiti.it/valgranda

Ristorante Al Borgo
via Anconetta 8
32100 Belluno
phone +39 0437.926755
info@alborgo.to www.alborgo.to

Trattoria da Ninetta
località Mezzocanale
32012 Forno di Zoldo (BL)
phone +39 0437.78240

dozza (emilia—romagna)

Hotel Monte del Re
via Monte del Re 43
40050 Dozza (BO)
phone +39 0542.678400
montedelre@tiscali.it

Ristorante Canè
via XX Settembre 27
40050 Dozza (BO)
phone +39 0542.678120
ristorantecane@tin.it

Cereria d'Autore
via XX Settembre 42
40050 Dozza (BO)
phone +39 0542.679010

I sogni nel cassetto
via XX Settembre 62
40050 Dozza (BO)
phone +39 0542.678008

elba island (tuscany)

Tourist Information
Calata Italia 35
57037 Portoferraio (LI)
phone +39 0565.914671
info@aptelba.it
www.arcipelago.turismo.toscana.it

Hotel Hermitage
località La Biodola
57037 Portoferraio (LI)
phone +39 0565.974811
info@hotelhermitage.it

Hotel Airone del Parco e delle Terme
località San Giovanni
57037 Portoferraio (LI)
phone +39 0565.929111
info@airone.info

Ristorante Capo Nord
Località La Fenicia, 69
57033 Marciana Marina (LI)
phone +39 0565.996983

Ristorante Publius
frazione Poggio, Piazza XX Settembre 6/7
57030 Marciana (LI)
phone +39 0565.99208

Ristorante Stella Marina
banchina Alto Fondale
via V. Emanuele II 1
57037 Portoferraio (LI)
phone +39 0565.915983

Ristorante Cantuccio
località Marina di Campo
via Garibaldi 2
57034 Campo nell'Elba (LI)
phone +39 0565.976775

Museo minerali elbani
57039 Rio nell'Elba (LI)
phone +39 0565.939294

Cose Belle
Calata Mazzini 12
57037 Portoferraio (LI)
phone +39 0565.917344

Giannini Valter
via Marconi 15
57036 Porto Azzurro (LI)
phone +39 0565.921064

este (veneto)

Ceramiche Estensi
via A. Volta 26
35042 Este (PD)
phone +39 0429.4848
info@ceramichestensi.it
www.ceramichestensi.it

fabriano (marche)

Tourist Information
corso della Repubblica 70
60044 Fabriano (AN)
phone +39 0732.625067
iat.fabriano@regione.marche.it

Hotel Gentile da Fabriano
via di Vittorio 13
60044 Fabriano (AN)
phone +39 0732.627190
info@hotelgentile.it

Ristorante Marchese del Grillo
località Rocchetta Bassa Nord est
60044 Fabriano (AN)
phone +39 0732.625690
info@marchesedelgrillo.com

Cartiera Miliani-Fabriano
via XIII Luglio
60044 Fabriano (AN)
phone +39 0732.23031
mail@cartieremilianifabriano.com

www.cartierefabriano.it
Cartiera Artem
via Corsi Lamberto 3
60044 Fabriano (AN)
phone +39 0732.23521
info@artemcarta.it
www.artemcarta.it

Museo della carta e della filigrana
largo F.lli Spacca 2
60044 Fabriano (AN)
phone +39 0732.709297
www.museodellacarta.com

faenza (emilia-romagna)

Tourist Information
piazza del Popolo 1
48018 Faenza (RA)
phone +39 054.625231
www.comune.faenza.ra.it

Hotel Cavallino
via Forlivese 185
48018 Faenza (RA)
phone +39 054.6634411

Ristorante Enoteca Astorre
piazza della Libertà 16/a
48018 Faenza (RA)
phone +39 054.6681407

Bottega d'Arte Ceramica Gatti
via Pampignoli 4
48018 Faenza (RA)
phone +39 054.6634301

Ceramiche Vitali
corso Mazzini 110 A
48018 Faenza (RA)
phone +39 054.625791

Ceramiche Artistiche Vignoli
via Fermi 30
48018 Faenza (RA)
phone +39 054.6621076

Maestri Maiolicari Faentini
via Granarolo 63
48018 Faenza (RA)
phone +39 054.6664139

**Museo internazionale
delle ceramiche**
via Campidori 2
48018 Faenza (RA)
phone +39 054.6697311
www.micfaenza.org

Arte Regalo
piazza del Popolo 6
48018 Faenza (RA)
phone +39 0546.21646

Ceramica Monti
via Pier Maria Cavina 22
48018 Faenza (RA)
phone +39 0546.25264

Ceramiche Mirta Morigi
via Barbavara 19/4
48018 Faenza (RA)
phone +39 0564.29940

Le Terre di Faenza
via Cavina 30
48018 Faenza (RA)
phone +39 0546.29440

farra di soligo (veneto)

Tessitura Bertazzon
via Faverei 14
31010 Farra di Soligo (TV)
phone +39 0438.900113

fidenza (emilia-romagna)

Bormioli Rocco & Figlio
viale Martiri della Libertà
43036 Fidenza (PR)
phone +39 0524.511200
Spaccio_brfcasa@bormiolirocco.com

fiorano modenese (emilia-romagna)

Collezione ceramiche sassolesi
villa Vigarani Guastalla
SS Est 3
41042 Fiorano Modenese (MO)
phone +39 0536.833111

Museo della ceramica
Castello di Spezzano
via del Castello 12
41042 Fiorano Modenese (MO)
phone +39 0536.845064
cultura@comune.fiorano-modenese.mo.it
www.comune.fiorano-
modenese.mo.it/cultura/museo.htm

florence (tuscany)

Tourist Information
via Cavour 1r
50100 Florence
phone +39 055.290832
infoturismo@provincia.fi.it
piazza della Stazione 4
phone +39 055.212245
turismo3@provincia.fi.it

Hotel The Westin Excelsior
piazza Ognissanti 3
50123 Florence
phone +39 055.27151
excelsiorflorence@westin.com

Hotel Continentale
vicolo dell'Oro 6r
50123 Florence
phone +39 055.27262
continental@lungarnohotels.com

Ristorante Enoteca Pinchiorri
via Ghibellina 87
50122 Florence
phone +39 055.242777
ristorante@enotecapinchiorri.com
www.enotecapinchiorri.com

Trattoria Del Fagioli
corso Tintori 47
50122 Florence
phone +39 055.244285

Trattoria Alla Vecchia Bettola
viale V. Pratolini 3/7
50124 Florence
phone +39 055.224158

Beltrami
via dei Panzani 1r
50123 Florence
phone +39 055.212661

Calzaturificio Buccioni
via Aretina 403d
50136 Florence
phone +39 055.2340271

Lori, Clara e Lorenzo
via De Nicola 15
50136 Florence
phone +39 055.6503204

Il Guardaroba
Borgo Albizi 78r
50123 Florence
phone +39 055.212661

**Galleria del costume
di Palazzo Pitti**
piazza Pitti
50125 Florence
phone +39 055.2388601

Passamaneria Toscana
piazza S. Lorenzo 12r
50100 Florence
phone +39 055.214670

Museo Ferragamo
via Tornabuoni 2
50100 Florence
phone +39 055.3360456
www.salvatoreferragamo.it

Gucci
via Tornabuoni 73
50100 Florence
phone +39 055.759221
www.gucci.com

Tessilarte
via P. Toselli 100
50100 Florence
phone +39 055.365182
info@tessilarte.it

Cotto Ref
via di Cappello, 26/4
50023 Impruneta (FI)
phone +39 055.2011013-2011606
fax +39 055 2313210
info@cottoref.it
www.cottoref.it

**Brandimarte argento
Uffici e Vendita**
via L. Ariosto 11/Cr
50124 Florence
phone +39 055.23041
fax +39 055.224081

Laboratorio
via Ugo Foscolo, 6
phone +39 055 2286242
fax +39 055.2276318
info@brandimarte.com
www.brandimarte.com

Baldini Ubaldo
via Palazzuolo 101/R
50123 Florence
phone +39 055.210933

Mercato delle pulci
(every last sunday of the month)
piazza dei Ciompi
50100 Florence
phone +39 055.23320

Calzature Mannina
via Guicciardini 16 r
50100 Florence
phone +39 055.282895

Oreria
Borgo Pinti 87°
50100 Florence
phone +39 055.244708

Mercato del porcellino
Piazza del Mercato Nuovo
50122 Florence

firenzuola (tuscany)

Museo della pietra serena
Rocca di Firenzuola, piazza don S. Casini 1
50033 Firenzuola (FI)
phone +39 0558.199437

Cooperativa Scalpellini
via Imolese 51
50033 Firenzuola (FI)
phone +39 055.819038
info@coopscalpellini.com

La Pietra Toscana
via Cornacchiaia 389
località Alberaccio
50033 Firenzuola (FI)
phone +39 055.819696
info@lapietratoscana.com

Comad
località San Pietro Santerno 7
50033 Firenzuola (FI)
phone +39 055.819462

fiuggi (lazio)

Tourist Information I.A.T.
via Gorizia, 4
03014 Fiuggi (FR)
phone +39 0775.515446

Hotel Palazzo della Fonte
via dei Villini 7
03014 Fiuggi (FR)
phone +39 0775.5081
information@palazzodellafonte.com
www.palazzodellafonte.com

Ristorante La Torre
piazza Trento e Trieste 29
03014 Fiuggi (FR)
phone +39 0775.515382
acimine@tin.it

Gioielleria Rosito
via Prenestina 13
03014 Fiuggi (FR)
phone +39 0775. 515626

fax +39 0775 504140
digilander.libero.it/rosito

follonica (tuscany)

Museo del ferro e della ghisa
ex Ilva
58022 Follonica (GR)
phone +39 0566.40762
comune.follonica.gr.it/museo

forlì (emilia—romagna)

Tourist Information
piazza Pacifici 2
47100 Forlì
phone +39 0543.712435
iat@comune.forli.fo.it

Hotel Globus City
via Traiano Imperatore 4
47100 Forlì
phone +39 0543.722215
info@hotelglobus.it

Hotel Masini
corso Garibaldi 28
47100 Forlì
phone +39 0543.28072
info@hotelmasini.com

Hotel Ramada Encore
viale Vittorio Veneto 3/e
47100 Forlì
phone +39 0543.22038
reservation@ramadaencoreforli.com

**Ristorante Casa Rusticale
dei Cavalieri Templari**
viale Bologna 275
47100 Forlì
phone +39 0543.701888

Arredamenti Cavallini
viale Roma 203
47100 Forlì
phone +39 0543.780780

frosolone (molise)

Tourist Information
via Farinacci 9
86170 Isernia
phone +39 0865.3992
www.comune.frosolone.is.it/

Rocco Petrunti
via Colozza 11
86095 Frosolone (IS)
phone +39 0874.890660
www.petrunticoltelli.com

Artigianato Forbici
via Dante 5
86095 Frosolone (IS)
phone +39 0874.890462

Nicola Francescone
via Monforte 24
86100 Campobasso
phone +39 0874.97304

Coltelleria Francesco Fraraccio
via Selva 1
86095 Frosolone (IS)
phone +39 0874.899910

Coltellerie Fratelli Paolucci
via Teste 1
86095 Frosolone (IS)
phone +39 0874.890120

Forbici Lupa
via Calvario 3
86095 Frosolone (IS)
phone +39 0874.890873

gallarate (lombardy)

Sergio Tacchini Factory Outlet
via Milano 169
21013 Gallarate (VA)
phone +39 0331.790347
www.sergiotacchini.com

gambettola (emilia—romagna)

Tourist Information
piazza Risorgimento 6
47035 Gambettola (FC)
phone +39 0547.45111
www.comune.gambettola.fc.it

Trattoria Locanda al Gambero Rosso
via G. Verdi 5
47026 San Piero in Bagno (FC)
phone +39 0543.903405
locanda.gamberorosso@libero.it
www.bagnodiromagnaturismo.it/locanda.
gambero.rosso

Fratelli Pascucci 1826
via Verdi 18
47035 Gambettola (FC)
phone +39 054.753105
www.pascucci1826.it

Bertozzi
via Verdi 6
47035 Gambettola (FC)
phone +39 054.753105
info@stamperiabertozzi.it

gardone val trompia (lombardy)

Tourist Information
corso Zanardelli 38
25121 Brescia
phone +39 030.45052
promobs@tin.it
www.valletrompia.it

Fabbrica d'armi Pietro Beretta
via P. Beretta 18
25063 Gardone Val Trompia (BS)
phone +39 030.83411/8913826

Museo delle Armi Beretta
via P. Beretta 18
Gardone Valtrompia (BS)
phone +39 030.83411

Armeria Brignoli
via V. Alfieri 6
25063 Gardone Val Trompia (BS)

phone +39 030.8912295
www.brignoliarmi.com

Creative Art
via G. Matteotti 127
25063 Gardone Val Trompia (BS)
phone +39 030.8911807
www.creativeart.it

Bottega delle incisioni Giovannelli
Via X giornate 43
25063 Gardone Val Trompia (BS)
phone +39 030.8912909
fax +39 030.82296
www.giovannelliengraving.com

gavirate (lombardy)

Ristorante Tipamasaro
via Cavour 31
21026 Gavirate (VA)
phone +39 0332.743524

Museo della pipa
via del Chiostro 1
21026 Gavirate (VA)
phone +39 0332.743334

genoa (liguria)

Tourist Information
Stazione Piazza Principe
piazza Acqua Verde
16100 Genoa
phone e fax +39 010.2462633
iat.principe@apt.genova.it
Aeroporto Cristoforo Colombo
via Pionieri e Aviatori d'Italia
16100 Genoa
phone +39 010.6015247
iat.aeroporto@apt.genova.it

Hotel Savoia Majestic
piazza Stazione Principe
16100 Genoa
phone 010.261641
www.hotelsavoiagenova.it

Hotel Bristol Palace
via XX Settembre 35
16121 Genoa
phone +39 010.592541
info@hotelbristolpalace.com

Hotel Jolly Marina
via Molo Ponte Calvi 5
16124 Genoa
phone +39 010.25391
genova-marina.jollyhotels.com

Hotel City
via San Sebastiano 6
16123 Genoa
phone +39 010.5545
city.ge@bestwestern.it

Locanda di Palazzo Cicala
piazza San Lorenzo 16
16123 Genoa
phone +39 010.2518824
palazzocicala@mentelocale.it
www.palazzocicala.it

Ristorante La Bitta nella Pergola
località Foce
via G. Casaregis 52r
16129 Genoa
phone +39 010.588543
labittanellapergola@libero.it

Ristorante Edilio
corso A. De Stefanis 104r
16139 Genoa
phone +39 010.880501

Trattoria Maxelà
vico Inferiore del Ferro 9
16100 Genoa
phone +39 010.2474209

Ferrari Roberto
vicolo Casano 18r
16123 Genoa
phone +39 010.2474511

Lo Scampolo del negozietto
via Albaro 18r
16121 Genoa
phone +39 010.3626707

Magazzini del Cotone
via Morin 32r
16129 Genoa
phone +39 010.5704399

Maglificio Ferro
Lungobisagno Dalmazia 71/int 13
16141 Genoa
phone +39 010.8360380

Diffusione Tessile
località Genova Campi
16141 Genoa
phone +39 010. 6591235

Fiera Nautica
piazzale Kennedy 1
16100 Genoa
phone +39 010.8360380
fierage@fiera.ge.it
www.fiera.ge.it

Mercatino d'Antiquariato
(every first week-end of the month)
piazza Ducale
16100 Genoa
phone +39 010.588735

Museo della Filigrana
Museo della Filigrana
Via della giustizia 1
16013, Campo Ligure (GE)
phone +39 010.920099
www.museofiligrana.org

ghiffa (piedmont)

Hotel Ghiffa
corso Belvedere 88
28823 Ghiffa (VB)
phone +39 0323.59285
info@hotelghiffa.com

Museo dell'arte del cappello
corso Belvedere 279
28823 Ghiffa (VB)
phone +39 0323.59209
museocappelloghiffa@libero.it

giano dell'umbria (umbria)

La Forgia
zona Industriale
località Bastardo
06030 Giano dell'Umbria (PG)
phone +39 0742.99384

giaveno (piedmont)

Calza di cuoio
piazza Scopis 6
10094 Giaveno (TO)
phone +39 01119.364044

gignese (lombardy)

Museo dell'ombrello e del parasole
via Golf Panorama 12
28836 Gignese (VB)
phone +39 0323.208061
www.gignese.it/museo

gorizia (friuli–venezia giulia)

Tourist Information
via Roma 5
Palazzo della Regione
34170 Gorizia
phone +39 0481.3862225
arpt-go1@regione.fvg.it

Ristorante Majda
via Duca d'Aosta 71
34170 Gorizia
phone +39 0481.530906

Museo della moda e delle arti applicate
Borgo Castello 13
34170 Gorizia
phone +39 0481.533926

gorle (lombardy)

Vercos Vetrate
via Buonarroti 30
24020 Gorle (BG)
phone +39 035.290330
info@vercos.com
www.vercos.com

grandate (lombardy)

Museo del cavallo giocattolo Chicco
via Tornese 10
22070 Grandate (CO)
phone +39 031.382912
infomuseo@artsana.it
www.museodelcavallogiocattolo.it

grazzano visconti (emilia–romagna)

Tourist Information
piazza Cavalli
29100 Piacenza
phone +39 0523.329324
iat@comune.piacenza.it

Hotel City
via Emilia Parmense 154

29100 Piacenza
phone +39 0523.579752
info@hotelcitypc.it

Ristorante Antica Osteria del Teatro
via Verdi 16
29100 Piacenza
phone +39 0523.323777
menu@anticaosteriadelteatro.it
www.anticaosteriadelteatro.it

Ristorante Vecchia Piacenza
via San Bernardo 1
29100 Piacenza
phone +39 0523.305462
www.ristorantevecchiapiacenza.it

Istituzione Giuseppe Visconti di Modrone
piazza Gian Galeazzo Visconti 8
Grazzano Visconti
29020 Vigolzone (PC)
phone +39 0523.870205

grignasco (piedmont)

Filatura di Grignasco
via Dante Alighieri 2
28075 Grignasco (NO)
phone +39 0163.4101
www.filgri.it

grosseto (tuscany)

Tourist Information
viale Monterosa 206
58100 Grosseto
phone +39 0564.462611
info@lamaremma.info

Grand Hotel Bastiani
piazza Gioberti 64
58100 Grosseto
phone +39 0584.20047
info@hotelbastiani.com

Ristorante Canapone
piazza Dante 3
58100 Grosseto
phone +39 0564.24546

Il Riccio
via Damiano Chiesa 36
58100 Grosseto
phone +39 0564.4494796

grottaglie (puglia)

Tourist Information
corso Umberto I, 113
74100 Taranto
phone +39 099.4532392
infoaptta@libero.it

Castello Episcopio
74023 Grottaglie (TA)
phone +39 099.5623866
phone +39 800.545333

Hotel Europa
via Roma 2
74100 Taranto
phone +39 099.4525994
info@hoteleuropaonline.it

Ristorante Gesù Cristo
via C. Battisti 10
74100 Taranto
phone +39 099.7772589

Museo della ceramica
Castello Episcopio
74023 Grottaglie (TA)
phone +39 099.5620222

Museo didattico delle maioliche
via Jacopo della Quercia
74023 Grottaglie (TA)
phone +39 099.5666521

Ceramiche Giuseppe Fasano
via F. Crispi 27
74023 Grottaglie (TA)
phone/fax +39 099.5661640
www.giuseppefasano.it

Le ceramiche di Trani Anna
via Crispi 81
74023 Grottaglie (TA)
phone +39 099.5628154
ceramichetrani@libero.it

Ceramica Puparieddu
via Caravaggio 14
74023 Grottaglie (TA)
phone +39 099.5622890
pupariedduceramica@libero.it

Cooperativa Modulo Zero Sud
via Ionio 4
74023 Grottaglie (TA)
phone +39 0995.622951

La Bottega dei Fischietti
via Crispi 55
74023 Grottaglie (TA)
phone +39 0995.661033

Studio d'Arte Ligorio
via Crispi 46
74023 Grottaglie (TA)
phone +39 0995.623199

Vaserie Artistiche Mediterranee
via Fogazaro 10
74023 Grottaglie (TA)
phone +39 0995.612051

**La Ceramica "Vincenzo Del Monaco"
di Giuseppe Del Monaco**
Via S. Sofia 2/4
74023 Grottaglie (TA)
phone +39 99.5661023
fax +39 99.5667522
www.ceramistidigrottaglie.it/delmonaco

guardea (umbria)

La Bottega del Ferro
via dell'Arcale 2A
05025 Guardea (TR)
phone +39 0744.903721

Varasi Pascuccio
via Luzzi
05025 Guardea (TR)
phone +39 0744.903649

guardiagrele (abruzzo)

Ristorante Villa Maiella
via Sette Dolori 30
66016 Guardiagrele (CH)
phone +39 0871.809362
info@villamaiella.it

Domenico di Sciascio
via Maruccina
66016 Guardiagrele (CH)
phone +39 0872.83011

Auriti
via Campo Sportivo 52
66016 Guardiagrele (CH)
phone +39 0871.800595

gubbio (umbria)

Tourist Information
piazza Oderisi 6
06024 Gubbio (PG)
phone +39 075.9220693
info@iat.gubbio.pg.it

Hotel Relais Ducale
via Galeotti 19
06024 Gubbio (PG)
phone +39 0759.220157

Ristorante Federico da Montefeltro
via della Repubblica 35
06024 Gubbio (PG)
phone +39 0759.273949

Museo comunale
Palazzo dei Consoli
piazza Grande
06024 Gubbio (PG)
phone +39 0759.274298
www.comune.gubbio.pg.it/musei

Ceramiche da Mastro Giorgio
via Tifernate 10
06024 Gubbio (PG)
phone +39 0759.273616

La fornace del bucchero
via Federico da Montefeltro 10
06024 Gubbio (PG)
phone +39 075.9277216
info@bucchero.it
www.bucchero.it

Artigianato Ferro Artistico
via Baldassini 22
06024 Gubbio (PG)
phone +39 0759.273079

Medioevo
Zona industriale Ponte d'Assi
06024 Gubbio (PG)
phone +39 0759.221396

Ceramica Aldo Fumanti
località Zappacenere
06024 Gubbio (PG)
phone +39 0759.276413

Ceramica Grilli
via della Zecca 21
06024 Gubbio (PG)
phone +39 0759.275120

Rampini ceramiche
via Leonardo da Vinci 94
06024 Gubbio (PG)
phone +39 0759.272963

guidonia (lazio)

Laura Biagiotti Outlet
via Marco Simone 82
00012 Guidonia (RM)
phone +39 0774.401311
info@laurabiagiotti.it
www.laurabiagiotti.it

guspini (sardinia)

Coltelleria artigianale Guspinese
Zona Artigianale, SS 126 km 85
09036 Guspini (CA)
phone +39 347.6186893
spiga.efisio@tiscali.it
www.coltellosardo.com

imola (emilia—romagna)

Hotel Donatello Imola
via Rossini 25
40026 Imola (BO)
phone +39 0542.680800
info@imolahophoneit

Ristorante San Domenico
via Sacchi 1
40026 Imola (BO)
phone +39 0542.29000
sandomenico@sandomenico.it

La Fenice
via Baviera Maghinardo 17
40026 Imola (BO)
phone +39 0542.33494

Controluce
vicolo Troni 2
40026 Imola (BO)
phone +39 0542.27719

**Museo delle armi e delle maioliche
della Rocca Sforzesca**
p.le G. dalle Bande Nere
40026 Imola (BO)
phone +39 0542.602609
www.comune.imola.bo.it/museicomunali/

Museo della cooperativa ceramica di Imola
via V. Veneto 3
40026 Imola (BO)
phone +39 0542.601601
www.imolaceramica.it

impruneta (tuscany)

Tourist Information
via Mazzini 1
50023 Impruneta (FI)
phone +39 055.2313729

Relais Villa Olmo
via Impruneta 19
50023 Impruneta (FI)
phone +39 055.2311311
florence.chianti@dada.it

Cotto Chiti
via Chiantigiana 169
50023 Impruneta (FI)
phone +39 055.207030

isernia (molise)

Tourist Information
via Farinacci 9
86170 Isernia
phone +39 0865.3992

Grand Hotel Europa
SS per Campobasso
86170 Isernia
phone +39 0865.411450
grandhot@tin.it

Castiello
via Testa 49
86170 Isernia
phone +39 086.53994

Sassi Buccigrossi
corso Risorgimento 75
86170 Isernia
phone +39 086.5415142

islands of sicily (sicily)

Tourist Information
piazza Saturno
91100 Trapani
phone +39 0923.29000
apttp@maill.cinet.it
corso Vittorio Emanuele 202
98055 Lipari (ME)
phone +39 090.9880095
aasteolie@netnet.it
infoaast@netnet.it
www.netnet.it/aasteolie

Hotel Ericusa
località Berciato
via Regina Elena
98050 Alicudi (ME)
phone +39 090.9889902

Hotel Villa Meligunis
via Marte 7
98055 Lipari (ME)
phone +39 090.9812426
info@villameligunis.it
www.villameligunis.it

Hotel Quartara
via San Pietro 15
98050 Panarea (ME)
phone +39 090.983027
info@quartarahophonecom

Ristorante Da Modesta
via San Pietro
98050 Panarea (ME)
phone +39 090.983306

Hotel Bellavista
località Santa Marina Salina
via Risorgimento 242
98050 Leni-Isola di Salina (ME)
phone +39 090.9843009

Hotel Signum
via Scalo 15
98050 Malfa-Isola di Salina (ME)
phone +39 090.9844375
salina@hotelsignum.it

La Sirenetta Park Hotel
località Ficogrande
via Marina 33
98050 Stromboli (ME)
phone +39 090.986025
info@lasirenetta.it

Hotel Les Sables Noir
località Porto di Ponente
98050 Vulcano (ME)
phone +39 090.9850
reservation.lsn@framonhotels.it

Ristorante E Pulera
via Isabella Conti Vainicher
98055 Lipari (ME)
phone +39 090.9811158
filippino@filippino.it

Ristorante Da Franco
via Belvedere 8
98050 Santa Marina di Salina (ME)
phone +39 090.9843287
info@ristorantedafranco.com

Ristorante Porto Bello
via Bianchi 1
98050 Santa Marina di Salina (ME)
phone +39 090.9843125
teonadari@hotmail.com

Ristorante Punta Lena
località Ficogrande
via Marina
98050 Stromboli (ME)
phone +39 090.986204

Trattoria A' Tana
via Porto
98050 Filicudi (ME)
phone +39 090.9889089

Hotel Grotta Azzurra
contrada S. Ferlicchio
90010 Ustica (PA)
phone +39 0918.449048

Ristorante La Nicchia
contrada Scauri Basso
91017 Pantelleria (TP)
phone +39 0923.916342

lamoli (marche)

Museo dei colori naturali
via dell'Abbazia 7
località Lamoli
61049 Borgo Pace (PS)
oasi@info-net.it
www.museipartecipati.net

lanciano (abruzzo)

Mercantico d'Abruzzo
(every second sunday of the month)
corso Trento e Trieste
66034 Lanciano (CH)
phone +39 085.7672513

l'aquila (abruzzo)

Tourist Information
piazza S. Maria di Paganica 5
67100 L'Aquila
phone +39 0862.410808
presidio.aquila@abruzzoturismo.it
via XX Settembre 8
67100 L'Aquila
phone +39 0862.22306
iat.aquila@abruzzoturismo.it
www.regione.abruzzo.it

Albergo Diffuso
67020 Santo Stefano di Sessanio (AQ)
phone +39 0862.8999116
info@sextantio.it
www.sextantio.it

Hotel Parco delle Rose
località Paganica SS 17 bis
67016 L'Aquila
phone +39 0862.680128
hotelpdr@inwind.it

Hotel Duomo
via Dragonetti 10
67100 L'Aquila
phone +39 0862.410893

Ristorante Elodia
località Camarda
SS 17 bis del Gran Sasso 37
67010 L'Aquila
phone +39 0862.606219
elodia@tin.it

Ristorante La Grotta di Aligi
viale Rendina 2
67100 L'Aquila
phone +39 0862.65260

Selleria De Santis
Via Cembalo dei Colantonii, 9
67100 L'Aquila
phone +39 0862.413425
web.tiscali.it/selleria_desantis

Terre d'Abruzzo
via de Navelli 3A
67100 L'Aquila
phone +39 0862.65872

Le mani d'oro
corso V. Emanuele 23
67100 L'Aquila
phone +39 0862.410971

larciano (tuscany)

Francesco Tani fiori secchi
via Marconi 964
51036 Larciano (PT)
phone +39 0573.81276

la spezia (liguria)

Tourist Information
viale Mazzini 45
19100 La Spezia
phone +39 0187.770900
info@aptcinqueterre.sp.it

Hotel Ghironi
via Tino 62
19100 La Spezia
phone +39 0187.504141

Ristorante Parodi
viale Amendola 210
19100 La Spezia
phone +39 0187.715777

Cantieri Baglietto
via S. Bartolomeo 414
19138 La Spezia
phone +39 0187.59831
www.baglietto.com

Museo tecnico navale
viale Amendola 1
19100 La Spezia
phone +39 0187.783016
www.museotecniconavale.it

Museo del sigillo
Palazzina delle Arti
Via Prione 236
19121 La Spezia
phone +39 0187.778544
www.castagna.it/museodelsigillo/

Ferretti S.p.A.
Divisione Ferretti Yachts
Via Ansaldo, 9/B
Zona Industriale Villa Selva
47100 Forlì
phone +39 0543.474411
fax +39 0543.782410
info@ferretti-yachts.com
www.ferretti-yachts.com

la valle (trentino–alto adige)

Tessitura artistica Nagler
Zona artigianale Pederoa 13
39030 La Valle /Wengen (BZ)
phone +39 0471.843188

laveno (lombardy)

Museo della ceramica
località Cerro di Laveno
Lungolago Perabò 5
phone +39 0332.666530

lecce (puglia)

Tourist Information
corso Vittorio Emanuele 24
73100 Lecce
phone +39 0832.248092
aptlecce@pugliaturismo.com
www.pugliaturismo.com
via Monte San Michele 20
phone +39 0832.2314117
www.puglia.it

Hotel Patria Palace
piazzetta G. Riccardi 13
73100 Lecce
phone +39 0832.245111
info@patriapalacelecce.com

Hotel Delle Palme
via di Leuca 90
73100 Lecce
phone +39 0832.347171
hdellepalme@tiscalinet.it

Hotel President
via Salandra 6
73100 Lecce
phone +39 0832.436111
www.hotelpresidentlecce.it

Trattoria Osteria degli Spiriti
via Battisti 14
73100 Lecce
phone +39 0832.246274
info@osteriadelispiriti.it

Trattoria Cucina Casareccia (Le Zie)
via Col. A. Costadura 19
73100 Lecce
phone +39 0832.245178

Artefare
corso V. Emanuele 14
73100 Lecce
www.artefare.it

Galleria de Tommasi
via dei Mocenigo 7
73100 Lecce
phone +39 0832.242684
www.detommasi.com

Eugenio Galli
Corte dei Castromediano 8
73100 Lecce
phone +39 0832.303870

Arte della cartapesta
via Cerrate Casale
73100 Lecce
phone +39 0832.304488

Arredi d'arte in pietra
via Umberto 125
73100 Lecce
phone +39 0832.301260
infoline@arrediinpietra.it

legnano (lombardy)

Dolce & Gabbana
via Rossini 72
20025 Legnano (MI)
phone +39 0331.545888
www.dolcegabbana.it

leinì (piedmont)

Ditta Verde
via Carlo Alberto 64
10040 Leinì (TO)
phone +39 011.9988016

lerma (piedmont)

Museo storico dell'oro italiano
piazza Genova 2,
15070 Lerma (AL)
phone +39 0143.882289
www.oromuseo.com

259

lissone (lombardy)

Damber Italia
viale Repubblica 67
20035 Lissone (MI)
phone +39 0394.81085

lipari (sicily)

L'Ossidiana
via Porto Levante Vulcano
98055 Lipari (ME)
phone +39 090.9852215

Grazia Famularo
via V. Emanuele 80
98055 Lipari (ME)
phone +39 090.9812491

Bartolo Lauria Ceramiche
via Melignues 1
98055 Lipari (ME)
phone +39 090.9812847

Stefano Panza
via Roma 1
98055 Lipari (ME)
phone +39 090.9812021

lodi (lombardy)

Ceramica artistica Vecchia Lodi
via S. Fereolo 9
26900 Lodi (LO)
phone +39 0371.32575
www.calvecchialodi.it

Il Vasaio
via Marsala 45
26900 Lodi (LO)
phone +39 0371.422177

longobucco (calabria)

Mario Celestino
via Monaci 14
87066 Longobucco (CS)
phone +39 0983.371048

lorsica (liguria)

De Martini Damaschi
via Scaletta 78
16045 Lorsica (GE)
phone +39 0185.977302

lucca (tuscany)

Tourist Information
piazza Santa Maria 35
55100 Lucca
phone +39 0583.919931
info@lucca.turismo.it
www.lucca.turismo.toscana.it

Hotel Ilaria e Residenza dell'Alba
via del Fosso 26
55100 Lucca
phone +39 0583.47615
info@hotelilaria.com

Hotel Villa Agnese
viale A. Marti 177
55100 Lucca
phone +39 0583.467109
info@villagnese.it

Hotel Piccolo Puccini
via di Poggio 9
55100 Lucca
phone +39 058.355421

Locanda l'Elisa
frazione Massa Pisana - SS 12r
via Nuova per Pisa
55050 Massa Pisana (LU)
phone +39 0583.379737
info@locandaelisa.it

Ristorante La Mora
località Ponte a Moriano
via Sesto di Moriano 1748
55029 Sesto di Moriano (LU)
phone +39 0583.406402
info@ristorantelamora.it
www.ristorantelamora.it

Ristorante La Buca di Sant'Antonio
via della Cervia 1/5
55100 Lucca
phone +39 0583.55881
la.buca@lunet.it

**Ristorante Osteria
Al Ritrovo del Platano**
località Ponte di Campia
55027 Gallicano (LU)
phone +39 0583.766142

Antica Farmacia Massagli
Piazza S. Michele 36
55100 Lucca
phone +39 0583.496067

Club Amici del Toscano
via del Casale di S. Nicola 53
00123 Roma
phone +39 800853335
www.amicidellatoscana.it

Michel Alain Eggimann
via Anfiteatri 23
55100 Lucca
phone +39 0583.955813

Mercato Antiquariato
(every fourth week-end of the month)
piazza S. Martino
55100 Lucca

Antica Farmacia Massagli
Piazza S. Michele 36
55100 Lucca
phone +39 0583.496067

Litografia Angeli
via della Zecca 55
55100 Lucca
phone +39 0583.467337

Massimo Bonino
via Fatinelli 7
55100 Lucca
phone +39 0583.494388

Nadia Caselli
c/o Museo di Palazzo Mansi
via Galli Tassi 43
55100 Lucca
phone +39 0583.962244

macerata (marche)

Tourist Information
piazza della Libertà 12
62100 Macerata
phone +39 0733.234807
iat.macerata@regione.marche.it

Hotel Claudiani
vicolo Ulissi 8
62100 Macerata
phone +39 0733.261400
info@hotelclaudiani.it

Ristorante Le Case
Contrada Mozzavinci 16
62100 Macerata
phone +39 0733.231897
ristorantelecase@tin.it

Orfeo Borgani
via Ancona 6
62100 Macerata
phone +39 0733.237585

mandatoriccio (calabria)

Calabria Pipe
via Nazionale 119
87060 Mandatoriccio (CS)
phone +39 098.3994363

mandello del lario (lombardy)

Museo Guzzi
via E. Parodi 57
23826 Mandello del Lario (LC)
phone +39 0341.709111
www.motoguzzi.it

maniago (friuli–venezia giulia)

Consorzio Coltellinai
piazza Italia 11
33085 Maniago (PN)
phone +39 0427.71744
info@mkm.it
www.mkm.it

AE Coltellerie
via Cellina 17
33085 Maniago (PN)
phone +39 042.771029
www.aecolt.it

Museo dell'arte fabbrile
via Battiferri 1
33085 Maniago (PN)
phone +39 0427.733296

Lion Steel
via dei Fabbri 32
33085 Maniago (PN)
phone +39 0427.71984
www.lionsteel.it

mantova (lombardy)

Tourist Information
piazza A. Mantegna 6
46100 Mantova
phone +39 0376.328253
aptmantova@iol.it
www.turismo.mantova.it

Hotel San Lorenzo
piazza Concordia 14
46100 Mantova
phone +39 0376.220500
www.hotelsanlorenzo.it

Ristorante Aquila Nigra
vicolo Bonacolsi 4
46100 Mantova
phone +39 0376.327180
informazioni@aquilanigra.it

Fer Giochi
via Marmirolo 8
46100 Mantova
phone +39 0376.391237

manzano (friuli–venezia giulia)

Albergo Castello di Spessa
via Spessa 1
34070 Capriva del Friuli (GO)
phone +39 0481.808124
info@castellospessa.com
www.castellospessa.com

Sedialand
via Udine 26
33044 Manzano (GO)
phone +39 0432.745547
sedialand.ud@crabo.it
www.crabo.it

maranello (emilia–romagna)

Planet Hotel
via Verga 22
41053 Maranello (MO)
phone +39 0536.946782
planethotel@planethophoneorg

La Locanda del Mulino
via Nuova Estense 3430
41053 Maranello (MO)
phone +39 0536. 948895

Galleria Ferrari
via Dino Ferrari 43
41053 Maranello (MO)
phone +39 053.6949713
www.ferrari.com

marcon (veneto)

La Murrina
via Alta 28
30020 Marcon (VE)
phone +39 041.5951140

maremma (tuscany)

Tourist Information
viale Monterosa 206

58100 Grosseto
phone +39 0564.462611
info@lamaremma.info
www.grosseto.turismo.toscana.it

Bastiani Grand Hotel
piazza Gioberti 64
58100 Grosseto
phone +39 0564.20047
info@hotelbastiani.com
www.hotelbastiani.com

Hotel della Fortezza
piazza Cairoli
58018 Sorano (GR)
phone +39 0564 632010
fortezzahotel@tin.it

Hotel Granduca
via Senese 170
58100 Grosseto
phone +39 0564.453833
info@hotelgranduca.com

Agriturismo Pian dei Casali
località Pianetti
58050 Montemerano (GR)
phone +39 0564.602625
info@piandeicasali.it
www.piandeicasali.it

Ristorante Canapone
piazza Dante 3
58100 Grosseto
phone +39 0564.24546

Ristorante Lorena
via Mameli 23
58100 Grosseto
phone +39 0564.22695

Ristorante Terzo Cerchio
piazza Castello 2
58040 Istia d'Ombrone (GR)
phone +39 0564.409235
terzocerchio@virgilio.it

Ristorante Da Caino
via Canonica 3
58050 Montemerano (GR)
phone +39 0564.602817
caino@dacaino.it

Antica Sartoria di Maremma
via del Colle
località Pancole
58050 Scansano (GR)
phone +39 0564.503029
confbrema@interfree.it
www.confezionibrema.com

Maremma Antiquaria Mercato
(every third sunday of the month)
Lungomare
58046 Marina di Grosseto (GR)
phone +39 0572.478269

Marco Bedini
viale XX Settembre 300 bis
Marina di Carrara (MS)
phone +39 0585.856260

Hotel Due Mori
corso Mazzini 73
36063 Marostica (VI)
phone +39 0424.471777
info@duemori.com

Ristorante La Rosina
via Marchetti 4
località Valle San Floriano
36063 Marostica (VI)
phone +39 0424.470360

Alla Vecia Botega
via Vajenti 23
36063 Marostica (VI)
phone +39 0424.73674

Museo del cappello di paglia
piazza Castello Inferiore 1
36063 Marostica (VI)
phone +39 0424.479120

Ecomuseo della paglia
via Sisemo 1
36060 Crosara di Marostica (VI)
phone +39 0424.72357

Spaccio Belfe
via Ing. Festa/corso della Ceramica 76
36063 Marostica (VI)
phone +39 0424.470709
www.belfe.it

Mercatino dell'Antiquariato
(every first sunday of the month)
piazza del Castello Inferiore
36063 Marostica (VI)
phone +39 0424.72127

Ceramica ai Due Tosin
via Montello 52
36063 Marostica (VI)
phone +39 0424.780619

Ceramiche Porcellane Flavia
via Marsan
36063 Marostica (VI)
phone +39 0424.77209

Soffieria Parise
via della Ceramica 18
36063 Marostica (VI)
phone +39 0424.75035

Outlet Diadora Invicta
via E. Fermi 1
31010 Maser (TV)
phone +39 423.950887
sport1@diadora.it
www.diadora.it
www.invicta.it

Tourist Information
via De Viti De Marco 9
75100 Matera
phone +39 0835.331983
info@aptbasilicata.it

Albergo Locanda di San Martino
via San Martino 22
75100 Matera
phone +39 0835.256600
info@locandadisanmartino.it
www.locandadisanmartino.it

Albergo La Casa di Lucio
via San Piero Caveoso 66
75100 Matera
phone +39 0835.312798
nfo@lacasadilucio.com
www.lacasadilucio.com

Sassi Hotel
via San Giovanni Vecchio 89
75100 Matera
phone +39 0835.331009
hotelsassi@virgilio.it

Hotel Del Campo
via Lucrezio ang. via Gravina
75100 Matera
phone +39 0835.388844
info@hoteldelcampo.com

**Ristorante Casino del Diavolo
da Francolino**
via La Martella 48
75100 Matera
phone +39 0835.261986
info@casinodeldiavolo.com
www.casinodeldiavolo.com

Ristorante Le Botteghe
piazza San Pietro Barisano 22
75100 Matera
phone +39 0835.344072

Pantasuglia Michele
via Stigliani 56
75100 Matera
phone +39 0835.262043

Festa Nicola
Rione Casalnuovo
75100 Matera
phone +39 0835.314139

Gurrado Pietro
via Duomo 5
75100 Matera
phone +39 0835.330447

Geppetto
Piazza del Sedile 19
75100 Matera
phone +39 0835 331857

Arte Decorativa
via S. Francesco 15
75100 Matera
phone +39 0835.334206

Tourist Information
corso della Libertà 45
39012 Merano (BZ)
phone +39 0473.272000
info@meraninfo.it

Grand Hotel Palace-Schloss Maur
via Cavour 2
39012 Merano (BZ)

phone +39 0473.271000
info@palace.it

Castel Rundegg Hotel
via Scena 2
39012 Merano (BZ)
phone +39 0473.234100
info@rundegg.com

Ristorante Sissi
via Galilei 44
39012 Merano (BZ)
phone +39 0473.231062

Runggaldier Gerta
via Portici 276
39012 Merano (BZ)
phone +39 0473.237454

Oberrauch-Zitt
via Portici 273
39012 Merano (BZ)
phone +39 0473.270464

Mercato di Merano
piazza della Stazione
39012 Merano (BZ)

Laguna Palace
viale Ancona 2
30172 Mestre Venezia
phone +39 041.8296111
info@lagunapalace.com

Ristorante Marco Polo
Via Forte Marghera 67
30173 Mestre Venezia
leonardi.marcopolo@libero.it

Benetton
piazza Ferretto 50
30172 Mestre Venezia
phone +39 041.971521
www.benetton.com

Tourist Information
via G. Marconi 1
20100 Milan
phone +39 02.72524301
aptinfo@libero.it
Stazione Centrale Galleria di Testa 1
phone +39 02.72524360
20100 Milan
turismo@regione.lombardia.it
www.inlombardia.it

Hotel Excelsior Gallia
piazza Duca d'Aosta 9
20124 Milan
phone +39 02.67851
sales@excelsiorgallia.it

Hotel The Gray
via San Raffaele 6
20100 Milan
phone +39 02.7208951
info.thegray@sinahotes.it

Hotel Regency
via Arimondi 12
20155 Milan
phone +39 02.39216021
regency@regency-milano.com

Ristorante Il Luogo di Aimo e Nadia
via Montecuccoli 6
20147 Milan
phone +39 02.416886
info@aimoenadia.com
www.aimoenadia.com

Trattoria Tagiura
via Tagiura 5
20100 Milan
phone +39 02.48950613

Ristorante Savini
Galleria V. Emanuele II
20121 Milan
phone +39 02.72003433
savini@thi.it

Antico ristorante Boeucc
piazza Belgioioso 2
20121 Milan
phone +39 02.76020224

Antica Trattoria della Pesa
viale Pasubio 10
20154 Milan
phone +39 02.6555741

Da Berti
via Algarotti 20
20100 Milan
phone +39 02.6694627

Dmagzine Outlet
via Montenapoleone 26
20121 Milan
phone +39 02.76006027
www.dmagazine.it

Emporio Isola
via Prina 11
20154 Milan
phone +39 02.3491040
www.emporioisola

Griffes Diffusion
via Rizzoli 9
20132 Milan
phone +39 02.26305305
www.griffesdiffusion.it

Visa
via Jenner 29
20159 Milan
phone +39 02.69311985

Krizia Industria
via Lago d'Iseo 2
20098 San Giuliano Milanese (MI)
phone +39 02.98284057
www.krizia.it

**Museo del giocattolo
e del bambino**
via Pitteri 56
20134 Milan
phone/fax +39 02.26411585
www.museodelgiocattolo.it

Grassi Vetrate Artistiche
via Piranesi 39
20137 Milan
phone +39 02.70102804
vetrateg@tin.it

Borsalino
via Verri ang. via Bigli
20100 Milan
phone +39 02.76398539
www.borsalino.com

Fendi
via Barozzi 3
20100 Milan
phone +39 02.764291
www.fendi.com

Ferragamo
via Borgospesso 2
20100 Milan
phone +39 02.77111441
www.ferragamo.it

Versace
via Manzoni 38
20100 Milan
phone +39 02.760931
www.versace.com

Valentino
via Montenapoleone 20
20100 Milan
phone +39 02.76006182
www.valentino.it

Pucci
Foro Bonaparte 71
20100 Milan
phone +39 02.86464818
www.emiliopucci.com

Emporio Armani
via Borgonuovo 11
20100 Milan
phone +39 02.723181
www.emporioarmani.com

Loro Piana
via Bigli 22
20100 Milan
phone +39 02.778021
www.loropiana.com

Albert Bijoux
via Adige 14
20100 Milan
phone +39 02.55011104
albertbijoux@infinito.it
www.paginegialle.it/albertbijoux

Il Borsino del Cordusio
(sunday morning: coins, stamps, medals)
via and Galleria Cordusio
20100 Milan
phone +39 02.725421

Arflex
corso Europa 11
20122 Milan
phone +39 02.76318162
www.arflex.it

Artemide
corso Monforte 19
20122 Milan
phone +39 02.76006930
monforte@artemide.com
www.artemide.it

Arzigozzoviglieria
Alzaia Naviglio Grande 8
20144 Milan
phone +39 02.58111567

Cassina
via Durini 16
20122 Milan
phone +39 02.76020745
www.cassina.it

Danese
via Canova 34
20145 Milan
phone +39 02.34537900
www.danesemilan.com

Fornace Curti
via Tobagi 8
20100 Milan
phone +39 02.8135049
www.fornacecurti.it

Marzona
Alzaia Naviglio Grande 4
20144 Milan
phone +39 335.7479318
info@marcellamarzona.it
www.marcellamarzona.it

Naviglio In
Alzaia Naviglio Grande 44
20144 Milan
phone +39 02.8375460
q_guille@hotmail.com

Poltronafrau
via P. Cossa 2
20122 Milan
phone +39 02.77807711
www.poltronafrau.it

Cappellini
via Santa Cecilia 4
20122 Milan
phone +39 02.76003889
s.cecilia@cappellini.it

Guzzini
via San Damiano 3
20122 Milan
phone +39 02.7621161
www.fratelliguzzini.com

Tisettanta
via Visconti di Modrone 12
20122 Milan
phone +39 02.794330

Fornasetti
Via Manzoni 45
20121 Milan
phone+39 02.6592341
fax +39 02.6592244
showroom@fornasetti.com
www.fornasetti.com

Franco Maria Ricci
via Durini, 19
20122 Milan
phone +39 02.798444
www.fmrspa.it

modena (emilia–romagna)

Tourist Information
via Scudari 12
41100 Modena
phone +39 059.206660
iatmo@comune.modena.it
www.comune.modena.it

Hotel Real Fini
via Emilia Est 441
41100 Modena
phone +39 059.2051530
booking@hrf.it

Hotel Canalgrande
corso Canalgrande 6
41100 Modena
phone +39 059.217160
info@canalgrandehophoneit

Ristorante Fini
rua Frati Minori 54
41100 Modena
phone +39 059.223314
ristorante.fini@hrf.it

Hosteria Giusti
vicolo Squallore 46
41100 Modena
phone +39 059.222533

Osteria Francescana
Via Stella 22
41100 Modena
phone +39 059.210118

moena (trentino–alto adige)

Tourist Information
via Manci 2
38100 Trento
phone +39 0461.983880
informazioni@apt.trento.it
www.apt.trento.it
piazza C. Battisti 33
38035 Moena (TN)
phone +39 0462.573122
infomoena@fassa.com

Hotel Adige
frazione Mattarello
via Pomeranos 2
38100 Trento
phone +39 0461.944545
adigehotel@cr-surfing.net

Hotel Buonconsiglio
via Romagnosi 16/18
38100 Trento
phone +39 0461.272888
hotelhb@tin.it
www.hotelbuonconsiglio.it

Hotel Maria
via dei Colli 7
38035 Moena (TN)
phone +39 0462.573265
info@hotelmaria.com

Ristorante Malga Panna
via Costalunga 56
località Sorte
38035 Moena (TN)
phone +39 0462.573489

Fabio Vettori
via R. Löwy 16/A
38035 Moena (TN)
phone/fax +39 0462.573327
fabio@fabiovettori.com
www.fabiovettori.com

mogoro (sardinia)

Cooperativa Tessitrici Su Trobasciu
via Antonio Gramsci, 1
Mogoro (OR)
phone +39 0783.990581
fax +39 0783.997177
www.sutrobasciu.com
mail@sutrobasciu.com

monastier (veneto)

Sartorial Homme
via Vallio 15
31050 Monastier (TV)
phone +39 0422.898068
info@sartorialhomme.com
www.sartorialhomme.com

monsummano terme (tuscany)

Hotel Crotta Giusti Terme
via Crotta Giusti 1411
51015 Monsummano Terme (PT)
phone +39 0572.90711
info@crottagiustispa.com

Nuova T4 Pelletterie
via C. Battisti 989/c
51015 Monsummano Terme (PT)
phone +39 0572.82609

Calzaturificio Parlanti
via Barni 80
51015 Monsummano Terme (PT)
phone +39 0572.924617

Calzaturificio Lunik
via Francesca 669
51015 Monsummano Terme (PT)
phone +39 0572.51507

Studio Chironi
via Buozzi 34
51015 Monsummano Terme (PT)
phone +39 0572.952222

montappone (marche)

Chaday Complit
via S. Giorgio 2
63020 Montappone (AP)
phone +39 0734.760712

montebelluna (veneto)

Hotel Bellavista
via Zuccareda 20
località Mercato Vecchio
31044 Montebelluna (TV)
phone +39 0423.301031
infobellavista@tin.it

Ristorante Al Tiglio d'oro
località Mercato Vecchio
31044 Montebelluna (TV)
phone +39 0423.22419

Sport Outlet
via Feltrina Sud 160
31044 Montebelluna (TV)
phone +39 0423.303667
sportoutlet@libero.it

Fondazione museo dello scarpone e della calzatura sportiva
Villa Binetti, vicolo Zuccareda 5
31044 Montebelluna (TV)
phone +39 0423.303282
www.museoscarpone.it

Tecnica
Via Fante D'Italia 56
31040 Giavera del Montello (TV)
phone + 39 0422.8841
fax + 39 0422.775178
info@tecnica.it
www.tecnica.it

montecatini terme (tuscany)

Tourist Information
viale Verdi 66
51016 Montecatini (PT)
phone/fax +39 0572.772244
info@montecatini.turismo.toscana.it

Grand Hotel e La Pace
via della Torretta 1
51016 Montecatini (PT)
phone +39 0572.9240
info@grandhotellapace.it

Ristorante San Francisco
corso Roma 112
51016 Montecatini (PT)
phone +39 0572.79632
info@sanfrancisco.it

Legatoria del Bino
via Puglie 24
51016 Montecatini (PT)
phone +39 0572.74538

montegalda (veneto)

Museo delle campane
Villa Fogazzaro-Colbachini
via Fogazzaro 3
36047 Montegalda (VI)
phone +39 0444.737526
www.fonderiacolbachini.it

montegranaro (marche)

Borsettificio Lara San Paul
contrada Vallone 119
63014 Montegranaro (AP)
phone +39 0734.889298
www.larasnc.com

Marilungo
via Manzoni 51
63014 Montegranaro (AP)
phone +39 0734.891570
www.marilungo.it

RDB Dino Bigioni
via Veregrense 310
63014 Montegranaro (AP)
phone +39 0734.891259

Calzaturificio Spring
via F. Turati 4
63014 Montegranaro (AP)
phone +39 0734.890584
www.mariobruni.it

Zeis Escelsa
via Elpidiense Sud 195
63014 Montegranaro (AP)
phone +39 0734.8914354
www.zesexcelsa.it

monza (lombardy)

Hotel de la Ville
viale Regina Margherita 15
20052 Monza (MI)
phone +39 039.382581
info@hoteldelaville.com

Ristorante Derby Grill
viale Regina Margherita 15
20052 Monza (MI)
phone +39 039.382581

Anna Venturi
via Taccona 41B
20052 Monza (MI)
phone +39 039.741611
www.annaventuri.it

morbegno (lombardy)

Osteria del Crotto
via Pedemontana 22
23017 Morbegno (SO)
phone +39 0342.614800
info@osteriadelcrotto.it

Ruffoni
via Rivalta 45
23017 Morbegno (SO)
phone +39 0342.610806
members.xoom.it/ruffoni

Artistica
via Artigianato 11
23017 Morbegno (SO)
phone +39 0342.614673

murano (veneto)

Tourist Information
Stazione Santa Lucia
30121 Venice
phone +39 041.5298711
info@turismovenezia.it
Aeroporto Marco Polo, Tessera
phone +39 041.2606111

Ristorante Busa alla Torre
piazza S. Stefano 3
30141 Murano (VE)
phone +39 041.739662

Promovetro
30141 Murano (VE)
phone +39 041.5275074
www.promovetro.com

Museo dell'arte vetraria
Fondamenta Giustinian 8
30141 Murano (VE)
phone/fax +39 041.739586
www.comune.venezia.it/museicivici

La Murrina
phone +39 800.307101
www.lamurrina.com

Arte Vetraria Muranese
Fondamenta Vetrai 33
30141 Murano (VE)
phone +39 041.739173

Gambaro & Poggi
calle Vivarini 6
30141 Murano (VE)
phone +39 041.736576
www.gambaroepoggiglass.com

Vetreria Artistica Ballarin
Campo S. Bernardo 18
30141 Murano (VE)
phone +39 041.736703

Galliano Ferro
Fondamenta Vetrai 43
30141 Murano (VE)
phone +39 041.739477
www.gallianoferro.it

Luigi Fornasier
calle del Paradiso 14
30141 Murano, Venice
phone +39 041.736176
www.fornasier.it

Nason & Moretti
calle Dietro gli Orti 12
30141 Murano (VE)
phone +39 041.739020
www.nasonmoretti.it

Vetri d'arte Striulli
fondamenta S. Giovanni dei Battuti 10
30141 Murano (VE)
phone +39 041.736263
www.striullivetriarte.it

Vetreria Artistica Seguso
fondamenta Serenella 3
30141 Murano (VE)
phone +39 041.739005
seguso@seguso.it
www.seguso.it

Aureliano Toso
Fondamenta Radi 24
30141 Murano (VE)
phone +39 041.739388
fax +39 041.739386
info@auretoso.it
www.auretoso.it

CAM vetri d'arte srl
Piazzale Colonna 1/B
30141 Murano (VE)
phone +39 041.739944
fax +39 041.739882
www.cam-murano.com

Barbini Alfredo
Fondamenta Venier 44
30141 Murano (VE)
phone +39 041.739270
fax +39 041.739265
e-mail info@barbinimurano.com
www.barbinimurano.com

Fratelli Toso
Fondamenta Colleoni 7
30141 Murano (VE)
phone +39 041.739060
fax +39 041.739688
fratelli.toso@iol.it
www.fratellitoso.it

Signoretto Lampadari
Fondamenta da mula 148
30141 Murano (VE)
phone/fax +39 041.5274593
www.signorettolampadari.com

Venini
Fondamenta Vetrai 50
30141 Murano (VE)
phone +39 041.2737211
fax +39 041.2737223
venini@venini.it
www.venini.it

naples (campania)

Tourist Information
via San Carlo 9
80100 Naples
phone +39 081.402394
info@inaples.it
piazza del Gesù Nuovo 7
80100 Naples
phone +39 081.5223328
Stazione Margellina
80100 Naples
phone +39 081.7612102

Grand Hotel Vesuvio
via Partenope 45
80121 Naples
phone +39 081.7640044
info@vesuvio.it
www.vesuvio.it

Hotel San Francesco al Monte
corso Vittorio Emanuele 328
80135 Naples
phone +39 081.4239111
info@hotelsanfrancesco.it

Ristorante Ciro a Santa Brigida
via Santa Brigida 73
80132 Naples

phone +39 081.5524072
www.cirosantabrigida.it

**Ristorante Pizzeria
L'Europeo di Mattozzi**
via Campodisola 4
80133 Naples
phone +39 081.5521323

Ristorante Al Poeta
piazza S. Di Giacomo 134
80123 Naples
phone +39 081.5756936

Fratelli Sinno
largo Barone Marinelli 4
80134 Naples
phone/fax +39 081.417973
ciro.cinno@libero.it

Ulderico Pinfildi
via Camaldolilli 50
80100 Naples
phone +39 081.417973

Il mondo della ceramica
corso Secondigliano 562G
80144 Naples
phone +39 081.5430378

Ranieri pietra lavica
via Diaz 8
80100 Naples
phone +39 081.8284992
www.ranieripietralavica.it

Raffaele Cacace
via S. Domenico Maggiore 9
80100 Naples
phone +39 081.5515983

Ospedale delle bambole dal 1800
via S. Biagio dei Librai 81
80138 Naples
www.ospedaledellebambole.it

Museo del corallo
Angiporto Galleria Umberto I
piazzetta M. Serao 19
80132 Naples
napoli@ascione.com
www.ascione.com

Fiera Antiquaria Napoletana
(every third week-end of the month)
via Dorhn
80100 Naples
phone +39 081.7612541

Marinella
Via Riviera di Chiaia 287A
80100 Naples
phone +39 081.2451182
www.marinellanapoli.it

Consorzio Antico Borgo Orefici
phone +39 081.5523708
www.borgoorefici.it

Tina Canzano
via Sciaoia 17
80100 Naples
phone +39 081.202340

Kika
via Scialoia 20
80100 Naples
phone +39 081.5538938

L'arte del presepio
via dei Tribunali 304
80100 Naples
phone +39 081.447279

Arte presepiale
via Tribunali 86
80100 Naples
phone +39 081.4420792

La Scarabattola
Via Tribunali 50
80138 Naples
phone/fax +39 081.291735
info@lascarabattola.it
www.lascarabattola.it

Fratelli Capuano
via S. Gregorio Armeno 23
80100 Naples
phone +39 081.5519651

Officina della Tammorra
Vico San Severino, 14
80143 Naples
phone +39 081.4206024
info@officinadellatammorra.com
www.officinadellatammorra.com

Omega
via Stella 12
80100 Naples
phone +39 081.299041
omegant@tin.it
www.omegasrl.com

Lucio Monti
via B. Cellini 3
80133 Naples
phone +39 081.204619
info@luciomontioriegioie.it
www.luciomontioriegioie.it

nichelino (piedmont)

Museo di storia, arte e ammobiliamento
Palazzina di caccia
località Stupinigi
piazza Principe Amedeo 7
10042 Nichelino (TO)
phone +39 011.3581220
www.mauriziano.it/stupinigi/stupini.htm

nizza monferrato (piedmont)

Metalart
corso Acqui 150
14049 Nizza Monferrato (AT)
phone +39 0141.721771

novara (piedmont)

Tourist Information
Baluardo Quintino Sella 40
28100 Novara
phone +39 0321.394059
novaratl@tin.it

Hotel Italia
via P. Solaroli 8
28100 Novara
phone +39 0321.399316
italia@panciolihotels.it

Ristorante Tantris
località Vignale Nord
28100 Novara
phone +39 0321.657343
tantris.ristorante@starnova.it

Museo dell'università dei calzolai
viale Ferrucci 23
28100 Novara

nove (veneto)

Ceramiche Alessi
via Brenta 2
36055 Nove (VI)
phone +39 0424.590031
www.alessiceramiche.com

Ceramiche Rita dal Prà
via Munari 102
36055 Nove (VI)
phone +39 0424.590001

Ceramiche Barettoni
via Molini7
35042 Este (PD)
phone +39 0429.590013
barettonigiuliana+@libero.it
www.barettoni.it

Museo civico della ceramica
piazza de Fabris 5
36055 Nove (VI)
phone/fax +39 0424.829807
www.comune.nove.vi.it

Collezione Cecchetto
via Munari 2
36055 Nove (VI)
phone +39 0424.590015

La ceramica VBC
via Molini 45
36055 Nove (VI)
phone +39 0424.590026

Ceramiche Rigoni
via Molini 46
36055 Nove (VI)
phone +39 0424.590303

olbia (sardinia)

Tourist Information
Apt Olbia
via Castello Piro 1
07026 Olbia (SS)
phone +39 0789.21453
aastol@regionesrdegna.it

Cerasarda
07026 Olbia (SS)
SS per Palau Km. 2,800
phone +39 0789.50032
fax +39 0789.50421
info@cerasarda.it
www.cerasarda.it

Hotel Cavour
via Cavour 22
07026 Olbia (SS)
phone +39 0789.204033
hotelcavour@tiscalinet.it
www.cavourhotel.it

Stefania
località Pittulongu
07026 Olbia (SS)
phone +39 0789.39027
hotel.stefania@tiscalinet.it

Ristorante Gallura
corso Umberto 145
07026 Olbia (SS)
phone +39 0789.24648

ome (lombardy)

Ristorante Villa Carpino
via Maglio 15
25050 Ome (BS)
phone +39 030.652114

Maglio Averoldi
via Maglio 51
25050 Ome (BS)
phone +39 030.8912493

ora (trentino–alto adige)

Hotel Amadeus
via Capitello 23
39040 Ora (BZ)
phone +39 0471.810053
office@hotel-amadeus.it

Sigrid Pernter
via dei Campi 4
39040 Ora (BZ)
phone +39 0471.810286

oristano (sardinia)

Tourist Information
piazza Eleonora 19
09170 Oristano
phone +39 0783.36831
enturismo.oristano@tiscalinet.it

Hotel Mistral Due
via XX Settembre 34
09170 Oristano
phone +39 0783.210389
hmistral@tiscali.it

Ristorante Cocco & Dessì
via Tirso 31
09170 Oristano
phone +39 0783.300720
coccoedessi@tiscalinet.it

Ristorante Il Faro
via Bellini 25
09170 Oristano
phone +39 0783.70002
info@ristoranteilfaro.net

ortisei (trentino–alto adige)

Tourist Information
strada Rezia 1
39046 Ortisei (BZ)
phone +39 0471.796513
ortisei@valgardena.it

Hotel La Perla
via Digon 8
39046 Ortisei (BZ)
phone +39 0471.796421
www.laperlahophoneinfo

Ristorante Tubladel
località Trebinger 22
39046 Ortisei (BZ)
phone +39 0471.796879
info@tubladel.com
www.tubladel.com

Galaria Unika
via Arnaria 9
Roncadizza
39046 Ortisei (BZ)
phone +39 339.1792227
www.unika.org

Andreas Moroder
strada Rasciesa 53
39046 Ortisei (BZ)
phone +39 0471.798110
www.val-gardena.com/moroder-andreas

Markus Perathoner
strada Doss 12
39046 Ortisei (BZ)
phone +39 0471.796661

Georg Demetz
strada Doss 11
39046 Ortisei (BZ)
phone +39 0471.797743

Herbert Kostner
strada Cuca 27
39046 Ortisei (BZ)
phone +39 0471.798019

Livio Comploi
strada Sacun 20
39046 Ortisei (BZ)
phone +39 0471.796763

ortona (abruzzo)

Mercantico d'Abruzzo
(every second saturday of the month)
Passeggiata Orientale
66026 Ortona (CH)
phone +39 085.7672513

orvieto (umbria)

Tourist Information
piazza Duomo 24
05018 Orvieto (TR)
phone +39 0763.341772
info@iat.orvieto.tr.it
www.iat.orvieto.tr.it

Hotel Villa Ciconia
SS 71, via dei Tigli 69
05018 Orvieto Scalo (TR)
phone +39 0763.305582
villaciconia@libero.it
www.hotelvillaciconia.com

Hotel Palazzo Piccolomini
piazza Ranieri, 36
05018 Orvieto (TR)
phone +39 0763.341743
piccolomini.hotel@orvienet.it
www.hotelpiccolomini.it

Albergo Filippeschi
via Filippeschi 19
05018 Orvieto (TR)
phone +39 0763.343275
albergofilippeschi@tiscalinet.it

Ristorante I Sette Consoli
piazza Sant'Angelo 1/a
05018 Orvieto (TR)
phone +39 0763.343911

Trattoria L'Asino d'Oro
vicolo del Popolo 9
05018 Orvieto (TR)
phone +39 0763.344406

L'Albero
corso Cavour 108
05018 Orvieto (TR)
phone +39 0763.342478

ozzano dell'emilia (emilia–romagna)

Le maioliche di Silvia
via Fosse Ardeatine 4
40064 Ozzano dell'Emilia (BO)
phone +39 051.790031

padua (veneto)

Tourist Information
Stazione FS
35131 Padua
phone +39 049.8752077
infostazione@turismopadova.it

Hotel Grand'Italia
corso del Popolo 81
35131 Padua
phone +39 049.8761111
info@hotelgranditalia.it
www.hotelgranditalia.it

Ristorante Antico Brolo
corso Milano 22
35139 Padua
phone +39 049.664555

Ristorante La Vecchia Enoteca
via S. Martino e Solferino 32
35122 Padua
phone +39 049.8752856

Benetton
via E. Filiberto 26
35100 Padua
phone +39 049.8360969
info@benetton.it
www.benetton.com

Mercatino dell'Antiquariato
(every third sunday of the month)
Prato della Valle
35100 Padua
phone +39 049.8205856

palermo (sicily)

Tourist Information
piazza Castelnuovo 34
90100 Palermo
phone +39 091.583847
info@palermotourism.com
Salita Belmonte 1
phone +39 091.6398011
info@aziendaturismopalermomonreale.it

Grand Hotel Villa Igiea
Salita Belmonte 43
90142 Palermo
phone +39 091.6312111
villaigiea-agent@cormorano.net
www.cormorano.net/sgas/villaigiea

Grand Hotel et des Palmes
via Roma 398
90100 Palermo
phone +39 091.6028111
www.grandhoteletdespalmes.it

Hotel Principe di Villafranca
via G. Turrisi Colonna 4
90100 Palermo
phone +39 091.6118523
info@principedivillafranca.it

Hotel Residenza D'Aragona
via Ottavio D'Aragona 25
90139 Palermo
phone +39 091.6622222
residenzadaragona@libero.it

Ristorante La Scuderia
Viale del Fante 9
90146 Palermo
phone +39 091.520323
lascuderia@tiscalinet.it

Il Ristorantino
piazza De Gasperi 19
90100 Palermo
phone +39 091.512681

Trattoria Il Delfino
via Torretta 80
90100 Palermo
phone +39 091.530282
trattoriaildelfino@virgilio.it

Trattoria Il Mirto e La Rosa
via Principe di Granatelli 30
90100 Palermo
phone +39 091.324353
www.ilmirtoelarosa.com

Associazione Figli d'Arte Cuticchio
via Bara dell'Olivella 95
90100 Palermo
phone +39 091.323400

Museo Internazionale delle Marionette
via Butera 1
90100 Palermo
phone +39 091.328060
www.museomarionettapalermo.it

Aris
via Monte Pellegrino 149
90142 Palermo
phone +39 091.546088
arissrl@arissrl.it

Sicily Folk
via V. Emanuele 450
90100 Palermo
phone +39 091.6512787

De Simone Ceramiche
via G. Lanza di Scalea 960
90100 Palermo
phone +39 091.6711005
info@ceramicadesimone.com
www.ceramicadesimone.co

La coppola storta
via dell'Orologio 25
90100 Palermo
www.lacoppolastorta.com

Mercato La Vucciria
piazza Caracciolo
90100 Palermo
phone +39 0784.30343

pancole (tuscany)

Antica sartoria di Maremma
Confezioni Brema
via del Colle
58050 Pancole (GR)
phone +39 0564.503029
www.confezionibrema.com

parabiago (lombardy)

Ristorante da Palmiro
via del Riale 16
20015 Parabiago (MI)
phone +39 0331.552024

Fratelli Rossetti
via Cantù 24
20015 Parabiago (MI)
phone +39 0331.495217
spaccio@rossetti.it
www.rossetti.it

Calzaturificio Riccardo Banfi
via Monsignor Pogliani 2
20015 Parabiago (MI)
phone +39 0331.551335
riccardobanfi@tin.it

Parabiago Collezioni
via Caldara 4
20015 Parabiago (MI)
phone +39 0331.495007

Fashion Point
via De Amicis 24
20015 Parabiago (MI)
phone +39 0331.551526
fashionpoint@libero.it

pattada (sardinia)

Fogarizzu
via Fermi 3
07016 Pattada (SS)

phone +39 079.755227
www.fogarizzu.com

Sistigu
via Duca d'Aosta 20
07016 Pattada (SS)
phone +39 079.755410

pau (sardinia)

Museo dell'ossidiana
via San Giorgio
09090 Pau (OR)
phone +39 783.939002
comune.pau@tiscali.it
www.comune.pau.it

paularo (friuli–venezia giulia)

Confezioni Wally
via Roma 56
33027 Paularo (UD)
phone +39 0433.70078

pavia (lombardy)

Tourist Information
via Fabio Filzi 2
27100 Pavia
phone +39 0382.22156
info@apt.pv.it
www.apt.pv.it

Hotel Moderno
viale Vittorio Emanuele 41
27100 Pavia
phone +39 0382.303402
info@hotelmoderno.it

Hotel Excelsior
piazza Stazione 25
27100 Pavia
phone +39 0382.28596
info@excelsiorpavia.com

Ristorante Locanda Vecchia Pavia al Mulino
via al Monumento 5
27012 Certosa di Pavia PV
phone +39 0382.925894
vecchiapaviaalmulino@libero.it

Osteria del Naviglio
via Alzaia 39/b (p.le San Giuseppe)
27100 Pavia
phone +39 0382.460392
www.osteriadelnaviglio.it

Ristorante Villaglori al Sanmichele
vicolo San Michele 4
27100 Pavia
phone +39 0382.20716

Ristorante Antica Osteria del Previ
località Borgo Ticino
via Milazzo 65
27100 Pavia
phone +39 0382.26203

Dellera Pellicce
via Zecca 4
27100 Pavia
phone +39 0382.304639
www.dellera.com

Mazzocchi Pellicce
corso Cavour 9
27100 Pavia
phone +39 0382.25174

Castelfur
via Gragnani 12
27100 Pavia
phone +39 0382.527158

Pellicceria Annabella
corso Cavour 1
27100 Pavia
phone +39 0382.21122/21761
www.annabella.it

perugia (umbria)

Tourist Information
piazza 4 Novembre 3
06123 Perugia
phone +39 075.5736458
info@iat.perugia.it

Hotel Le Tre Vaselle
via Garibaldi 48
06089 Torgiano (PG)
phone +39 075.9880447
3vaselle@3vaselle.it
www.3vaselle.it

Hotel Castello dell'Oscano
località Cenerente
strada Forcella 37
06070 Perugia
phone +39 075.584371
info@oscano.com

Hotel Brufani
piazza Italia 12
06121 Perugia
phone +39 075.5732541
reservationsbrun@sinahotels.it

Ristorante Giò Arte e Vini
via R. D'Andreotto 19
06124 Perugia
phone +39 075.5731100
hotelgio@interbusiness.it
www.hotelgio.it

Osteria del Bartolo
via del Bartolo 30
06100 Perugia
phone +39 0755.731561

Ristorante Lungarotti
corso V. Emanuele 31
06089 Torgiano (PG)
phone +39 075.9880200
www.lungarotti.it

Bottega d'arte Ceccucci
corso Vannucci 38
06100 Perugia

Luisa Spagnoli
Strada S. Lucia 35
06100 Perugia
phone +39 075.4591
www.luisaspagnoli.it

Confezioni Ikebana
via Penna-S.Sisto
Zona Industriale S. Andrea

06100 Perugia
phone +39 075.286154

Sterne International
via Manna 75
Zona Industriale S. Andrea
06100 Perugia
phone +39 075.5289810

Giuditta Brozzetti
Via T. Berardi 5/6
06123 Perugia
phone +39 075.40236
fax +39 075.500236
email@brozzetti.com
www.brozzetti.com

pescara (abruzzo)

Mercantico d'Abruzzo
(every first sunday of the month)
strada Parco Colli Innamorati
Corso Manthoné
65100 Pescara
phone +39 0857.672513

pescia (tuscany)

Cooperativa Gli antichi mestieri
via Val di Torbaia 54
località S. Quirico
51017 Pescia (PT)
phone +39 0572.400045

pianello del lario (lombardy)

Museo della barca lariana
località Calozzo
via statale 139
22010 Pianello del Lario (CO)
phone +39 0344.87235

pietra ligure (liguria)

Mercatino dell'Artigianato
(every last sunday of the month)
piazza S. Nicolò
17027 Pietra Ligure SV
phone +39 019.6299003

pietrasanta (tuscany)

Tourist Information
Lungomare Vespucci 24
57037 Marina di Massa (MS)
phone +39 0585.240063
info@aptmassacarrara.it
www.turismo.toscana.it
piazza Statuto
55044 Pietrasanta (LU)
phone +39 0584.283284
info@pietrasantaemarina.it

Hotel Carrara
via E. Petacchi 21
54031 Avenza (MS)
phone +39 0585.857616
info@hotelcarrara.it

Hotel Cavalieri del Mare
via Verdi 23
54039 Ronchi (MS)
phone +39 0585.868010
info@cavalieridelmare.com

Hotel Mediterraneo
via Genova 2/h
54030 Marina di Carrara (MS)
phone +39 0585.785222

Ristorante Ninan
via L. Bartolini 3
54033 Carrara (MS)
phone +39 0585.74741
ninan@tiscalinet.it

Museo dei Bozzetti
via S. Agostino 1
55045 Pietrasanta (LU)
phone +39 0584.795500
www.museodeibozzetti.com

Fratelli Galeotti
via della Cisa 10
55045 Pietrasanta (LU)
phone +39 0584.792920

Pelletti & Simonetti
via Col di Nava 2
55045 Pietrasanta (LU)
phone +39 0584.793345

Bacci Marmi
località Vallecchia
via Pescarella 24
55045 Pietrasanta (LU)

Cervietti Franco & C
Via Sant'Agostino 53
55045 Pietrasanta
phone +39 0584.790454
fax +39 0584.790925
www.cervietti.com

pieve di cadore (veneto)

Museo dell'occhiale
via degli Alpini 39
32044 Pieve di Cadore (BL)
phone +39 0435.500213
www.eyesway.com

pinasca (piedmont)

Museo del mobile
corso R. Gagliano 2
10060 Pinasca (TO)
phone +39 0121.809101
abitareinvalle@tiscalinet.it
www.abitareinvalle.it

pioraco (marche)

Museo della carta e della filigrana
largo G. Leopardi 1
62025 Pioraco (MC)
phone +39 0733.232218

pisa (tuscany)

Tourist Information
piazza Miracoli
56126 Pisa
phone +39 050.560464
pisa.turismo@traveleurope.it
Aeroporto G. Galilei
56100 Pisa
phone +39 050.503700

Hotel Relais dell'Orologio
via della Faggiola 12
56126 Pisa
phone +39 050.830361
info@hotelrelaisorologio.com
www.hotelrelaisorologio.com

Ristorante A Casa Mia
via Provinciale Vicarese 10
56010 Ghezzano (PI)
phone +39 050.879265
ristoranteacasamia@supereva.it
TM
piazza S. Stefano 12
56024 Ponte a Egola (PI)
phone +39 0571.485158
info@verapelle.it
www.verapelle.it

Mercato dell'Antiquariato
(every second week-end of the month)
piazza Cavalieri
56100 Pisa

pistoia (tuscany)

Tourist Information
Palazzo dei Vescovi
piazza del Duomo
51100 Pistoia
phone +39 0573.21622
aptpistoia@tiscalinet.it

Albergo La Volpe e l'Uva
Villa Vannini
via di Villa 6
51030 Villa di Piteccio (PT)
phone +39 0573.42031
info@volpe-uva.it

Ristorante Corradossi
via Frosini 112
51100 Pistoia
phone +39 0573.25683
loriscorradossi@virgilio.it

Trattoria La Bottegaia
via del Lastrone 17
51100 Pistoia
phone +39 0573.365602

Re.Bi
via Sansoni 7
51100 Pistoia
phone +39 0573.31901

Rose Barni
via del Castello 5
51100 Pistoia

Vivai Capecchi
via Pratese 185a
51100 Pistoia

Magni Piante
via Fiorentina 424
51100 Pistoia
phone +39 0573.380065
magnipiante@tin.it

Tesi Ubaldo
via Girone 29
51100 Pistoia
phone +39 0573.532318
tesivivai@tin.it

Angori Rossella
via Traversa del Pillone 4
51100 Pistoia
phone +39 0573.380490

Arte del ferro
via Lucchese 486
51100 Pistoia
phone +39 0573.51332
info@forgediron.it

Mercato dell'Antiquariato
(every second week-end of the month)
via Roma
51100 Pistoia

piuro (lombardy)

Roberto Lucchinetti
via alla Chiusa 5
località Prosto
23020 Piuro (SO)
phone +39 03423.35905

pont canavese (piedmont)

Ceretto Castigliano
10085 Pont Canavese (TO)
phone +39 0124.85189

Museo etnografico di antichi mestieri
Via F.O. Rossio 1
10085 Pont Canavese (TO)
phone +39 0124.85484

pontedera (tuscany)

Tourist Information
via Nenni 24
56124 Pisa
phone +39 050.929777
aptpisa@pisa.turismo.toscana.it
www.pisa.turismo.toscana.it

Hotel Armonia
piazza Caduti 11
56025 Pontedera (PI)
phone +39 0587.278511
reception@hotelarmonia.it
www.hotelarmonia.it

Ristorante Aeroscalo
via Roma 8
56025 Pontedera (PI)
phone +39 0587.52024

Arte in Ceramica
via Veneto 77
56025 Pontedera (PI)
phone +39 0587.56007

ponte nossa (lombardy)

Museo dei magli
via dei Magli
24028 Ponte Nossa (BG)
phone +39 035.701054
www.comune.ponte-nossa.bg.it

ponte san giovanni (umbria)

Big Bertha Outlet
via dell'Industria 19
Zona Industriale Molinaccio
06087 Ponte S. Giovanni (PG)
phone +39 075.5997572

ponti (piedmont)

Ebanisteria Reale
Regione Oltre Bormida 9
15010 Ponti (AL)
phone +39 0144.596403

ponzano veneto (veneto)

Benetton
Villa Minelli
31050 Ponzano Veneto (TV)
phone +39 0422.519111
fax +39 0422.969501
info@benetton.it
www.benetton.com

pordenone (friuli–venezia giulia)

Tourist Information
corso Vittorio Emanuele II 38
33170 Pordenone
phone +39 0434.21912
arpt-pn1@regione.fvg.it

Palace Hotel Moderno
viale Martelli 1
33170 Pordenone
phone +39 0434.28215
info@palacehotelmoderno.it

Hotel Villa Luppis
località Rivarotta
via San Martino 34
33087 Pasiano di Pordenone (PN)
phone +39 0434.626969
hotel@villaluppis.it
www.villaluppis.it

Ristorante Casetta
località Palse Sud
via Colombo 35
33080 Porcia (PN)
phone +39 0434.922720
fab.casetta@inwind.it

Trattoria La Vecia Osteria del Moro
via Castello 2
33170 Pordenone
phone +39 0434.28658

Ristorante Novecento
via C. Menotti 62
33072 Casarsa della Delizia (PN)
phone +39 0434.86203
www.ristorante900.it

Zava Flora Ceramica
via Spallanzani 14
33170 Pordenone
phone +39 436.571754

Museo Civico d'Arte
Corso Vittorio Emanuele II, 51
phone +39 0434.392312
fax +39 0434.522507
museo.arte@comune.pordenone.it

pove del grappa (veneto)

Ars Oro
viale Europa 20
36020 Pove del Grappa (VI)
phone +39 0424.80571
arsmail@tin.it

Museo dello scalpellino
viale Marconi
36020 Pove del Grappa (VI)
phone +39 0424.80659

prato (tuscany)

Tourist Information
piazza delle Carceri15
59100 Prato
phone +39 0574.24112
apt@prato.turismo.toscana.it

Hotel Giardino
via Magnolfi 4
59100 Prato
phone +39 0574.606588
info@giardinohophonecom
www.giardinohotel.com

Arthotel
viale della Repubblica 289
59100 Prato
phone +39 057.45787
www.arthotel.it

Ristorante Da Delfina
località Artiminio
Via della Chiesa 1
59015 Carmignano (PO)
phone +39 055.8718074
posta@dadelfina.it

Gruppo Osvaldo Bruni
via Galcianese 67
59100 Prato
phone +39 0574.607591

Machattie
via Cortesi 29a
59100 Prato
phone +39 0574.400838

Monteferrato
via Toccafondi 24
59100 Prato
phone +39 0574.603648

Nieri
via Frescobaldi 23
59100 Prato
phone +39 0574.813774
lucianonieri@virgilio.it

Fabric Stock House
via Lungo Ficarello 6
59100 Prato
phone +39 0574.815453
info@fabricstockhouse.com

Alexander
via Caserane 18c
59100 Prato
phone +39 0574.812393

Geronimo
via Traversa Fiorentina 34b
59100 Prato
phone +39 0574.546124
www.geronimo.it

Futura Trade
via De Gasperi 15
59100 Prato
phone +39 0574.571340
futura@futuratrade.it

Museo del tessuto
piazza del Comune 9
59100 Prato
phone +39 0574.611503
www.po-net.prato.it/tessuto

premana (lombardy)

Tourist Information
via N. Sauro 6
23900 Lecco
phone +39 0341.362360
info@aptlecco.com

Hotel Don Abbondio
piazza Era 10
23900 Lecco
phone +39 0341.366315

Hotel Alberi
Lungo Lario Isonzo 4
23900 Lecco
phone +39 0341.350992
info@hotelalberi.lecco.it

Ristorante Cermenati
corso Matteotti 71
23900 Lecco
phone +39 0341.283017

Osteria Olga
località Maggianico, via Poncione 7
23900 Lecco
phone +39 0341.422030
www.osteriaolga.it

Da Ceko il Pescatore
piazza Era 8
23900 Lecco
phone +39 0341.284101

Consorzio Premax
via Giabbio
23834 Premana (LC)
phone +39 0341.818003
www.premax.it

Coltelleria Art
via Roma 6
23834 Premana (LC)
phone +39 0341.890432
www.coltelleria-art.com

Pinin
via Risorgimento 28
23834 Premana (LC)
phone/fax +39 0341.890181
www.pinin.com

quarna (lombardy)

Rampone e Cazzani
piazza S. Rita 2
28896 Quarna (VB)
phone +39 0323.826134

Museo dello strumento musicale a fiato
via Roma
28896 Quarna (VB)
phone +39 0323.89622
www.lagodorta.net

ravello (campania)

Museo del corallo
piazza Duomo 9
84010 Ravello (SA)
phone +39 089.857461

ravenna (emilia—romagna)

Tourist Information
via Salara 8
48100 Ravenna
phone +39 0544.35404
ravennaintorno@mail.provincia.ra.it

Jolly Hotel
piazza Mameli 1
48100 Ravenna
phone +39 0544.35762
ravenna@jollyhotels.it
www.jollyhotels.it

Hotel Diana
via Rossi 47
48100 Ravenna
phone +39 0544.39164
info@hoteldiana.ra.it

Antica Trattoria al Gallo 1909
via Maggiore 87
48100 Ravenna
phone +39 0544.213775

Trattoria vecchia Falegnameria
via Faentina 54
48100 Ravenna
phone +39 0544.501870
vecchiafalegnameria@libero.it

Arredomosaic
via Guerrini 70
località Sant'Alberto
48100 Ravenna
phone +39 0544.528714

Artemosaico
viale Baracca 5
48100 Ravenna
phone +39 0544.66007

Cooperativa Mosaicisti Ravenna
via Fiandrini 13
48100 Ravenna
phone +39 0544.34799

art@coopmosaico.it
www.coopmosaico.it

Dimensione Mosaico
via Ricci Curbastro 12
località Fornace Zarattini
48100 Ravenna
phone +39 0544.502493

Mosaici Antichi e Moderni
via Mariani 9
48100 Ravenna
phone +39 0544.35448

Mostra Mercato di Antiquariato e Artigianato
(every third week-end of the month)
piazza del Popolo
48100 Ravenna
phone +39 0544.482111

recanati (marche)

Tourist Information
piazza della Libertà 12
62100 Macerata
phone +39 0733.234807
iat.macerata@regione.marche.it

Moretti Pipe
vicolo dell'Olmo 7
62019 Recanati (MC)
phone +39 071.7570063
www.pipemoretti.com

Castagnari Fisarmoniche
via Risorgimento 77
62019 Recanati (MC)
phone +39 071.7574294

Antica Bottega Amanuense
via Villa Collardo Mels
62019 Recanati (MC)
phone +39 0717.574393

rocca bianca (emilia—romagna)

Giovanni Ferrari
località Fontanelle
via Babilana 10
43010 Roccabianca (PR)
phone +39 0521.1870111

rolo (emilia—romagna)

Museo della tarsia
corso Repubblica 39
42047 Rolo (RE)
phone +39 0522.666112
info@comune.rolo.re.it
www.comune.rolo.re.it

rome (lazio)

Tourist Information
via Parigi 5
00100 Rome
phone +39 06.36004399
Stazione Termini
00100 Rome
phone +39 06.47825194

Hotel Hassler Villa Medici
piazza Trinità dei Monti 6
00100 Rome
phone +39 06.600340
booking@hotelhassler.it

Hotel De Russie
via del Babuino
00100 Rome
phone +39 06.328881
reservation@hotelderussie.it

Hotel The Inn at the Spanish Steps
via dei Condotti 85
00100 Rome
phone +39 06.69925657
spanishstep@tin.it

Hostaria dell'Orso di Gualtiero Marchesi
via dei Soldati 25/c
00100 Rome
phone +39 06.68301192
info@hdo.it

Ristorante Da Pancrazio
piazza del Biscione 92
00100 Rome
phone +39 06.6861246
dapancrazio@tin.it

**Trattoria Giggetto
al Portico d'Ottavia**
via del Portico d'Ottavia 21
00100 Rome
phone +39 06.6861105

Ristorante Il Sanpietrino
piazza Costaguti 15
00100 Rome
phone +39 06.68806471
www.ilsanpietrino.it

Bulgari Outlet
via Aurelia 1052
00166 Rome
phone +39 06.6617071
www.bulgari.com

Discount delle Firme
via dei Serviti 27
00187 Rome
phone +39 06.4827790

Marzotto Factory Store
via Carnevale 74
località La Romanina
00173 Rome
phone +39 06.72630021
www.marzotto.it

Megastore Sergio Tacchini
via Tiburtina 1115
00100 Rome
phone +39 06.41205558
www.sergiotacchini.com

**Vetrate artistiche
Paolo Corpetti**
viale Jonio 127
00141 Rome
phone +39 06.8175381
info@vetrateartistiche.com
www.vetrateartistiche.com

Bottega Mortet
via dei Portoghesi 18

00100 Rome
phone +39 06.6861629

Stilvetro
via Frattina 56
00100 Rome
phone +39 06.6790258

Stockhouse Parioli
via Parioli 23
00100 Rome
phone +39 06.8079549

The Outlet Factory
via Ponte Piscina Cupa 118
00129 Rome
phone +39 06.50576542

Www.fashionstock-house.it
via Anastasio II 146
00100 Rome
phone +39 06.6380520

Mercato Porta Portese
(sunday)
Trastevere
00100 Rome
phone +39 06.58233114

Libri con gusto
largo dei Librai 84
00100 Rome
phone +39 06.68804600
www.libricongusto.it

Picta
Campo dei Fiori 11
00100 Roma
phone +39 06.68300248

Arte Orafa Romana
via Condotti 23a
00187 Roma
phone +39 06.6784153
info@arteorafaromana.it

Campanile
via Condotti 58
00187 Roma
phone +39 06.6790731

La Casa di Flora
via S. Salvatore in Campo 53
00100 Rome
phone +39 06.68806330

Laurenti
via dei Pompieri 30
00100 Rome

Sciam
via del Pellegrino 55
00186 Rome
phone +39 06.68308957

Fratelli Viganò
via Minghetti
00100 Rome
phone +39 06.6795147

Mercatino delle stampe
piazza Borghese
00100 Rome

romagnano sesia (piedmont)

Ristorante alla Torre
via 1° Maggio 75
28078 Romagnano Sesia (NO)
phone +39 0163.826411

Lanificio Loro Piana
via per Novara 484
28078 Romagnano Sesia (NO)
phone +39 0163.826875
www.loropiana.com

ronco canavese (piedmont)

Museo fucina da rame
località Castellaro
10080 Ronco Canavese (TO)
phone +39 3386326627

saint pierre (valle d'aosta)

Cooperativa La Grolla
località Cognein 44
11010 St. Pierre (AO)
phone +39 0165.903403

sala bolognese (emilia–romagna)

Il Navile carte d'arte
via Matteotti 44
40010 Sala Bolognese (BO)
phone +39 051.829220

saluzzo (piedmont)

Tourist Information
via Roma 28
12100 Cuneo
phone +39 0171.693258
atl@cuneotourism.com
www.cuneotourism.com
via Torino 51
12100 Cuneo
phone +39 0175.46710
iat@comune.saluzzo.cn.it

Hotel Astor
piazza Garibaldi 39
12037 Saluzzo (CN)
phone +39 0175.45506
astor@mtrade.com

Albergo Real Castello
via Umberto I 9
12060 Verduno (CN)
phone +39 0172.470125
castellodiverduno@castellodiverduno.com
www.castellodiverduno.com

Palazzo Lovera Hotel
via Roma 37
12100 Cuneo
phone +39 0171.690420
info@palazzolovera.com

La Gargotta del Pellico
piazzetta Mondagli 5
12037 Saluzzo (CN)
phone +39 0175.56833

Il Rustico
via Ruata Re 1
12037 Saluzzo (CN)
phone +39 0175.43679

Fratelli Coccolino
via Monviso 7
12037 Saluzzo (CN)
phone +39 0175.43307

san donato milanese (lombardy)

Gusella Discount
via XXV Aprile 11
20097 S. Donato Milanese (MI)
phone +39 02.513511

Mercato Pulci
Capolinea MM3
20097 S. Donato Milanese
phone +39 02.725421

san fermo della battaglia (lombardy)

Giovannini
via Belvedere 13
22020 S. Fermo (CO)
phone +39 031.211060
www.handpaintedties.net

san genesio (trentino–alto adige)

Kaufmann
via Paese 3
39050 S. Genesio (BZ)
phone +39 0471.354595
info@kaufmannwalker.it
www.kaufmannwalker.it

san giorgio a cremano (campania)

Clipeus Art
via Giosuè Carducci 35
80046 S. Giorgio a Cremano (NA)
phone +39 081.5749281
clipeusart@libro.it

Alfonso Esposito
via Picenna 39
80046 San Giorgio a Cremano (NA)
phone +39 081.475132
dittaespositoalfonso@virgilio.it

san giovanni in fiore (calabria)

G. Battista Spadafora
via Roma 3
87055 San Giovanni in Fiore (CS)
phone +39 0984.993968

Gioielleria Pertichini
via Roma 173
87055 San Giovanni in Fiore (CS)
phone +39 0984.970465
www.gioiellipertichini.it

Scuola Tappeti Caruso
via Gramsci 195
87055 San Giovanni in Fiore (CS)
phone +39 0984.992724
www.scuolatappeti.it

Centro artigianato Tiano
via Vallone 223
87055 San Giovanni in Fiore (CS)
phone +39 0984.991515

san leucio (campania)

Antico Opificio Serico De Negri
piazza della Seta 1
81020 S. Leucio (CE)
phone +39 0823.361290
info@aos.it
www.aos.it

I Sorrisi
via delle Matasse 5
81020 S. Leucio (CE)
phone +39 0823.305153
www.isorrisi.it

san marino (repubblica di)

Tourist Information
piazza della Libertà
47890 Repubblica di San Marino
phone +39 0549.882914

Grand Hotel San Marino
via A. Onofri 31
47890 Repubblica di San Marino
phone +39 0549.992400
info@grandhophonesm

Ristorante Righi La taverna
piazza della Libertà 10
47890 Repubblica di San Marino
phone +39 0549.990597
lataverna@omniway.sm

Angel Shop
via IV Giugno 103
località Serravalle
47890 Repubblica di San Marino
phone +39 0549.960450
www.pieroguidi.com

San Marino Factory Outlet
via 3 Settembre 3
località Serravalle
47890 Repubblica di San Marino
phone +39 0549.904014
www.outlet-spacci.it

Pro Racing Bike
strada Cardio 18
località Serravalle
47890 Repubblica di San Marino
phone +39 0549.908303
mail@prbike.com
www.prbike.com

san martino al tagliamento (friuli–venezia giulia)

Friul Mosaic
via S. Giacomo 42
33096 San Martino al Tagliamento (PN)
phone +39 0434.899217
www.friulmosaic.com

san paolo albanese (basilicata)

Tourist Information
via Cavour 15
85100 Potenza
phone +39 0971.411839/274485

Municipio
via F.lli Bandiera
85030 San Paolo Albanese (PZ)
phone +39 0973.94367/94261

san polo d'enza (emilia–romagna)

Arredamenti de Angeli
via Papa Giovanni XXIII 7
42020 San Polo D'Enza (RE)
phone +39 0522.873271

sanremo (liguria)

Tourist Information
largo Nuvoloni 1
18038 Sanremo (IM)
phone +39 0184.500295
infosanremo@rivieradeifiori.org

Royal Hotel
corso Imperatrice 80
18038 Sanremo (IM)
phone +39 0184.5391
reservations@royalhotelsanremo.com
www.royalhotelsanremo.com

Grand Hotel de Londres
corso Matuzia 2
18038 Sanremo (IM)
phone +39 0184.668000

Ristorante Paolo e Barbara
via Roma 47
18038 Sanremo (IM)

Lindita Decorazioni Floreali
via G. Borea 139
18038 Sanremo (IM)
phone +39 0184.501392
lindita.fiori@tin.it

Centro Bonsai
via Bussana Vecchia 102
18038 Sanremo (IM)
phone +39 0184.510638

A&G
via Valle Armea
18038 Sanremo (IM)
phone +39 0184.510844

santa cristina valgardena (trentino–alto adige)

Thomas Comploi
strada Mulin d'Odum 9
39047 Santa Cristina Valgardena (BZ)
phone +39 0471.793723

sant'agnello (campania)

Il Telaio dei Sogni
via Iommella Piccola 26
80065 Sant'Agnello (NA)
phone +39 081.5342928
www.iltelaiodeisogni.com

sant'elpidio a mare (marche)

Tourist Information
63019 Sant'Elpidio a Mare (AP)
phone +39 0734.810008
ufficioturistico@santelpidioamare.it

Calzaturificio Muzi
via Faleriense 2103
63019 Sant'Elpidio a Mare (AP)
phone +39 0734.810234
info@nandomuzi.it

Della Valle Outlet
via F. Della Valle
63019 Sant'Elpidio a Mare (AP)
phone +39 0734.871671

Museo della calzatura
piazzale Marconi 16
63019 Sant'Elpidio a Mare (AP)
phone +39 0734.810840
museodella calzatura@libero.it

santo stefano di camastra (sicily)

Tourist Information
via Palazzo 35
98077 Santo Stefano di Camastra (ME)
phone +39 0921.331110

Museo della ceramica
Palazzo Trabia
via Palazzo 35
98077 Santo Stefano di Camastra (ME)
phone +39 0921.331110

Merlo pietra lavica
via Passo Barone 10
98077 Santo Stefano di Camastra (ME)
phone. +39 0921.331786
www.merlovincenzo.it

Ceramica Insana
via Vittoria 3
98077 Santo Stefano di Camastra (ME)
phone +39 0921.331408

san valentino della collina (umbria)

Sposini
strada Marcianese
06050 San Valentino della Collina (PG)
phone +39 075.8784134
sposinitessutiumbri@libero.it

san vito di cadore (veneto)

Ottica de Lotto
corso Italia 44
32046 San Vito di Cadore (BL)
phone +39 0436.99212
otticadelotto@sunrise.it

saronno (lombardy)

Collezione di ceramiche e maioliche
via Carcano 9
21047 Saronno (Va)
phone +39 02.9602383

sassari (sardinia)

Tourist Information
Ept Sassari
viale Caprera 36
07100 Sassari
phone +39 0792.99544
ept.sassari@regione.sardegna.it

Ceramica Scassellati
via Buddi
07100 Sassari
phone +39 079.316711

Espressioni Sarde
via Roth 35
07100 Sassari
phone +39 079.293537

sasso marconi (emilia–romagna)

Trasparia
via dell'Industria 14
40037 Sasso Marconi (BO)
phone +39 051.6750452

sassuolo (emilia–romagna)

Ristorante La Paggeria
via Rocca 16
41049 Sassuolo (MO)
phone +39 0536.805190
www.ristorantelapaggeria.com

Museo delle piastrelle di ceramica
Palazzina della Casiglia
viale Monte Santo 40
41049 Sassuolo (MO)
phone +39 053.6818111

Brandoli Enrico
via Circonvallazione Nord Est 29
41049 Sassuolo (MO)
phone +39 0536.807191

Marazzi Ceramiche
viale Regina Pacis 39
41049 Sassuolo (MO)
phone +39 0536.860111

Ceramiche Provenza
Via 2 Giugno 13/15
41040 Spezzano (MO)
phone +39 0536.927611
fax +39 0536.927626
info@ceramicheprovenza.com
www.ceramicheprovenza.com

scapoli (campania)

Hotel Le Ginestre
via Terra Grande
località Filignano
86070 Scapoli (IS)
phone +39 0865.926444

Ristorante Terra Nostra
via Fonte la Villa 1
86070 Scapoli (IS)
phone +39 0865.954135

Arte e tradizione
Centro Storico
86070 Scapoli (IS)
phone +39 338.2933684

**Mostra permanente di zampogne
e cornamuse**
via Aldo Moro
86070 Scapoli (IS)
phone +39 0865.954002
www.zampogna.org

Museo della zampogna
Palazzo Mancini
vico S. Maria
86070 Scapoli (IS)
phone +39 0865.954270
www.museodellazampogna.it

Circolo della Zampogna
Piazza Martiri di Scapoli
86070 Scapoli (IS)
phone +39 0865.954002
fax +39 0865.954086
www.zampogna.org
circolo@zampogna.org

scarperia (tuscany)

Sonesta Resort & Country Club Tuscany
via S. Gavino 27
località Gabbiano
50038 Scarperia (FI)
phone +39 055.84350

Coltellerie Conaz
via Roma 8
50038 Scarperia (FI)
phone +39 055.8430270
www.conaz.com

Berti Coltellerie
via Roma 43
50038 Scarperia (FI)
phone +39 055.8469903
www.coltellerieberti.it

Coltelleria Saladini
via Solferino 19
50038 Scarperia (FI)
phone +39 055.8431010
www.coltelleriasaladini.it

Museo dei ferri taglienti
Palazzo dei Vicari
via Roma 137
50032 Scarperia (FI)
phone +39 0558.468165

schio (veneto)

Marzotto Factory Store
viale dell'Industria 126
36015 Schio (VI)
phone +39 0445.693478
www.marzotto.it

Spaccio Seventy
via Venezia 146
36015 Schio (VI)
phone +39 0445.5899539
www.seventy.it

Euromanteau
via Schio 92
36015 Schio (VI)
phone +39 0445.660038
euroconf@schio.nettuno.it

segrate (lombardy)

Spaccio Superga
via Olgia 18
20090 Segrate (MI)
phone +39 02.2133378
www.superga.it

selva di val gardena (trentino–alto adige)

Otto Piazza
strada Ruacia 14
39048 Selva di Val Gardena (BZ)
phone +39 0471.794526

seriate (lombardy)

Coin Outlet
via Tonale 101
24068 Seriate (BG)
phone +39 035.583281
www.coin.it

sesto fiorentino (tuscany)

Roberto Cavalli Factory Outlet
via Volturno 3/3
50019 Sesto Fiorentino (FI)
phone +39 055.317754
factoryoutlet@robertocavalli.it
www.robertocavalli.it

sinnai (sardinia)

Coltelleria Monni Roberto
via Ninasuni 45
09048 Sinnai (CA)
phone +39 070.780660

siracusa (sicily)

Tourist Information
via S. Sebastiano 43
96100 Siracusa
phone +39 0931. 481200
info@apt.siracusa.it

Grand Hotel Ortigia
viale Mazzini 12
96100 Siracusa
phone +39 0931.464600

Ristorante Don Camillo
via Maestranza 96
96100 Siracusa
phone +39 0931.67133

Museo del papiro
via Teocrito 66
96100 Siracusa
phone +39 0931.22100
www.sistema.it/museopapiro

Istituto del papiro
via 20 settembre 19
96100 Siracusa
phone +39 0931.483342
info@papiro.it
www.papiro.it

Papyrus
via Scala Greca 445
96100 Siracusa
phone +39 0931.750981

Carolina de Santis
via Antioco 11
96100 Siracusa
phone +39 0931.65902

Oro design
via Roma 30
96100 Siracusa

solofra (campania)

Tourist Information
via Due Principati 5
83100 Avellino
phone +39 0825.74731
infi@eptavellino.it
www.eptavellino.it

Hotel De la Ville
via Palatucci 20
phone +39 0825.780911
83100 Avellino
info@hdv.av.it
www.hdv.av.it

Ristorante La Maschera
Rampa S. Modestino 1
phone +39 0825.37603
83100 Avellino
ristorantelamaschera@virgilio.it

Euro Moda
via Misericordia 21
83029 Solofra (AV)
phone +39 0825.581319

Confezioni Anna
via Misericordia 21
83029 Solofra (AV)
phone +39 0825.583697

New Age Leather
via Melito centro Asi
83029 Solofra (AV)
phone +39 0825.535434

Pelle d'oro
via Misericordia 21
83029 Solofra (AV)
phone +39 0825.583194

Conceria Gaeta Nicola
via Celentane
83029 Solofra (AV)
phone +39 0825.581574
gaeta@solofra.com
www.leather-in-italy.com/gaeta

Conceria De Maio
via Consolazione
83029 Solofra (AV)
phone +39 0825,581423

solomeo (umbria)

Tourist Information
piazza IV novembre 3
00123 Perugia
phone +39 075.5736458
info@iat.perugia.it

Brufani Palace
piazza Italia 12
06121 Perugia
phone +39 075.5732541
reservationsbrun@sinahotels.it

Locanda Solomeo
piazza C.A. dalla Chiesa 1
06073 Solomeo (PG)
phone +39 075.5293119
solomeo@tin.it

Brunello Cucinelli
Piazza C.A. della Chiesa 6
06070 Solomeo (PG)
phone +39 075.5293121
cucinelli@brunellocucinelli.it
www.brunellocucinelli.it

Gunex
via dell'Industria 5
06070 Solomeo (PG)
phone +39 075.529491
gunex@gunex.it
www.gunex.it

Rivamonti
via dell'Industria 5
06070 Solomeo (PG)
phone +39 075.697071
rivamonti@rivamonti.it
www.rivamonti.it

Ellesse
località Ellera Umbra
via F. Turati
06070 Solomeo (PG)
phone +39 075.5171523
uni.sport@tiscali.it
www.unisport.it

soncino (lombardy)

Museo della stampa
via Lanfranco 8
26029 Soncino (CR)
phone +39 0374.83171
www.museodellastampasoncino.it

sondrio (lombardy)

Tourist Information
via C. Battisti 12
23100 Sondrio
phone +39 0342.512500
aptvaltellina@provincia.so.it
www.valtellinaonline.com

Hotel Europa
Lungo Mallero Cadorna 27
phone +39 0342.515010
info@hoteleuropa.com
www.albergoeuropa.com

Ristorante dei Castelli
via Crocifisso 10
località Montagna in Valtellina
23100 Sondrio
phone +39 0342.380445

Floriana Palmieri
via Visconti Venosta 5
23100 Sondrio
phone +39 0342.212005

sorrento (campania)

Tourist Information
via de Maio 35
80067 Sorrento (NA)
phone +39 081.8074033
info@sorrentotourism.com

Grand Hotel Excelsior Vittoria
piazza Tasso 34
80067 Sorrento (NA)
phone +39 081.8071044
exvitt@exvitt.it
www.exvitt.it

Grand Hotel Ambasciatori
via Califano 18
80067 Sorrento (NA)
phone +39 081.8782025
ambasciatori@manniellohotels.it
www.ambasciatorisorrento.com

Ristorante Caruso
via S. Antonino 12
80067 Sorrento (NA)
phone +39 081.8073156
info@ristorantemuseocaruso.com

Ristorante Il Buco
Rampe Marina Piccola 5
80067 Sorrento (NA)
phone +39 081.8782354
info@ilbucoristorante.it

Carlo de Nicola
via T. Tasso 55
80067 Sorrento (NA)
phone +39 081.8781051

Giuseppe Esposito
via S. Renato 3
80067 Sorrento (NA)
phone +39 081.8071684

Francesco Maione
vicolo il Fuoro 11
80067 Sorrento (NA)

Museobottega della tarsia lignea
Palazzo Pomarici Santomasi
via S. Nicola 28
80067 Sorrento (NA)
phone/fax +39 081.8771942
www.alessandrofiorentinocollection.it

sottoguda (veneto)

La Fosina De Biasio
via Pian 11
località Sottoguda
32020 Rocca Pietore (BL)
phone +39 0437.722021
www.lafosina.com

sotto il monte (lombardy)

Le bambole di Angy
via Don Carlo Valtellina 7
24039 Sotto il Monte (BG)
phone +39 035.784133

spilimbergo (friuli–venezia giulia)

Tourist Information
corso V. Emanuele II, 38
33170 Pordenone
phone +39 0434.21912
arpt_pn1@regione.fvg.it

Palace Hotel Moderno
via Martelli 1
33170 Pordenone
phone +39 0434.28215
info@palacehotelmoderno.it
www.eahotels.it/moderno_ita

Ristorante La Torre
piazza Castello 8
33097 Spilmbergo (PN)
phone +39 0427.50555
info@ristorantelatorre.net
www.ristorantelatorre.net

Osteria da Afro
via Umberto I 14
33097 Spilimbergo (PN)
phone +39 0427.2264
osteriadaafro@tin.it

Cristina Cancian
via 2 Giugno 4
33097 Spilimbergo (PN)
phone +39 042.72084

spoleto (umbria)

Tourist Information
piazza Libertà 7
06049 Spoleto (PG)
phone +39 0743.238921
info@iat.spoleto.pg.it

Albornoz Palace Hotel
viale Matteotti
06049 Spoleto (PG)
phone +39 0743.221221
info@albornozpalace.com
www.albornozpalace.com

Ristorante Il Tartufo
piazza Garibaldi 24
06049 Spoleto (PG)
phone +39 0743.40236
truffles@libero.it

Arcarosa di Mastro Raphael
via dei Duchi 5
06049 Spoleto (PG)
www.arcarosa.com

Mastro Raphael
località Santo Chiodo 161
06049 Spoleto (PG)
phone +39 0743.230859
info@mastroraphael.com
www.mastroraphael.com

stradella (lombardy)

Tourist Information
piazzale Trieste
27049 Stradella (PV)
phone +39 0385.245912

Fabbrica armoniche Mariano Dellapè
via Mazzini 12
27049 Stradella (PV)
phone +39 0385.48627

Fratelli Crosio
via Garibaldi 66
27049 Stradella (PV)
phone +39 0385.245822

Lucchini & C.
via Martiri Partigiani 32
27049 Stradella (PV)
phone +39 0385.48651

Museo della fisarmonica Dallapè
Palazzo Garibaldi
via Montebello 2
27049 Stradella (PV)
phone +39 0385.42069

sulmona (abruzzo)

Tourist Information
corso Ovidio 208
67039 Sulmona (AQ)
phone/fax +39 0864.53276

Hotel Santacroce
SS 17
67039 Sulmona (AQ)
phone +39 0864.251696
meeting@arc.it
www.hotelsantacroce.com

Ristorante Gino
piazza Plebiscito 12
67039 Sulmona (AQ)
phone +39 0864.52289
marcoallega@virgilio.it

Ristorante Clemente
vico Quercia 5
67039 Sulmona (AQ)
phone +39 0864.52284
www.ristoranteclemente.com

Museo dell'arte e della tecnologia confettiera Pelino
via Introdacqua 55
67039 Sulmona (AQ)
phone +39 0864.210047
www.pelino.it

Confetteria d' Alessandro
corso Ovidio 77
67039 Sulmona (AQ)
phone +39 0846.55888
www.confettidalessandro.it

susegana (veneto)

Mercatino del giunco
strada Ponte della Priula 20
31058 Susegana (TV)
phone +39 0438.895205

taranto (puglia)

Tourist Information
corso Umberto I 113
74100 Taranto
phone +39 099.4532392
infoaptta@libero.it
www.puglia.it

Hotel Europa
via Roma 2
74100 Taranto
phone +39 099.4525994
info@hoteleuropaonline.it

Ristorante Il Caffè
via T. D'Aquino 8
74100 Taranto
phone +39 099.4525097

tarquinia (lazio)

Tourist Information
via Romiti (Stazione Porta Romana)
01100 Viterbo
phone +39 0761.304795
infoviterbo@apt.viterbo.it
Barria S. Giusto 23
01016 Tarquinia (VT)
phone +39 0766.849282
comunetarquinia@tarquinia.net

Ristorante Arcadia
via Mazzini 6
01016 Tarquinia (VT)
phone +39 0766.855501
arcadiaristorante@libero.it
www.on-web.it/arcadia

L'Ultimo Etrusco
via della Ripa 33
01016 Tarquinia (VT)
phone +39 0766.855175

Todini sculture
via Leonardo da Vinci
lotto 29
01016 Tarquinia (VT)
phone +39 0766.858294

telese terme (campania)

Adam vetrate
via Lamparelli 12
82037 Telese Terme (BN)
phone +39 0824.901007
adam_art@tin.it
www.adamart.it

terrasini (sicily)

Ristorante Primafila
via Sapuito 8
90049 Terrasini (PA)
phone +39 091.8684422

Museo del carretto siciliano
90049 Terrasini (PA)
phone +39 091.8685636
museo.carretto@regione.sicilia.it

thiene (veneto)

Oblò Ricami
via Corso Campagna 56
36016 Thiene (VI)
phone +39 0445.314844

tolentino (marche)

Nazareno Gabrielli
contrada Cisterna 63
62029 Tolentino (MC)
phone +39 0733.9021
ng@nazarenogabrielli.it
www.nazarenogabrielli.it

Pelletteria Elia Feliziani
via Colombo 114
62029 Tolentino (MC)
phone +39 0733.930588

Grazia Pelletteria
via Terme S. Lucia 24
62029 Tolentino (MC)
phone +39 0733.969720

Valigeria La Rancia
via Sacharov 24
62029 Tolentino (MC)
phone +39 0733.971371

tollegno (piedmont)

Filatura Lana Gatto
via Roma 16
13818 Tollegno (BI)
phone +39 015.2429228
www.tollegno1900.it

tolmezzo (friuli–venezia giulia)

Rossitti Giobatta e fratelli
via Giralba 39
Tolmezzo (UD)
phone +39 0433.43925

turin (piedmont)

Tourist Information
piazza Solferino
10100 Turin
phone +39 011.535181
info@turismotorino.org
Aeroporto Torino Caselle
10100 Turin
phone +39 011.5678124
www.turismotorino.org

Grand Hotel Sitea
via Carlo Alberto 35
10123 Turin
phone +39 011.5170171
sitea@thi.it www.thi.it
www.sitea.thi.it

Hotel Victoria
via N. Costa 4
10123 Turin
phone +39 011.5611909
reservation@hotelvictoria-torino.com
www.hotelvictoria-torino.com

Ristorante Del Cambio
piazza Carignano 2
10123 Turin
phone +39 011.543760
cambio@thi.it

Ristorante Al Gatto Nero
corso F. Turati 14
10100 Turin
phone +39 011.590477
info@gattonero.it
www.gattonero.it

Osteria Antiche Sere
via Cenischia 9
10100 Turin
phone +39 011.3854347

Quill
via Monte di Pietà 17
10122 Turin
phone +39 011.5628267
quilltorino@virgilio.it

Gibus
via Luigi Cibrario
10143 Turin
phone +39 011.746754

Stilografiche Monasterolo
via Cernaia 24
10122 Turin
phone +39 011.541744

Torino Penna
via XX Settembre 4
10121 Turin
phone +39 011.542962

Aurora Due
strada comunale Bertolla
all'Abbadia di Stura 200
10156 Turin
phone +39 011.2734186
aurora@aurorapen.it
www.aurorapen.it

Atelier della ceramica
corso Bramante 14A
10156 Turin
phone +39 011.3196782

L'Artigiano dell'ottone
via Vanchiglia 24
10156 Turin
phone +39 011.872813

Atelier d'arte orafa
via dei Mercanti 15C
10156 Turin
phone +39 011.5627680

Orafa Artigiana
via Cocconato 8
10156 Turin
phone +39 011.9187446

Redivivus (liuteria)
via Bava 32
10156 Turin
phone +39 011.8171667
info@maribyredivivus.it
www.maribyredivivus.it

**Castello di Rivoli Museo d'Arte
Contemporanea**
piazza Mafalda di Savoia
10098 Rivoli (TO)
phone +39 011.9565222
fax +39 011.9565230
www.castellodirivoli.it
info@castellodirivoli.org

torre del greco (campania)

Tourist Information
piazza dei Martiri 58
80121 Naples
phone +39 081.405311
ept@netgroup.it
www.ept.napoli.it

Hotel Sakura
via de Nicola 26
80059 Torre del Greco (NA)
phone +39 081.8493144
info@hotelsakura.it

Hotel Grillo Verde
piazza Imbriani 19
80058 Torre Annunziata (NA)
phone +39 081.8611019
hgv@hotelgrilloverde.it

Ristorante La mammola
via B. Croce 20
80059 Torre del Greco (NA)
phone +39 081.8492168
marad@marad.it

Museo del Corallo
piazza Palomba 6
80059 Torre del Greco (NA)
phone +39 0818.811360
www.museodelcoralloedelcammeo.it

Petrosino Preziosi
via S. Vito 87
80059 Torre del Greco (NA)
phone +39 081.8816336
www.oromare.com

Vesuvio Coralli
via Calamarino traversa Fosso S. Michele 2
80059 Torre del Greco (NA)
phone +39 0818.813841

Giuseppe Petrucci
via dei Bazzellai
80059 Torre del Greco (NA)
phone +39 0818.492363

Coralli Del Gatto
via E. de Nicola 25
80059 Torre del Greco (NA)
phone +39 0818.814191

De Luca Brothers
via Montedoro 23
80059 Torre del Greco (NA)
phone +39 0818.824666

Fratelli Iacobelli
via Misericordia 20
80059 Torre del Greco (NA)
phone +39 0818.491349

trento (trentino–alto adige)

Tourist Information
via Manci 2
38100 Trento
phone +39 0461.983880
informazioni@apt.trento.it

Boscolo Grand Hotel Trento
via Alfieri 1
38100 Trento
phone +39 0461.271000
reservation@trento.boscolo.com
www.boscolohotels.com

Ristorante Scrigno del Duomo
piazza Duomo 29
38100 Trento
phone +39 0461.220030
info@scrignodelduomo.com

Ceramica Cicuttin
via Valsugana 67
38100 Trento
phone/fax +39 0461.983741
ceramica.cicuttin@dnet.it
www.ceramicacicuttin.com

Cereria Ronca
via della Cooperazione 13
località Mattarello
38100 Trento
phone +39 0461.946030
info@cereriaronca.it
www.cereriaronca.it

Mercatino dei Gaudenti
(every second saturday of the month)
piazza Garzetti
38100 Trento
phone +39 0461.235062

Mercatino di antiquariato
(every fourth saturady of the month)
centro storico
38060 Villalagarina (TN)
phone +39 0464.494222

Artigianato Artistico
vicolo Vò 21
38100 Trento
phone +39 0461.983571

Jolly B
via Gandhi 2
38100 Trento
phone +39 0461.924796

Tiziana Zeni
via Caneppele 20/2
38100 Trento
phone +39 0461.991628

Renzo Lazzarin
via Soccampo 21
32012 Forno di Zoldo (BL)
phone +39 0437.78469

valenza (piedmont)

Tourist Information
via Gagliaudo 2
15100 Alessandria
phone +39 0131.234794
iat@comune.alessandria.it

Hotel Europa
via Palestro 1
15100 Alessandria
phone +39 0131.236226

Ristorante La Fermata
via Vochieri 120
15100 Alessandria
phone +39 0131.251350

La Fabbrica dell'oro
via Circonvallazione Ovest 14
15048 Valenza (AL)
phone +39 0131.943195
info@fabbricadelloro.it
www.fabbricadelloro.it

MC Gold
via Pellizzari 29
15048 Valenza (AL)
phone +39 0131.942078

Orostaff Preziosi
via Falteria 15
15048 Valenza (AL)
phone +39 0131.947909

Alessandro Gioielli
via 29 Aprile 30
15048 Valenza (AL)
phone +39 0131.941961

Fratelli Canepari
piazza Gramsci 15
15048 Valenza (AL)
phone +39 0131.942061

valgrisenche (Valle d'Aosta)

Cooperativa Les Tisserands
11010 Valgrisenche (AO)
phone +39 0165.97163
www.ivat.org

valstrona (lombardy)

Artek
località Fornero
via Strona 33
28020 Valstrona (VB)
phone +39 0323.387110

Mastro Geppetto
via Consorzio 3
località Piana di Fornero
28020 Valstrona (VB)
phone +39 0323.387274

Museo dell'artigianato
Frazione Forno
28020 Valstrona (VB)
phone +39 0323.885133

valtellina (lombardy)

Tourist Information
via C. Battisti 12
23100 Sondrio
phone +39 0342.512500
aptvaltellina@provincia.so.it
corso Vittorio Emanuele II 2
23022 Chiavenna (SO)
phone +39 0343.36384
aptchiavenna@provincia.so.it

Hotel Europa
Lungo Mallero Cadorna 27
23100 Sondrio
phone +39 0342.515010
info@htleuropa.com

Albergo Ristorante della Posta
via Dogana 8
23020 Montespluga (SO)
phone +39 0343.54234
salafaustoenoteca@tiscalinet.it

Hotel Aurora
località Campedello Est
via Rezia 73
23022 Chiavenna (SO)
phone +39 0343.32708
info@albergoaurora.it
www.albergoaurora.it

Ristorante Al Cenacolo
via Pedretti 16
23022 Chiavenna (SO)
phone +39 0343.32123

Ristorante Passerini
via Dolzino 128
23022 Chiavenna (SO)
phone +39 0343.36166
info@ristorantepasserini.com

Ristorante Sassella
via Roma 2
23033 Grosio (SO)
phone +39 0342.847272

valtrompia (lombardy)

Tourist Information
località Lavone, via don Piotti 12
25063 Gardone Val Trompia
phone +39 030.9220338
www.valtrompiaturismo.it

vandoies (trentino–alto adige)

Tourist Information
via Stazione 9
39042 Bressanone (BZ)
phone +39 0472.836401
info@brixen.org
www.brixen.org
via J.A. Zoller 1
39030 Vandoies di Sotto (BZ)
phone +39 0472.869100
info@vandoies.com

Hotel Ristorante Elephant
via Rio Bianco 4
39042 Bressanone (BZ)
phone +39 0472.832750
info@hotelelephant.com
www.hotelelephant.com

Hotel Lodenwirt
via Pusteria 1
39030 Vandoies (BZ)
phone +39 0472.867000
info@lodenwirt.it
www.lodenwirt.it

Hotel Dominik
via Terzo di Sotto 13
39042 Bressanone (BZ)
phone +39 0472.830144
info@hoteldominik.com
www.hoteldominik.com

Hotel Grüner Baum
via Stufles 11
39042 Bressanone (BZ)
phone +39 0472.274100
info@gruenerbaum.it

Ristorante Sunnegg
via Vigneti 67
39042 Bressanone (BZ)
phone +39 0472.834760
gasthof.sunnegg@rolmail.net

Ristorante Tillia
39030 Vandoies di Sopra (BZ)
phone +39 0472.868185
info@chris-oberhammer.com

Museo del loden Oberrauch Zitt
39030 Vandoies (BZ)
phone +39 0472.868540
info.lodenwelt@oberrauch-zitt.com

varallo sesia (piedmont)

Tourist Information
corso Roma 38
13019 Varallo Sesia (VC)
phone +39 0163.564404

Hotel Sacro Monte
località Sacro Monte 14
13019 Varallo Sesia (VC)
phone +39 0163.54254

Ristorante Delzanno
località Crosa
13019 Varallo Sesia (VC)
phone +39 0163.51439

varese (lombardy)

Tourist Information
via Carrobbio 2
21100 Varese
phone +39 0332.283604
apt-va@libero.it

Ristorante Al Vecchio Convento
viale Borri 348
località Bizzozero
21100 Varese
phone +39 0332.261005
www.alvecchioconvento.it

Ristorante Il Sole
piazza Venezia 5
21030 Ranco (VA)
phone +39 0331.976507

De Santi
via Giordani 42
21100 Varese
phone +39 0332.212515

Arte Ceramiche
via Belforte 154
21100 Varese
phone +39 0332.331300

Santambrogio & C.
Via al Lago, 8
21026 Groppello di Gavirate (Va)
phone/fax +39 0332 743077
santambrogio.fumarelapipa.com

venice (veneto)

Tourist Information
calle Ascensione-San Marco 71
30100 Venice
phone +39 041.5297811
info@turismovenezia.it
Aeroporto Marco Polo, Tessera
30100 Venice
phone +39 041.5298711

Hotel Cipriani
Isola della Giudecca 10
30133 Venice
phone +39 041.5207744
info@hotelcipriani.it
www.hotelcipriani.com

Hotel Danieli
Riva degli Schiavoni 4196
30122 Venice
phone +39 041.5226480
danieli@luxurycollection.com
www.danieli.hotelinvenice.com

Hotel Quattro Fontane
via Quattro Fontane 16
30126 Lido di Venezia, Venice
phone +39 041.5260227
www.quattrofontane.com

Ristorante Caffè Quadri
piazza San Marco 120
30124 Venice
phone +39 041.5222105
quadri@quadrivenice.com
www.quadrivenice.com

Ristorante Da Fiore
calle del Scaleter, San Polo 2202/A
30125 Venice
phone +39 041.721308
reservation@dafiore.com
www.dafiore.com

Naranzaria osteria
San Polo 130
30125 Venezia
phone/fax + 39 041.72 41 035
naranzaria@naranzaria.it
www.naranzaria.it

Trattoria Bancogiro Osteria da Andrea
Campo San Giacometto, San Polo 122
30125 Venice
phone +39 041.5232061

Laboratorio Artigiano di Maschere
Santa Croce 1164
30135 Venice
phone +39 041.717898

Mondonovo Maschere
Dorsoduro 3063
30123 Venice
phone +39 041.5212633
www.mondonovomaschere.it

**Museo di storia del tessuto e del costume
di Palazzo Mocenigo**
Santa Croce 1992
30135 Venice
phone +39 041.721798
www.comune.venezia.it/museicivici

Venetia Studium
San Marco 2425
30124 Venice
phone +39 041.5236953
fax +39 041.5227353
info@venetiastudium.com
www.venetiastudium.com

Benetton
via Mercerie 2 Aprile
30100 Venice
phone +39 041.2960493
info@benetton.it
www.benetton.com

Jesurum
Cannaregio 3219, Fondamenta della Sensa
30121 Venice
phone +39 041.5242540
fax +39 041.5242542
San Marco, 4856, Mercerie del Capitello
phone +39 041.5206177
www.jesurum.it

Venini
San Marco 314, Piazzetta Leoncini
30124 Venice
phone/fax +39 041.5224045
venezia@venini.it

Carlo Moretti
San Marco 1468, Campo San Moisè
30124 Venice
phone +39 041.5231973
fax +39 041.5223118
venezia@carlomoretti.com

Galleria Marina Barovier
San Marco 3216, Salizada San Samuele
30124 Venice
phone +39 041.5236748
fax +39 041.2447042
info@barovier.it
www.barovier.it

Nicolao Atelier
Cannaregio 2590
30121 Venice
phone +39 041.5207051
fax +39 041.716797
atelier@nicolao.com
www.nicolao.com

Tessitura Luigi Bevilacqua
Santa Croce 1320
30135 Venezia
phone +39 041.721566
fax +39 041.5242302
bevilacqua@luigi-bevilacqua.com
luigi-bevilacqua.com

Annelie
Dorsoduro 2748
30100 Venice
phone +39 041.5203277

Cenerentola
calle dei Saoneri 2718 San Polo
30100 Venice
phone +39 041.5232006

Remèr de Venexia
Giudecca 681/A
30133 Venice
phone/fax +39 041.5289463
pregno123@hotmail.com
www.forcolavenezia.com

verbania (lombardy)

Tourist Information
corso Zanitello 6
28922 Pallanza (VB)
phone +39 0323.503249
turismo@comune-verbania.it

Alessi
via Privata Alessi, 6
28882 Crusinallo (VB) Italia
phone +39 0323.868611
www.alessi.com

Hotel Pallanza
viale Magnolie 8
28922 Pallanza (VB)
phone +39 0323.503202
belvedere@pallanzahotels.com

Hotel Ancora
corso Mameli 65
28921 Intra (VB)
phone +39 0323.53951
info@hotelancora.it

Ristorante Il Torchio
via Manzoni 20
28922 Pallanza (VB)
phone +39 0323.503352

Ristorante La Tavernetta
via S. Vittore 22
28921 Intra (VB)
phone +39 0323.402635

M & SI
via Martiri 42
località Fordo
28924 Verbania
phone +39 0323.586850
maffioliadolfosas@libero.it

Laboratorio PRG
via De Notaris 75A
28924 Verbania
phone +39 0323.553839

verona (veneto)

Tourist Information
via degli Alpini 9
37100 Verona
phone +39 045.8068680
iatbra@tiscali.it
Aeroporto Villafranca
phone +39 045.8619163
iataeroporto@tiscali.it

Albergo Villa del Quar
località Pedemonte
Via Quar 12
37029 San Pietro in Cariano VR
phone +39 045.6800681
info@villadelquar.it
www.hotelvilaldelquar.it

Hotel Due Torri Baglioni
piazza Sant'Anastasia 4
37121 Verona
phone +39 045.595044
duetorri.verona@baglionihotels.com
www.baglionihotels.com

Ristorante 12 Apostoli
Corticella San Marco 3
37100 Verona
phone +39 045.596999
dodiciapostoli@tiscali.it

verres (valle d'aosta)

Ristorante Chez Pierre
via Martorey 75
11029 Verres (AO)
phone +39 0125.909376

Luciano Savin
via degli Artigiani 5
11029 Verres (AO)
phone +39 0125.929374

verrone (piedmont)

Fila Store
SS Trossi 8
13871 Verrone (BI)
phone +39 015.5821541
www.fila.com

verzegnis (friuli–venezia giulia)

Nella Fantasia
via V. Veneto 7
33020 Verzegnis (UD)
phone +39 0433.40678

viareggio (tuscany)

Tourist Information
viale Carducci 10
55049 Viareggio (LU)
phone +39 0584.962233
viareggio@versilia.turismo.toscana.it

Grand Hotel Principe di Piemonte
piazza Puccini 1
55049 Viareggio (LU)
phone +39 0584.4011
info@principedipiemonte.com

Hotel Excelsior
viale Carducci 88
55049 Viareggio (LU)
phone +39 0584.50726
info@excelsior-viareggio.it

L'Oca Bianca
via Coppino 409
55049 Viareggio (LU)
phone +39 0584.388477

Ristorante Romano
via Mazzini 120
55049 Viareggio (LU)
phone +39 0584.31382
info@romanoristorante.it

Euro Sailer
via Virgilio 164
55049 Viareggio (LU)
phone +39 0584.971069
www.eurosailer.it

Effebi
via Virgilio 234
55049 Viareggio (LU)
phone +39 0584.384361
www.effebivtr.it

SuperYachts
via dei Pescatori 56
55049 Viareggio (LU)
phone +39 0584.944955
info@vsy.it
www.vsy.it

Mercato dell'Antiquariato
(every fourth week-end of the month)
piazza d'Azeglio
55049 Viareggio (LU)
phone +39 0584.962350

Perini Navi
Via Coppino 114
55049 Viareggio
phone +39 0584.4241
fax +39 0584.424210
info@perininavi.it
www.perininavi.it

vicenza (veneto)

Tourist Information
piazza Matteotti 12
36100 Vicenza
phone +39 0444.320854
aptvicenza@ascom.vi.it

Jolly Hotel Tiepolo
viale S. Lazzaro 110
36100 Vicenza
phone +39 0444.954011
vicenza-tiepolo@jollyhotels.com
www.jollyhotels.com

Antico Ristorante agli Schioppi
Contrà Piazza del Castello 26
36100 Vicenza
phone +39 0444.5437014
info@ristoranteaglischioppi.com

Orobase
Contrà Porta Nova 11
36100 Vicenza
phone +39 0444.504222

orobase@orobase.it
www.orobase.it

Cash & Gold
viale della Scienza 14
Zona Industriale
36100 Vicenza
phone +39 0444.965947
www.cashgold.it

Mercatino del Collezionismo
(every second sunday of the month)
piazza dei Signori
36100 Vicenza
phone +39 0444.323863

Pianegonda
Via De Gasperi 82-84
36040 Grisignano (VI)
phone +39 0444.613000
fax +39 0444.613099
www.pianegonda.com
info@pianegonda.com

Vincenzo Galante
via Molini 82
36100 Vicenza
phone +39 044.4504222

Giuseppe Rossi
viale Trieste 78
36100 Vicenza
phone +39 044.4507630

vietri sul mare (campania)

Tourist Information
corso Umberto
84019 Vietri sul Mare (SA)
phone +39 089.763811
www.comune.vietri-sul-mare.sa.it

Hotel Lloyd's Baia
via de Marinis 2
84019 Vietri sul Mare (SA)
phone +39 089.210145
lloydsbaia@sogliahotels.com
www.sogliahotels.com

Ristorante La Locanda
corso Umberto 152
84019 Vietri sul Mare (SA)
phone +39 089.761070

Museo provinciale della ceramica
via Nuova Raito
località Raito
84010 Vietri sul Mare (SA)
phone +39 089.211835

Ceramica artistica Solimene
via Madonna degli Angeli 7
shop: via Costiera 10
84019 Vietri sul Mare (SA)
phone +39 089.212539 - 210243
solimene@amalficoast.it
www.solimene.com

F.lli Perotti Vetrate
via Nazionale Costiera Amalfitana 32
84019 Vietri sul Mare (SA)
phone +39 089.211545
www.perotti.it

Ceramica CE.AR
via De Marinis 26
località Molina
84019 Vietri sul Mare (SA)
phone +39 089.211743

Ceramica Vietri Scotto
via Pellegrino 56.
località Marina
84019 Vietri sul Mare (SA)
phone +39 089.210197

Ceramica Pinto
corso Umberto I 21
84019 Vietri sul Mare (SA)
phone +39 089.210271

vigevano (lombardy)

Tourist Information
corso V. Emanuele 29
27029 Vigevano (PV)
phone +39 0381.299282
www.comune.vigevano.pv.it

Ristorante I Castagni
via Ottobiano 8/20
27029 Vigevano (PV)
phone +39 0381.42860
ristoranteicastagni@libero.it

Ristorante da Maiuccia
via Sacchetti 10
27029 Vigevano (PV)
phone +39 0381.83469
info@damaiuccia.it

Museo della calzatura P. Bartolini
corso Cavour 82
27029 Vigevano (PV)
phone +39 0381.690373
www.comune.vigevano.pv.it/turismo/museo

Palco
via Novara 173
27029 Vigevano (PV)
phone +39 0381.20657

Centro Commerciale Ducale
via Industria 225
27029 Vigevano (PV)
phone +39 0381.347212

Asti Domenico
via V. Alfieri 30
27029 Vigevano (PV)
phone +39 0381.348933

Calzaturificio di Vigevano
via Gravellona 15
27029 Vigevano (PV)
phone +39 0381.20072

Calzaturificio Cesare Martinoli - Caimar
Via Montevecchio 21-23
27029 Vigevano (PV)
phone +39 0381.82031
fax +39 0381.74429
www.cesaremartinoli.it

vigo di cadore (veneto)

Ottica Metal Dream
SS per Auronzo
località Campopiano 1
32040 Vigo di Cadore (BL)
phone +39 435.77129
www.metaldream.com
metaldream@libero.it

*villanova di bagnacavallo
(emilia–romagna)*

Ecomuseo delle erbe palustri
largo Tre Giunchi 1
48020 Villanova di Bagnacavallo (RA)
phone +39 0545.47122
barangani@racine.ra.it
www.racine.raerbepalustri/

vimercate (lombardy)

Marzotto Factoy Store
via Bolzano 3
20059 Vimercate (MI)
phone +39 039.6084675
marzottod_vi01@tin.it
www.marzotto.it

volpago del montello (veneto)

Garmont
via Spineda 12
31040 Volpago del Montello (TV)
phone +39 0423.8726
www.garmont.com

volterra (tuscany)

Tourist Information
piazza Miracoli
56126 Pisa
phone +39 050.560464
pisa.turismo@traveleurope.it
piazza dei Priori
56048 Volterra (PI)
phone/fax +39 0588.87257
info@volterra.it

Hotel Royal Victoria
Lungarno Pacinotti 12
56126 Pisa
phone +39 050.940111
mail@royalvictoria.it

Park Hotel Le Fonti
via di Fontecorrenti
56048 Volterra (PI)
phone +39 0588.85219
info@parkhotellefonti.com

Hotel Villa Nencini
Borgo S. Stefano 55
56048 Volterra (PI)
phone +39 058.886386

Vecchia Osteria dei Poeti
via Matteotti 55
56048 Volterra (PI)
phone +39 0588.88537

Alab'Arte
via Orti S. Agostino 28
56048 Volterra (PI)
phone +39 0588.87968
www.alabarte.com

Soc. Coop. Artieri Alabastro
piazza dei Priori 5
56048 Volterra (PI)
phone +39 0588.87590

Gloria Giannelli
via di Sotto 2
56048 Volterra (PI)
phone +39 0588.84030
gkglory@virgilio.it

Paola Colvicchi
via Porta all'Arco 25
56048 Volterra (PI)
phone +39 347.6969413

Fabula Etrusca
via Lungo le Mura del Mandorlo 10
56048 Volterra (PI)
phone +39 0588.86401
www.fabulaetrusca.it

zoagli (liguria)

Ristorante L'Arenella
Lungomare dei Naviganti
16030 Zoagli (GE)
phone +39 0185.359393

Velluti e seterie Cordani
via S. Pietro 21
16030 Zoagli (GE)
phone +39 0185.259141
cordani-zoagli@libero.it
www.seteriecordani.com

SUGGESTED READING

ART AND DESIGN

Cogeval, Guy and Giampiero Bosoni, eds. *Il Modo Italiano: Italian Design and Avant-Garde in the 20th Century*. (Skira, 2006).

Ferro Sims, John. *Handmade in Italy: A Celebration of Italian Artisans Working in Ceramics, Textiles, Glass, Stone, Metal and Wood*. (New York: Watson-Guptill Publications, 2003).

Heller, Stephen and Louise Fili. *Italian Art Deco: Graphic Design between the Wars*. (New York: Chronicle Books, 1993).

Helman Minchilli, Elizabeth and Susie Cushner. *Deruta: A Tradition of Italian Ceramics*. (New York: Chronicle Books, 1998).

SHOPPING

Gershman, Suzy. *Suzy Gershman's Born to Shop Italy: The Ultimate Guide for Travelers Who Love to Shop*. (New York: Frommers, 2006).

Morelli, Laura. *Made in Italy: A Shopper's Guide to the Best of Italian Tradition*. (New York: Universe Publishing, 2003).

Seveso, Mario. *The Antique and Flea Markets of Italy*. (The Little Bookroom, 2003).

FASHION

Steele, Valerie. *Fashion, Italian Style*. (New Haven: Yale University Press, 2003).

Mulassano, Adriana. *The Who's Who of Italian Fashion*. (Spinelli & Co.: Florence, 1979).

Ricamo Nella Moda. *Embroidery: Italian Fashion*. (Diamani, 2006).

Seeling, Charlotte. Fashion; *The Century of the Designer*. (Konemann, 2000).

TRAVEL

Italy: The Best Travel Writing from the New York Times. Various contributors. (New York: Harry N. Abrams, 2005).

Lazzarin, Paolo. *One Hundred and One Beautiful Towns in Italy: Food and Wine*. (New York: Rizzoli, 2005).

Podesta, Gina. *The Romantic's Guide to Italy*. (Ten Speed Press, 2004).

PHOTO CREDITS

First published in the United States of America in 2007
by Rizzoli International Publications, Inc.
300 Park Avenue South
New York, NY 10010
www.rizzoliusa.com

© 2007 Rizzoli International Publications

Production: Colophon srl, Venice, Italy

Editorial Direction: Andrea Grandese

Editor in Chief: Rosanna Alberti

Layout: Colophon, Venice

Design Concept: Stephen Fay

English Translation: Judith Goodman

2007 2008 2009 2010 2011 / 10 9 8 7 6 5 4 3 2 1

Printed in Italy

ISBN-10: 0-8478-2840-9
ISBN-13: 978-0-8478-2840-1

Library of Congress Control Number: 2006939240